THE NATURAL HISTORY OF AN ENGLISH FOREST

The Wild Life of Wyre

From Wyre Forest to the centre of Birmingham is just a fraction over 20 miles: it is even nearer to the greater part of the industrial 'Black Country' of Smethwick and Dudley. Yet, away from the Midlands, it is so little known—6000 acres of glades and woodland on the boundary of Worcestershire and Shropshire, with Bewdley as its main point of access.

Here is one of the old English Forests, not remote, but with its own air of isolation: held within a strait-jacket of industrial activity yet still containing almost 3000 acres of its original 'old oak', thanks to a policy of conservation that was embarked upon before 'conservation' became a meaningful word.

It was fifty years ago, as a young boy, that Norman Hickin first visited the forest from his Birmingham home and, ever since, he has observed, recorded and sketched the wild life and beauty of Wyre. In this book he presents a portrait of the Forest as he has come to know it over half-a-century: intimately, sympathetically, and with the rare insight of an entomologist of international repute. Nearly 200 drawings by the author bring vividly to mind the flora and fauna of Wyre: the alder kitten and white-barred clearwing moth, the pied flycatcher and the dipper: the woodcock and the wild aquilegia, and the whitty pear and long-leaved helleborine. All these beautiful and extra-ordinary plants and animals are still to be found in Wyre, together with many thousands of species of living things which go to form the complex, reticulated pattern of a great English Forest.

By the same Author

CADDIS—Field Study Books

WOODWORM—Its Biology and Extermination

FOREST REFRESHED

CADDIS LARVAE

AFRICAN NOTEBOOK

Rentokil Library Series

   INSECT FACTOR IN WOOD DECAY

   THE WOODWORM PROBLEM

   THE DRY ROT PROBLEM

   HOUSEHOLD INSECT PESTS

   THE CONSERVATION OF BUILDING TIMBERS

   TERMITES—A WORLD PROBLEM

THE NATURAL HISTORY OF AN ENGLISH FOREST

The Wild Life of Wyre

Norman E. Hickin

ARROW BOOKS

ARROW BOOKS LTD
3, Fitzroy Square, London W1

AN IMPRINT OF THE ⬤ HUTCHINSON GROUP

London Melbourne Sydney Auckland
Wellington Johannesburg Cape Town
and agencies throughout the world

First published by
Hutchinson & Co (Publishers) Ltd 1971
Arrow edition 1972

Printed in Great Britain by
Flarepath Printers, St. Albans, Herts and bound by
William Brendon, Tiptree, Essex
ISBN 0 09 906240 2

To
Emma
whom I first met on the banks of Dowles

Contents

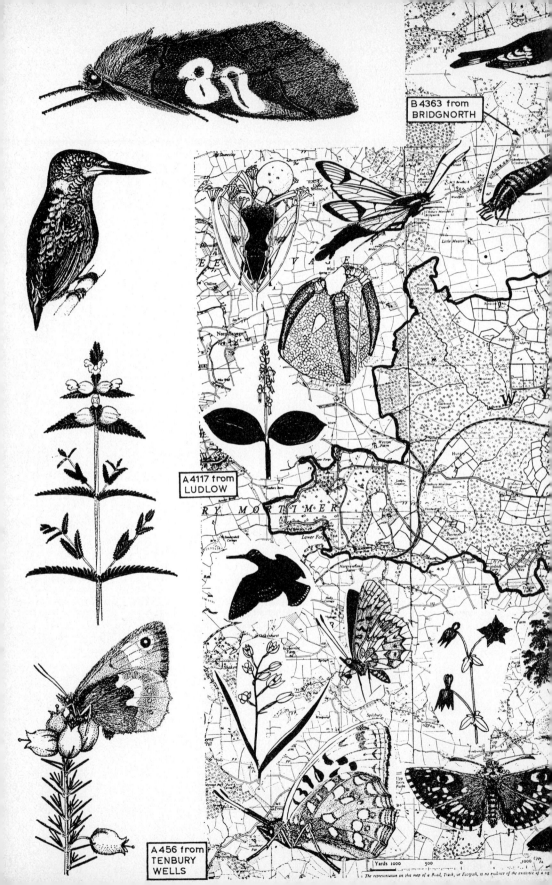

B 4363 from
BRIDGNORTH

A 4117 from
LUDLOW

A 456 from
TENBURY
WELLS

A456 from
KIDDERMINSTER

B 4194 from
STOURPORT

ACKNOWLEDGMENTS

How difficult it is to acknowledge the help given to me over a period of half a century in gathering information about the animals and plants of Wyre. It was in 1919 that I first walked through the forest with my Mother, Father, and brother. My early informants have long since passed on but I must mention F. W. Edwards, the then curator of the Birmingham Natural History Museum, S. E. Wace Carlier, an entomologist with a broad knowledge of many insect orders, and ColbranWainwright, the eminent dipterist, who identified a number of insects for me in the forest when I was a small boy. In recent years R. E. Young, Head Forester, and Edwin George of the Forestry Commission have taught me many things about trees and deer. John and Monica Betts of Goodmoor Grange for many kindnesses. They have helped considerably in many ways. Daphne Culpan identified a number of plants, and Robin Edwards determined a number of insect species from the forest. Hilda Maxwell carried out the various secretarial duties in connection with the book and produced the typescripts. I am very grateful to her. I would like to thank also, Martin and Doris Swansborough of Rudd's Bridge, Wyre Forest for the many ways in which they have helped my wife and I to live in two places.

Most of the material in this book was first published as a series of articles in the *Kidderminster Times* and I wish to thank Gilbert Smith, the editor, for permission to republish in this form.

1971.

FOREWORD

by Norman Riley CBE FRES FZS

This book really began when Norman Hickin, as a nine-year-old Birmingham lad, first strode into Wyre Forest from Bewdley. It has been growing ever since. The path he trod was the self-same path trodden by many earlier naturalists to whom he is a worthy successor. It was love at first sight, how deep and enduring is manifest in the essays that make up this volume, and even better perhaps in his recent autobiography, *Forest Refreshed*.

Mammals, birds, butterflies, beetles and other 'bugs', trees, shrubs and wild flowers all find their place in these tales of Wyre Forest, gathered together to paint an attractive and illuminating picture of an old English forest lying so close to Birmingham and the black country as to seem in these days almost an anachronism. 'Development' so often means destruction insofar as the country-side is concerned that the survival of Wyre Forest and its wild life, so near to these busy centres, is almost a miracle, a miracle of which Norman Hickin has taken full advantage. Observations spread over half a century of exploration of the forest and its wild life are recorded with accuracy and insight, and recounted with a sensitivity that the reader can hardly fail to share. And what a boon it is that the author is as good an artist as naturalist, able to illustrate his subject so faithfully and with such feeling. Some readers will have seen these drawings when originally published in the *Kidderminster Times*: they will appreciate their resurrection from those ephemeral pages to become a permanent joy.

It was many years ago that I first met Norman Hickin. He was then a young man evidently 'going places' but not quite sure of the route. Later, to satisfy his unbounded energy, he sought a leisure job, and I suggested he took a look at the lives of the caddis flies. Now, with a long list of publications behind him and many satisfying achievements in other fields, he tells me that he is making his home permanently where his heart belongs, in Wyre Forest.

NORMAN RILEY

INTRODUCTION

BEFORE IT IS TOO LATE

When one draws a map it is almost always for the benefit of human beings. But the map we show here is different. It is primarily for the benefit of all the wild life that still lives within the broad boundary, and that is its only significance. We are still to be counted fortunate that in spite of all the mounting pressures acting against the continuation of the wild life pattern that has existed in Wyre Forest for so many years, so much of it still remains. How has it survived? There are probably a number of reasons. It cannot be said to be remote, but one gets the sense of comparative isolation, although the area is within twenty miles of one of the greatest conurbations in Britain. Perhaps the lack of publicity about the region is of importance.

As far as the people of Britain, as a whole, are concerned, Wyre Forest has never been as well known as Epping Forest and the New Forest. This is probably because the emerging industrialisation of the West Midlands made heavy demands on the timber for fuel and thus caused a great decrease in the extent of the forest-lands at a much earlier period. The 1581 map of Worcestershire shows this in a local context. Feckenham Forest and Malvern Chase are shown as much more extensive than Wyre. One may mention Wyre Forest to acquaintances who would possess a fair knowledge of British geography, only to be followed by a blank expression of ignorance as to its where-abouts. It is often confused in conversation with the river Wye!

The Forest of Wyre lies on the boundary of Worcestershire and Shropshire. It, thus, lies partly in north-west Worcestershire and partly in south-east Shropshire. The county boundary through the forest is the Dowles Brook which, formed by the junction of the Lem Brook, Baveney Brook and Mad Brook, runs for the most part from west to east and enters the river Severn just less than one mile to the north of the town of Bewdley. The river Severn is, for the most part, the forest boundary to the east. Eymore Wood, however, lying on the east side of the Severn can properly be considered as part of the Forest of Wyre and points a finger as far as Shatterford to the north-east.

The Municipal Borough of Bewdley (population 5,190) lies 125 miles to the north-west of London, three miles from Kidder-minster and 15 from Worcester. Bewdley has usually been the point of access to the forest and, indeed, many references to Wyre Forest in both literature and science are given as Bewdley Forest. It was formerly of great importance. Lying on the river

Severn it had access at one time to the sea and had considerable industry. The nearest town on the west side of the forest is Cleobury Mortimer in Shropshire. About eight miles from Bewdley, it is reached on the A.4117 road to Ludlow. This road, which loops southwards on its way to the west forms the general boundary to the south of the forest, except for Rock Coppice and Ribbesford Woods on the east, and in addition it seems right to include the area of old orchard country as far south as Rock Common, to include Gorst Hill and rejoining the A.4117 road again near Finger Post.

Immediately to the north of the forest the road B.4194 runs north-westerly from Bewdley to the village of Kinlet. Then the B.4363 runs south-westerly to Cleobury Mortimer. A short road, B.4199, from Catsley to Bradley cuts the corner. Considerable forest areas, however, lie to the north of the B.4194, the 'Buttonoak Road'. Thus, to the north lie Gibbonswell, Coldwell, Dinglespout, Broadhurst and Blackgraves Coppices, the Pound Green and Hurst Coppice area, and to the south-east Cliff Wood, Seckley Wood, Graft Wood, Horsepool Coppice, Hawk-batch Valleys, Spike Copse and Skeys Wood.

From Wyre Forest to the centre of Birmingham is just a fraction over 20 miles. It is much less to the greater part of the so-called Black Country including Dudley, Brierley Hill, Smethwick, Oldbury and Halesowen.

Let us now turn our attention to the location of Wyre Forest in relation to England as a whole. If a line is drawn between Chester and Gloucester, the Forest would lie to the east of it, but it would touch the line. It lies rather nearer to Gloucester than to Chester. Although the name of Welch Gate in Bewdley is indicative of the nearness of Wales and, indeed, Tickenhill Palace also in Bewdley, was historically of importance as a residence of the Earls of the Marches, it is some 25 miles to present-day Wales, to the Radnor or Montgomeryshire boundaries. If a line is drawn from Aberystwyth to Cambridge, the forest lies to the north of it, but would just touch it.

The Whitty pear, long-leaved helleborine, alder wood wasp, land caddis fly, the kentish glory, alder kitten and white-barred clearwing moth, the pied flycatcher and the dipper, the wood-cock and the wild aquilegia; all these beautiful and extraordinary plants and animals are still to be found in the Forest of Wyre, together with many thousands of species of living things which go to form the complex reticulated pattern of a great English forest.

THE TREES OF WYRE

THE TWO OAKS

When Sir E. J. Salisbury carried out his survey of the vegetation of Wyre Forest in the years immediately following the first World War, he was able to state that it was one of the larger areas of natural woodland still remaining in Britain. He also said that it was possible to traverse over five miles of almost continuous woodland from Dowles, on the east (he had in mind Dowles Church at the joining of Dowles Brook with the Severn—but he would be hard put to find Dowles Church now, even the Bridge of Dowles over Severn where the water crowfoot grows thick, is reduced to a set of stumps) to Cleobury Mortimer, on the west, or nearly five miles of woodland from Coppicegate, on the north, to Burnt Wood, on the south. But also it was the firm belief of Salisbury that Ribbesford Woods to the south of Bewdley on the west bank of Severn, and Eymore and Arley to the north-east, and the woods adjacent to Kinlet Park, belonged properly to the Forest of Wyre itself.

Of course, it is still possible to make the selfsame traverses and it would be mostly woodland through which one made one's way, but I doubt if all the woodland could rightly be called 'natural'. Six thousand acres of Wyre woodland and just over half, 3,300 acres, are held by the Forestry Commission, but it is to the credit of a number of the private owners of the remaining 2,700 acres that much of the 'old oak' of Wyre remains. This is, indeed, all the more creditable in that the woodland owners' policy of conservation was embarked upon long before 'conservation' had become a meaningful word. They looked upon their woods of Wyre as an imperishable amenity and long may the people around Wyre think and believe the same.

But what of the oaks of Wyre, the individual trees that make the forest, not the great trees the Mawley Oak or the Oak of Goodmoor, to which I refer on page 6.

Two kinds or species of oak tree grow in Wyre, and in addition a number of trees intermediate in many characters due to hybridisation.

There are two species native to Britain and to the Forest of Wyre as follows:

COMMON OAK, *Quercus robur*, known also as Pedunculate Oak, *Quercus pedunculata*

This species grows best on damp soil and was the main species in

Common oak, Quercus robur. *Long-stalked acorns, stalkless leaves (near Furnace Mill).*

the wealden forests. It dominates the limey soils but planting has often obscured the natural preferences. In characters of identification the branchlets of common oak are smooth and the buds are rather blunt. The leaf stalk is very short, or absent, and the leaf base is square and the edges are turned up into a pair of ear-like processes known as auricles. The lateral veins of the leaf run to the hollows between the lobes and the lower surface is hairless. The acorns are blunt at the end and are situated on long stalks.

DURMAST OAK, *Quercus petraea,* known also as Sessile Oak, *Quercus sessiliflora*

Growing best on drier soils it was the main species of the northern forests, especially of the Forest of Dean and Wyre. It is found growing naturally on soils that are more acidic. In characters of identification it is seen that the branchlets of durmast oak are hairy and the buds are more pointed, and likewise hairy. The leaf stalk is long and the leaf base tapers without auricles being present. Only rarely do the veins run as far as the hollows between the lobes, and brown hairs are present on the cover surface of the leaf, especially in the axils of the veins. The acorn is more pointed and is stalkless, or nearly so.

But in addition to these two species dominant in certain localities, as we shall describe later, a few rarer species occur to be found by those with the trained eye. A specimen or two of Turkey oak, *Quercus cerris,* grow along the old railway line and there are, of course, some other introduced species in grounds of private houses. The blaze of colour in October of the scarlet oak at Goodmoor Grange is quite exceptional.

Now, where in the forest are the two oaks, the common and the durmast, to be found in respect of their natural preferences?

Durmast oak, Quercus petraea. *Stalkless acorns and long-stalked leaves* (*Wyre Common*).

To give an adequate answer we should refresh our memories with regard to the geology of Wyre. Almost the whole area of the forest is on the Middle Coal Measures. These comprise sandstones, shale, and ironstones with sweet coal, and narrow bands of Spirorbis limestone occur in a few places, particularly near Button Oak. Soils of Upper Coal Measure origin occur in woodlands north of Button Oak. Thus, it is seen that almost throughout the forest the soil is derived from non-calcareous rocks. Furthermore, the forest is divided by the steep-sided valley of Dowles with its tributary streams. The dry elevated area, steep valley slopes and acidic soil give conditions very suitable for the durmast and is where this oak species is found. Indeed, the durmast is the dominant tree species of Wyre and pure stands also occur. The rate of growth of the durmast at Wyre also has been measured and found to be somewhat better than average, thus emphasising the suitability of the area for the species.

The common oak and hybrids with durmast occur at the lower edge of the slopes along the streams and on the alluvial soil of the wider parts of Dowles Valley. This is where the calcareous soils occur, leached out of the higher regions. Besides the oak species, other plants and trees serve as indications of soil types. Thus, on the high slopes the bilberry occurs almost everywhere—a plant of acid soils, but along the banks of Dowles you will find the bird cherry, the *montana* variety of wych elm and ash, all associated with non-acid soils.

When, in the autumn of a good acorn year, you walk along the Dowles and then make your way south up to Callow Hill or north to Button Oak, take a notebook and see if this all works out.

THE OAKS OF MAWLEY AND GOODMOOR

For several centuries the oaks of Wyre were coppiced to produce charcoal for the smelting of iron. This has meant that few of our standing oaks today have grown directly from an acorn, without having sprouted from the stump of a felled tree. The young coppice oak tree can be identified from a 'standard', that is, a tree grown directly from an acorn, by the pronounced bend at the base showing that it originated as a lateral bud emerging from the stump. This twisted base of the coppice tree can be seen even in trees of up to one hundred years of age, but after that it becomes more difficult. The old stump rots away (although such stumps are exceedingly durable objects and can commonly be seen throughout the forest), or it is enveloped. In this latter case the base of the trunk completely covers the old stump and then often looks like a standard but is, in fact, a 'false standard'. For this reason Wyre oaks are not generally looked upon as good timber trees. Heart and butt rots are legacies from the wood-rotting fungi attacking the old stump. Mature standards are more likely to be trees of the hedgerow and this appears likely to be the origin of the two outstanding oaks on the west side of the forest. These are the oaks of Mawley and Goodmoor. Both are durmast oaks with little, if any, stalk to the acorn and stalked leaves. This is as we should expect from their position on high ground where the soil is more acid. But that is where the similarity ends; in appearance they are very different trees. The Mawley Oak must either have been a lonely tree, it certainly did not have to fight its way up towards the light, or it was a pollard. The Goodmoor Oak most certainly had many other trees around it to produce its straight bole.

THE MAWLEY OAK

This tree is situated near the junction of the B.4202 road from Clows Top and the A.4117 road from Far Forest to Cleobury Mortimer. It stands but a few yards from the south-east corner and on the opposite side of the B.4202 road from where the modern garage now stands. It cannot fail to attract the attention of anyone standing at the road junction.

An opportunity was taken of examining and measuring the tree on 19th October 1968. Only a very few acorns were present. The girth at head height, over a very rough trunk, was 23-ft 6-in.

The Mawley oak. Girth at head height 23 ft. 6 in. In height, 86 ft., but the widely spreading branches cover well over a quarter of an acre.

giving a diameter of practically 7½-ft. The area on the ground covered by foliage was 1,417 square yards, well over a quarter of an acre.

Perhaps the most outstanding point about this tree is the very large number of main branches, although difficult to count these were made out as thirty and all arose from between 12 and 15-ft from the ground. So that the Mawley Oak has a broad but very short trunk but with a magnificent head. The height was reckoned at 86-ft. The bark was extremely crevassed to the extent that it held the nest of a wren and one small branch was rotten and a strong colony of honey bees were flying in and out of a hole in it.

In the past oaks were often used as boundary markers and possibly the Mawley Oak once functioned in this way, although its huge head and short bole probably signifies that it was once pollarded.

THE GOODMOOR OAK
This tree lies a few yards from the road from the old Wyre Forest station to the bridge on the Far Forest to Kinlet road, and a few yards from the old footpath that runs to Furnace Mill. It is

situated between Cherry Orchard House and Stepping Stones House. A light iron fence surrounds the trunk. The tree was examined and measured on 20th October 1968 and the girth at six feet was found to be 15-ft 6-in. This gives a diameter of almost 5-ft.

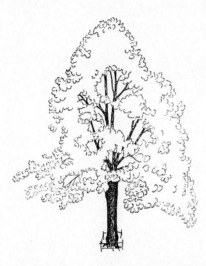

The Goodmoor oak is a pyramid 91 ft. high. The main trunk is 23 ft. high and the girth 15 ft. 6 in.

Several large burrs occurred at breast height indicating perhaps that it had been used as a fence at sometime in the past. After the burrs, the trunk is smooth and straight to about 23-ft when it divides into four large branches and a number of smaller ones. The total height of the tree was estimated to be about 90-ft, and the area on the ground covered by foliage was roughly 630 square yards, less than half that of the Mawley Oak. It had produced a fair crop of acorns in, generally, a good acorn year.

We have been able to find out practically nothing of the history of these trees so that any information concerning them and, indeed, about any other goodly trees of our forest, would be welcomed.

TURKEY OAK, *Quercus cerris*

Four species of oak are commonly found in Britain, the common oak, *Quercus robur*, and the durmast, *Quercus petraea*, being native, have already been discussed previously (pp. 3–5). The two other species, Turkey oak, *Quercus cerris*, and the holm oak or evergreen oak, *Quercus ilex*, are introduced, the former from

Europe and south-west Asia, and the latter from the Mediterranean region.

Turkey oak, although planted extensively as an ornamental has also become naturalised in southern England where the soil is acid. There is at least one specimen naturalised on the railway bank in the Forest. Perhaps an acorn fell into an open truck somewhere in its wide travels and it rolled out when it was near

Turkey oak (Blount Arms).

Cleobury Mortimer junction. The timber of the Turkey oak is of no value.

I know of no specimens of the evergreen oak within the Forest's precincts.

THE SECKLEY BEECH

Seckley Wood covers about 105 acres of the north-eastern edge of Wyre Forest and is an integral part of it. It is bounded on the north-east by an almost west-to-east sweep of the river Severn between the three islands and Folly Point, which is for the most part a steep cliff. To the south of Seckley Wood there is continuous woodland, Horsepool Coppice and Hawkbatch, until the Bewdley to Button Oak road, B.4194, is reached. To the south of this road, of course, there is also continuous woodland. On the west of Seckley lies an area of old Cherry orchard and some arable farmland until Pound Green Common and Pound Green Coppice are reached. The village of Arley lies about one mile to the north, and the town of Bewdley lies three miles to the south, both on the Severn.

In common with almost the whole of Wyre Forest, the underlying rock is of the Middle Coal Measures and whereas the wood generally possesses a shallow sandy soil, rocks outcrop at the cliffs on the river bank. Due to the presence of clay patches, one or more landslips are always in evidence, occasionally of some magnitude. A number of mature trees sometimes become uprooted and fall down the cliff forming an impenetrable tangle.

Flowing into the Severn at the Three Islands is a stream which has cut a steep valley down the cliff and it rises in the farmland on the plateau between Cherry Orchard and Woodhouse farms and is a significant trickle near the site of an old well which is marked on the largescale maps. Close by the well, and within a few yards of the stream, stands the Seckley Beech. This extraordinary tree is only a few yards from the modern forest road and is now screened from view by young trees and shrubs, from this road, which was made from the old path. Anyone wishing to find it will have to search for it but the directions which have been given above will ensure success.

On first sight the impression is not of a single tree but of a great clump of beeches growing from a single rootstock and there must be a number reading this who, when they were children, have counted the trunks like a game to see if the same result was obtained by everyone present. It is one of those difficult tasks when halfway through the counting one forgets whether a particular trunk has been counted or not.

In early July of 1969 a visit was made to the tree to see how it was faring and we ate our lunch under its extensive shade.

Twenty-six main trunks were counted but, in addition, there were a few smaller trunks of only a few inches diameter. There were four examples of trunks coalescing or growing into each other at some distance from the ground. The distance around all the trunks at five feet from the ground was thirty-eight feet. Two of the main trunks had been broken off, probably by some vandal action, but for what purpose it would be difficult to contemplate because considerable ingenuity and force would have been required to accomplish it. Several of the trunks curl over and spread their wide branches fairly close to the ground so that the two broken ones could have been used as swings. The cleavage is sharp and no fungal decay is present, but an extraordinary number of flight holes of the common furniture beetle are present covering the whole surface of the exposed sapwood and heartwood. Two other trunks show some fungal decay and appear to have offered some nesting facilities to woodpeckers, probably the greater spotted species, and in another trunk at some 30-ft from the ground there appear to be a number of nesting holes which could be those of the lesser spotted woodpecker. Bird life was evident everywhere. As the tree was examined a family group of long-tailed tits flitted through the branches, a wren sang fron nearby bushes and wood pigeons noisily fluttered around.

The dense shade caused by the tight leaf canopy causes the large area of the ground beneath to be bare of vegetation, a single holly struggles for existence, and at the time of the visit, the soil surface was dry and friable. It is strange that yet another example of a multi-trunked beech stands only about ten yards away and it possesses four trunks.

The Seckley Beech has, in the past, been the object of many country walks as the initial-scarred bark, up to 20-ft from the ground, so eloquently testifies, and it is hoped that this 'curiosity of Nature', as our forbears used to express it, will long remain to interest us.

BEECH, SWEET CHESTNUT AND THE OAKS

The beech, sweet chestnut, and the several species of oak are classified together in a single family, the Fagaceae. Members of this family are all trees and shrubs and have scaly buds. The flowers are of a single sex; those of the male sex being catkin-like, or in the form of tassels. The female flowers occur only in small groups, either singly, in pairs or in groups of three. Thus, in the beech, *Fagus sylvatica*, the male flowers are held erect on long-stalked tassels and there is usually a pair of female flowers at the base. In the sweet chestnut, *Castanea sativa*, the inflorescence is an erect catkin with numerous male flowers and female flowers at the base. In the oaks, of which four species are listed in the recent floras, the male flowers are in drooping catkins whilst the female flowers are solitary or in small spikes.

BEECH, *Fagus sylvatica*

Two thousand years ago, Julius Caesar wrote in his *De Bello Gallico* that the beech tree was absent from Britain, and this statement has been taken at its face value—that the beech is not an indigenous British tree—until comparatively recently. The growing expertise in the examination of peat and pollen deposits from the bottoms of lakes and in other situations, and their identification, has led us to reconsider and, indeed, in many instances, contradict previous opinions that have been unquestioned for, as in this case, centuries. Actually, there seems no doubt today that the beech tree was widespread over many parts of the southern half of Britain when the Romans came, and must have presented an appearance much as parts of the Chiltern Hills do today.

Beech. The developing fruit (Seckley).

The beech has been a popular tree for the forester, but it is not a pioneer. In its early life it needs some shelter, and to some extent, shade. It is extremely shade-tolerant and in Wyre it has been planted extensively amongst oak 'nurse' trees. The beech will eventually grow through the oak canopy and then its own dense foliage will kill its sheltering nurses. The shade cast by the beech is so dense that no other plants can thrive on the forest floor, except for a few which do not have to rely on their green chlorophyll and sunlight for their carbohydrate nutrition.

Beech is not a durable timber out-of-doors being susceptible to certain wood-rotting fungi, but indoors, it is most useful. Its warm fine and even grain commends it for furniture, especially for chair-legs, and it can be turned and steam-bent for manufacturing articles for a host of functions.

Beech can be seen in various stages of growth in the New Parks area of the Forest and there are some mature trees in Oxbind Coppice. Seckley Wood, however, is to be visited for observing the beech at its best in Wyre.

SWEET CHESTNUT or SPANISH CHESTNUT, *Castanea sativa*

This is an introduced tree although it is naturalised in south-east England. It is a native of southern Europe, North Africa, Asia Minor, the Caucasus and western Persia. It has been planted on a large scale in Britain on account of its useful timber. It grows into a large handsome tree with the dark brownish-grey bark heavily fissured, sometimes showing a spiral arrangement. Except for the gigantic tree at Kateshill there are few large trees of this species around the forest but anyone wishing to observe and admire a mature grove should visit Burwarton where the path along the base of Clee winds amongst them.

The sweet chestnut is readily identified by its long shining leaves edged with spines and its upright blossoms conspicuous on account of the bunches of cream-coloured stamens on upright stalks. These appear very late in the year, usually about August and it is only in exceptional years that a crop of chestnuts is produced. Our summer is not long enough.

Sweet chestnut is usually planted on good well-drained soil by the forester so that it can be coppiced. That is when the young trees are established they are cut down and from the resulting stool a number of saplings are produced. This, the sweet chestnut does very freely. At about 14 years of age these saplings produce an economic crop for cleft palings when twisted into wire; it is also valuable for hop-poles and general fencing purposes.

Sweet chestnut (Weston Plantation).

THE WHITTY PEAR, *Sorbus domestica*

The Whitty pear of Wyre must certainly lay claim to be one of the most highly documented trees in Britain. The first record of its existence is in the twelfth volume of the *Philosophical Transactions* for 1678 where an Alderman Edmund Pitts of Worcester described it in a note entitled 'Account of the *Sorbus pyriformis*'. He said of the fruit '. . . in September so rough as to be ready to strangle one. But being then gathered, and kept till October they eat as well as any medlar.' The verification of this reference in the original paper entailed a pleasant morning in the rooms of the Royal Society. Not unreasonably this august body did not allow their volume 12 to be long out of sight. Alderman Pitt

Sorbus domestica 40 feet high. *Lin: syst: nat: manured sorb*

The original Whitty pear as illustrated by Nash, 1781, *in* Collection for the History of Worcestershire.

considered the *Sorbus pyriformis* to be an old tree at the time he wrote but, in fact, the tree lingered on although decrepit until 1862 when the remnant of this hoary and gnarled old tree was burnt down by hooligans. George Jorden found the burnt-out trunk and some time afterwards sorrowfully gathered up the fragments. Indeed, one piece was exhibited at the Worcester Naturalists Club in 1862 and it was afterwards made into a silver-mounted cup and presented to William Mathews at a meeting of the Club on 25th October 1864. Incidentally, Jorden

The Whitty pear with pear-like flowers and ash-like leaf and, below, the cluster of pear-like fruits, but all arising from a single stem.

had already exhibited a flowering branch of the tree at the Club in June 1855.

However, several illustrations of the tree exist in the Worcestershire literature. Good figures of the tree, the flowers, leaves and fruit, appeared in the 'Collection for the History of Worcestershire' by T. R. Nash in 1781. It was then referred to as *Sorbus domestica* and its height was given as 40-ft. In 1831 there is a record of it in the 'Magazine of Natural History', Vol. 4, page 450, when it was stated that it was rapidly decaying and had come to the limit of its age. Then in Lee's 'Botany of Worcestershire' published in 1867 there appeared two illustrations of the tree one, in leaf, as seen in 1856, and another as it appeared many years before. From the latter it appears even more decrepit as there are no young shoots.

I notice from the Transactions of the Worcester Naturalists Club, 1898, that a field meeting took place on the 26th May and in the grounds of Arley Castle the members 'were especially interested in and admired a *Sorb tree* or Whitty pear (*Pyrus domestica*) now in full blossom, which is a graft from the famous old Sorb tree of Wyre Forest'. But in Amphlett and Rea, 1909,

The original Whitty pear obviously in decline and illustrated in Lee's Botany of Worcestershire *(1867).*

the two strong descendants of the tree flourishing in the grounds of Arley Castle are stated to have been raised from seed!

We see little directly in the literature about our tree until the planting of another from Arley Castle, a direct descendant of the Wyre specimen, in 1913. That is, with the exception of general books on British trees where remarks are often made about it, showing that the author has neither first-hand knowledge nor studied the references. My own humble account occurs in *Forest Refreshed* published in 1965.

The original Whitty pear as it was in 1856 and illustrated in Lee's Botany of Worcestershire (1867).

Some ceremony must have accompanied the planting of the present tree which is commemorated by a small bronze plaque set on to a white post. It states that the present sorb tree was a direct descendant of the 'original' tree and that it was presented by Robert Woodward of Arley Castle and planted by Mrs. Woodward in the presence of John Humphreys and F. T. Spackman. The Worcester Naturalists Club is not mentioned on the plaque but these gentlemen were its officers.

Now for the tree as anyone will find it.

The Whitty pear was measured on 12th April 1968. It would then have been planted 55 years. The girth at 54-in from the ground was found to be 46½-in, whilst the height to the first

The second Whitty pear as it stands today with a 22-feet pole alongside.

branch was 7-ft 9-in. The total height of the tree was about 50-ft. This is 10-ft higher than the original tree when it was measured in 1781. Presumably, it was a sapling of about 5 or

6-ft in height at the ceremonial planting so that it has increased in height, on average, something less than a foot a year.

The leaves are very much like those of the mountain ash, *Sorbus aucuparia*, but the tree is much stouter-looking, as the girth of nearly 4-ft would suggest. It has a very rough bark. It flowers from the middle of May to June and again the large flat inflorescence of many white flowers is not unlike that of the mountain ash. The fruits, however, instead of red berries resemble small pears, about one inch or so in length. When they have fallen from the tree they may be searched for among the rough grass and bracken, but I never found a young tree that had regenerated. Yet, I have heard of them being grown from seed but success never came my way.

It is a native of Southern Europe, North Africa and Asia Minor, so that one might well ask what such a tree was doing in the centre of a great wild forest in the seventeenth century. But it is pleasing to know that there are other descendants of the original tree, although as far as I know, not growing under truly wild conditions in the forest.

TREMULOUS ASPEN AND GLUTINOUS ALDER

The aspen is one of the poplars and thus also related to the willows. There are a number of characteristics shared in common by this large assemblage of tree species. They are both light and water-demanding; they are mostly of northern distribution with long daylight hours in summer, and they are found in wet soils. The inflorescence is always a catkin but whereas in the poplars nectaries are absent and wind pollination takes place; in the willows nectaries are present and pollination takes place by means of insects. All are easily propagated by cuttings, roots being formed with ease under damp conditions. In the Aspen, as with other poplars, propagation is seldom by means of seed but the tree produces numerous suckers which often produce dense thickets and, indeed, we can see an example of this along some of the rides in the New Parks Plantation.

The leaves of the Aspen are borne on very long slender stalks which are flattened vertically; this is the reason for the constant movement of the leaves, again a character shared by some of the poplars. The leaves are nearly circular. At first they are slightly hairy but later become quite smooth. There are two cup-shaped glands at the base. Actually the shape of the leaf is quite variable, especially in the suckers where the bottom leaves may be circular

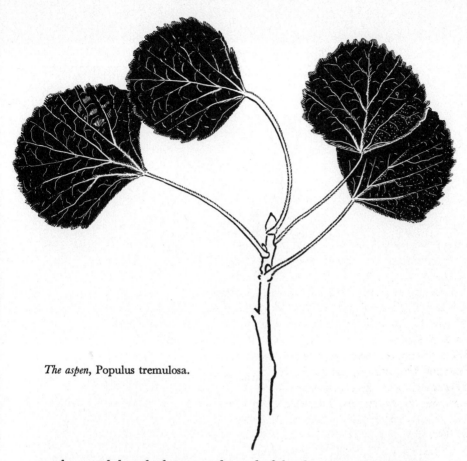

The aspen, Populus tremulosa.

and normal, but the leaves at the end of the shoot may be tapering and the stalks may be round and not flattened.

The catkins appear very early, often at the end of February and during March, before the leaves appear. Indeed, the aspen is one of the last trees to produce its leaves.

Whereas the aspen is found mainly on the higher ground of Wyre and is restricted to relatively few localities, the alder lines the banks of Dowles throughout its length, as well as many of its tributary streamlets. With but few exceptions it is not found far away from the lower ground.

The alder is even more water-demanding than the aspen and shows a number of adaptations to existence besides water-courses. Perhaps the most interesting of them is the construction of the seed which is small and so light that it requires nearly a quarter of a million of them to the pound. (Although not nearly so light as those of the silver birch, nearly three-quarters of a million being required to weigh a pound.) Each seed of alder, however, bears two minute air sacs or bladders enabling it to float and, thus, distribution of this tree is fairly quickly effected along watercourses. Another point of general interest concerns the abundance of characteristic nodules found on the roots. These contain bacteria of a special species (*Actinomycetes alni*) only known to be associated with the alder. It is presumed that, like similar nodule-bacteria found on the roots of leguminous plants, they possess the ability of converting the gas nitrogen from the air into water-soluble nitrogen salts capable of being assimilated by the tree and, of course, essential to its nutrition.

The leaves of alder are not unlike those of aspen but the stalks are not nearly so long nor is there the lateral thinning of the stalks. The bark is very different. That of aspen is usually rather

The alder, Alnus glutinosa.

smooth, at least in the younger trees, but that of alder is almost black, deeply fissured, and is very much like that of oak. Mistakes can be made unless a close examination is made. The alder, however, can always be identified even in mid-winter as the old fruiting cones or female catkins remain on the tree for a year or more whilst the forming male catkins, stalked and branched, can be easily identified.

None of the modern botany or tree books give us any indication as to why the specific name of *glutinosa* was given to the alder. Amphlett and Rea (1909), however, tell us that the alder foliage is 'glutinous', a quality our forefathers took advantage of, in the manner of the modern flypaper, 'to rid the chamber of those troublesome bedfellows'—fleas. The bark was also used as a medicine and the timber which is exceedingly durable under water was much used for clogs. The piles on which the ancient lake-village of Gastonbury was built, were made of alder.

The aspen, so far as I know, supports no rare or curious insects upon it in Wyre, but not so the alder. We are, indeed, fortunate that in Wyre a varied and rare fauna exists in association with the glutinous alder.

However, there comes a time in every year when the swelling alder buds feel the pressure of the rising sap and their damson-like bloom is one of the first signs of returning spring.

WILD SERVICE AND THE LIMES

Closely related to the Whitty pear tree (*Sorbus domestica*) is the wild service tree (*Sorbus torminalis*); at least they are placed in the same genus. The Whitty pear is also referred to as the service tree in botanical text books. The name 'Whitty pear', indeed, never receives a mention.

The wild service is an uncommon tree found only in southern and central England, very local in its distribution and it is said that where it does occur it is represented by only a few examples. Only three are known to me in Wyre, but maybe a few have been missed. He would be a boasting man who thought he knew every tree in the forest! All have their trunks within a few feet of Dowles. The wild service is a straggling tree but with wide-spreading branches, and in our Wyre trees they interlace with those of the oaks with which they dispute for the light.

The timber is tough and hard-wearing and within living memory the Dowles trees have been felled and sawn into suitable

Flowering shoot of the wild service tree from Dowles.

pieces for the cogs of wheels and other moving parts of milling machinery. None of these mills now contribute towards the human productivity of the forest. They only remain as names along Dowles such as Furnace, Coopers, Knowles and Town Mills.

If identification of the tree in winter is required then this is somewhat difficult. When the tree is young then the bark is grey, smooth and shiny, with conspicuous corky warts not unlike that of the rowan, but in the older tree the bark is darker, more rugged and somewhat scaly. It then more closely resembles the bark of the apple. The young twigs are rather woolly in appearance. In summer there are no identification problems. The leaves have long thin stalks and there are a number of clefts, increasingly deep the nearer they approach the stalk. The margin is toothed and when young the leaves are woolly beneath but as the leaves become mature the clothing of loose down is lost. Like the Whitty pear, the flowers appearing in April and May, are like those of the pear but borne in a cluster and the fruits are greenish-brown rather like haws. They can be eaten like medlars if they are kept until the onset of decay in November.

The word 'service' used in the popular name deserves some mention. It is not that they 'serve' men, but a drink made from the fermented fruits was known as service from the Latin 'cerevisia', a fermented drink. Perhaps, formerly, they were more abundant. One would be hard pressed today to find sufficient fruits with which to make a brew.

THE LIMES, *Tilia* spp.

Three distinct Lime trees can be distinguished in Britain. Two are separate species and the third is a hybrid between them. This latter is known as the common lime *Tilia cordata × platyphylla*, and indeed this is the tree most commonly found growing in parks and lining avenues. The sticky honey-dew raining from the aphid-infested leaves is a common and undesirable experience for those that park their cars beneath them. Strangely, although the common lime is of hybrid ancestry, it produces viable seed. Hybrids are usually sterile.

The Limes and their allies constitute a rather strange group of shrubs and trees. Jute is made from *Corchorus capsularis*, native to tropical Asia and is related to our limes.

The large-leaved lime, *Tilia platyphylla*, is only considered doubtfully to be of native stock. It is not usual for pollen of this species to be found in peat and other deposits. It has been planted extensively in a few counties of which Worcestershire is one. It is thought to have been naturalised, but usually it requires calcareous or base-rich soil, and it does well on limestone cliffs.

The large-leaved lime is identified by the woolly or downy appearance of the young twigs. The bark is more or less smooth and dark in colour and the leaves, as the common name implies, are large being from six to twelve cms in length. The leaves are also downy on the whole of the under-surfaces, as well as bearing tufts of whitish hairs in the axils of the veins. The inflorescence is a three-flowered cyme held erect.

The small-leaved lime, *Tilia cordata*, is a native British species and this is our Wyre lime. Like the wild service it is to be found along the banks of Dowles but, in addition, it constitutes a component of the old hedges enclosing the small fields. George Jorden, the well-known field botanist of Bewdley of the last century, considered that these old hedges perpetuate our native trees and shrubs which, in other environments, would have perished. Deer will browse on the young shoots if they can get at them.

The small-leaved lime is distinguished from the large-leaved species by, of course, its small leaves being only from three to six cms in length. The young twigs although at first downy soon become shiny. There are no hairs on the undersides of the longer-stalked leaves except for tufts of rusty hairs in the axils of the leaf veins.

The extremely even and fine texture of the timber of lime, together with its whiteness and softness makes it a desirable medium for the wood-carver (Grinling Gibbons used it extensively), and the toy-maker. Alas, today, these are rare accomplishments.

GEAN, *Prunus avium*

*'Loveliest of trees, the cherry now
is hung with bloom along the bough.'*

We, who are so fond of these lines of A. E. Housman from his poem in 'A Shropshire Lad', conjure into our mind a picture of the extraordinarily beautiful old cherry orchards around Wyre when they are covered with frothing bloom. But we should consider the next line which, with the last line, completes the sentence and the verse:

'And stands about the woodland ride
Wearing white for Eastertide.'

So that it was not the orchard tree which filled his mind with its beauty and stimulated the lines, but a cherry of the 'woodland ride'. This is the wild cherry or gean, *Prunus avium*, which is so abundant around Wyre. This is one of our native trees and one of the most beautiful constituents of mixed broadleaved woodlands. Widely distributed in Britain (and in Europe from Scandinavia to western Asia and southwards to North Africa) it generally grows to 40-ft in height but trees up to 60-ft in height and two feet in diameter are known. Surely the tree growing on sloping ground in the late Jack Brown's coppy (coppice) is in this latter category! To an extent it is light demanding so that with few exceptions it is to be found more on the edge of woodland than in the centre.

A flowering shoot of the gean or wild cherry (Button Oak).

The leaves are borne on long red stalks and a pair of glands on the stalk near the junction with the leaf, are said to be attractive to ants.

It is from the gean that the cultivated cherry has been evolved.

Three species of 'cherry' are more or less widely distributed in Britain. Firstly, the gean, or wild cherry, which is the subject of the notes above. Secondly, the bird-cherry, *Prunus padus*, which is a native British species but found only in Scotland and Northern England, but it is also found in Wales, where it grows up to an altitude of 2,000-ft. As far as I know it is not to be seen in Wyre, and Amphlett and Rea did not include it in the 'Botany of Worcestershire'. The cherry-like fruit is black and bitter and the stone is comparatively large. Birds will eat them but they are unpalatable to humans.

The bird-cherry tree is rather small being from 10 to 20-ft in height and the leaves are rather more elliptical than the other cherry species. A mechanism is present which favours cross-pollination. The flowers are erect when they open, and the stigmas mature first, then after the anthers mature the flowers droop. The bird-cherry should be identified with ease from flowering to fruiting time as the ten to forty flowers, and afterwards bluish-black bird-cherries, are borne on a pendulous stalk.

The third species is the sour or dwarf cherry, *Prunus cerasus*, which usually grows as a bushy shrub and wherever it grows a large number of suckers are produced. This has sometimes been taken as diagnostic but is unreliable as the gean will sometimes produce a veritable forest of suckers. The juice of the cherry of this species does not stain the fingers, distinguishing it from the gean, the fruit of which does stain. Another difference between these two species exists in the flowers. The petals of the gean are distinctly notched whilst in those of the sour cherry, a notch can scarcely be discerned.

The wood from the gean is very handsome with red-brown heartwood and yellow or pinkish sapwood, and is fine grained. It is sought after for high quality cabinet work because, in addition to these qualities, it can be compared with oak for strength and its working properties are excellent. But it is not for the timber that we value the gean in Wyre but for the white frosting of its flowers when the woodlands are viewed from a distance, the orange-red leaves of autumn and the shining grey cross-marked bark in winter.

THE SILVER BIRCH AND THE YEW

SILVER BIRCH, *Betula alba*

Who does not know the silver birch, the lady of the forest? There can be few who cannot identify this graceful tree of silver-white, slender trunk, and the tiny mobile serrated leaves set on stiff but cord-like black twigs. In Britain, it has an ancient history and the few tree species that can claim an earlier British distribution, would not normally be recognised as trees, but rather as stunted or ground-hugging shrubs that followed the retreating ice of the last glaciation.

A rather special rule operates with trees with regard to their designation as British native species. It is usual to consider only those species to be native that grew in Britain before the land bridge to continental Europe was washed away. This is thought to have taken place about 4500 B.C., so that no trees that have found their way to Britain within the last 6,500 years, are considered to be truly indigenous species.

The silver birch possesses a number of features which gives it pioneering status. Perhaps most important is the smallness and lightness of the seed; about three-quarters of a million go to make a pound! Under the best conditions only about one-fifth of the seed germinates, but what does that matter when it is produced so abundantly? It grows on almost every type of soil unless it is much too wet or much too acid, such as old heather peat. In Wyre it quickly regenerates, especially along the old timber paths. It is, however, a short-lived tree seldom exceeding 60 to 80 years before the fungus *Polyporus betulinus* attacks it, and before long the large light-coloured brackets can be seen standing out from the trunk.

In Britain, silver birch seldom grows straight and large enough for it to be utilised as timber although in Scandinavia it is an important timber for cutting into veneers, and then it is manufactured into plywood. It also turns well so that a large proportion of small wooden articles that are used in the home, are of birch. In British forestry, however, silver birch is of importance as a nurse or shade-tree, giving protection to young plantations for a few years. It is then cut and sawn up for firewood because it burns well. Longish, spindly timber is often used for rose pergolas on account of the attractive bark, but silver birch is so heavily attacked by wood-rotting fungi, out-of-doors, that it is a mistake to use it for any outside purpose.

Logs of silver birch, lying on the ground, are very quickly attacked by the fungus *Trametes rubescens*, the fruiting bodies of which quickly turn colour to pinkish-purple on being touched.

YEW, *Taxus baccata*

Scattered throughout the forest are the yews. Many are isolated and only in a few areas can one find several yews together. None of them are of large size and it is questionable whether many reach 30-ft in height. After all, the yew is more at home on the chalk of southern England where, both on the North and South Downs, there are a number of natural groves of substantial trees. The yew is not a tree of economic importance, although the timber is often of decorative value on account of the irregular growth-ring configuration, the practically white sapwood, and the sharply demarcated orange-brown to purplish-brown heart-wood. The wood also is often spotted and streaked with darker colours. Yew wood is heavy; indeed, it is the heaviest of all the softwoods, averaging something like 42-lb per cubic foot when seasoned. It is a timber now little appreciated in Britain but on the continent it has many uses in fine furniture, as well as for gateposts as it endures against the wood-rotting fungi of the soil. Before firearms, it was the timber of which the bow was made. The wood was split to give a thin layer of elastic sapwood on the outside and the low compressible heartwood was on the inside.

Our Wyre yews possess scarcely any bole, many consist of a number of gnarled distorted branches with their thin reddish-brown bark springing from near the ground and stretching outwards and downwards. Although the very dark green leaves arise from the stem in a spiral fashion, they form a row on each side. The foliage of yew is harmful to stock and is often fatal, and although some cattle know that it is best left alone it seems to be attractive if it is cut, when it grows in a hedge—with dire results.

Generally, the male and female flowers are borne on separate trees, and each female flower produces a single hard-coated seed surrounded, as in a cup, by a red fleshy outgrowth. This is known as an 'aril'.

There are very few young yew trees and although it is the policy of the Forestry Commission to leave the yews where they grow, until something is done about succession they must inevitably disappear, unless we do something about it!

Some trees on Breakneck Bank are heavily galled by a small fly, *Cecidomyia taxi*. The growth of the shoot tip stops, and the leaves form a tight cluster, the inner ones being nearly white. A single maggot is to be found in each gall, which emerges as a fly in July.

THE FOREST EXOTICS—DOUGLAS AND LARCH

Slightly over 3,000 acres, or rather more than half of the woodland area, of Wyre, is controlled by the Forestry Commission, and since 1928 considerable plantings have been carried out. During the first World War, what growing stocks of commercial timber we had were gravely depleted, many lives were lost and many ships sunk in bringing timber into Britain for essential purposes. A national organisation for growing timber on a vast commercial scale was put into operation and this is our Forestry Commission which today owns one and three quarter million acres of forest. The large number of forest compartments planned for the configuration of the land, and the diversity of tree species have contributed much towards maintaining the Wyre as an amenity for all who are privileged to walk along its quiet paths. Given that commercial timber had to be grown in Wyre, we have been well served by the Commission.

Amongst the exotic trees, that is, trees not native to Britain, Douglas fir and the larches, European and Japanese, have been planted most widely in Wyre.

DOUGLAS FIR, *Pseudotsuga taxifolia*

About 600 acres of this species have been planted in Wyre, the first in 1928. These latter will mature from 1980 to 1990, and the highest have already reached a height of 75-ft. In the fertile valleys they have grown well but have not done so well in the thin leached soils of the upland areas. The Douglas is an interesting tree with a history and a utility which makes it quite outstanding. It is found growing naturally on the Pacific coast of North America from British Columbia to California and it was first collected as a herbarium specimen in 1792 by Archibald Menzies who sailed with Captain Vancouver. It was David Douglas, however, a collector for the Royal Horticultural Society who first sent seeds home in 1825 (some textbooks say 1827) from Fort Vancouver on the Columbia River, and it was from these seeds that the first Douglas fir were grown in Britain. In its native land Douglas fir grows to an immense size, a number reaching a height of 300-ft and 40-ft in girth; its timber when imported is known as Oregon pine, British Columbian pine, red fir, or yellow fir. A number of trees in Britain are known of up to 170-ft in height and one at Powis Castle, Montgomery, is over 175-ft in height, and is thought to be the tallest tree in Britain.

As the Douglas fir in Britain does well, the forester expecting it to grow about two feet annually for 50 years, plantations in Britain are likely to increase in importance. We have to remember, however, that the timber imported into Britain is carefully selected timber growing in an area of several thousands of square miles, the great majority of the trees being passed over or used locally. It is doubtful if British plantation Douglas can compete on these terms until all the accessible high quality trees in

America have been felled. Douglas requires many prunings and
thinnings in our plantations and its timber is not won easily.

To see the Douglas fir as a timber tree at the peak of its
quality, the flagpole at Kew Gardens should be visited. It is
217-ft in height and was cut from a tree on Vancouver Island
in 1948. It replaced a pole 214-ft in height erected in 1919
which weighed 18 tons.

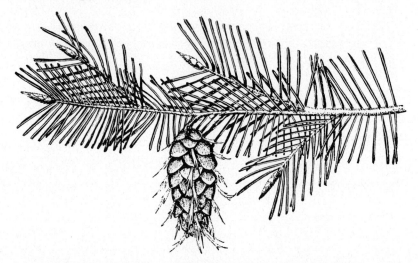

*A shoot of Douglas fir showing the long forked bracts emerging from the cone. There
are about 600 acres of this tree growing in Wyre, originating from the Pacific coast of
North America.*

The growing tree is of splendid aspect when growing in the
open. It is in the shape of a gigantic pyramid. The lowest branches
bend to the ground under their weight. Higher up the branches
are horizontal and feathery, but the topmost branches are
ascending. The smooth, dark grey bark of the young tree bears
resinous 'blisters' but in older trees the bark is rough and often
very thick. The long, pointed, red-brown buds are arranged in
whorls and bear a strong resemblance to those of beech. The
terminal bud is larger than the laterals. The inch-long needles
are parallel-sided but with the apex rounded and they arise in a
spiral fashion from the shoot but they twist round so as to form
a flat spray. The upper surfaces of the leaves are darker than the
lower. The male flowers are only about half-an-inch in length
and are inconspicuous. The female flowers are also small. The
cone is characteristic and it is three or four inches in length,

tapering towards the base and the apex. It hangs downwards from the stem and is light brown. The smooth, overlapping scales are arranged spirally but each is provided with a long three-pointed bract, the centre point of which is the longest and thickest.

EUROPEAN LARCH, *Larix decidua*

Altogether about 500 acres of the old oak coppice of Wyre has been replaced by planting European larch. This commenced in 1928 and the tallest of these older trees are about 48-ft in height. A long-term replacement programme is now in operation whereby over the next twenty-four years or so Douglas fir in the better soils, and Corsican pine, in the thinner soils, will take their place. They will not be clear-felled, but lines or individual trees will be taken out as appropriate, so that from a distance only a gradual change will be seen to take place.

European larch is a native of central and southern Europe where it ascends right up to the timber-line, 6,000-ft in Bavaria and 7,000-ft in Switzerland. It is known to have been introduced into England at some date prior to 1629. A hundred years later the second Duke of Atholl was experimenting with the planting of this species. Of two trees planted in the churchyard at Dunkeld one tree still remains. The fourth Duke of Atholl planted 27 million larch trees on 15,000 acres of poor land.

In spite of its susceptibility to various insect and fungal attacks European larch has proved a successful timber tree in many

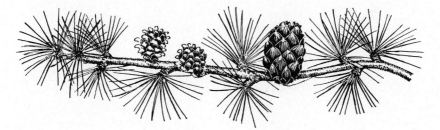

A shoot of European larch (above) *showing the young female flowers, young rosettes of leaves, and an old cone, and* (below) *a cone of Japanese larch showing recurved scales.*

parts of Britain. In Wyre, however, although it has proved useful, Douglas fir can produce about twice as much timber by volume. Wyre is notorious for its late spring frosts in the deep hollows and the soil is often dry and these are two factors which it is known are detrimental to the healthy growth of larch.

Larch is perhaps our easiest conifer to identify. It is deciduous and the bright emerald green rosettes of about 30 one-inch long needles borne on stumpy short shoots are a feature of early spring. The bark is light brown, thick and rough with deep vertical fissures in the older trees. The female flowers are bright fleshy red, scaly and upright, whilst the male flowers are small, yellow, and cylindrical. The cone is oval, erect and light warm brown in colour. The scales are smooth although the outer margins are slightly recurved.

The timber of larch is well sought after as it is very durable, even poles from 15 year old trees are of value. The heartwood is golden brown with a pale yellow, sharply differentiated sapwood.

JAPANESE LARCH, *Larix kaempferi*

About 200 acres of Japanese larch have been planted in Wyre. This species can be separated from European Larch by its distinctly reddish shoots compared with the yellowish of the latter, and in addition the cones are broader and the tips of the scales are more distinctly recurved. Not being an alpine tree where it is native, it can be grown in a rather wider variety of soils and situations than is the case with European Larch, and it is less susceptible to disease.

I wish to acknowledge the help of Mr. R. E. Young, head forester, Forestry Commission, in compiling this section of the book.

SCOTS PINE, *Pinus sylvestris*

No description of the trees of a British forest would be complete without reference to the Scots pine, *Pinus sylvestris*, even though it no longer grew there. That is not to say that we do not have good specimens of this species in Wyre, even though it is certain that they, or their immediate ancestors, would have been planted. But fashions change in the interpretation of those species which should be rightly included in a list of trees of our woodlands. Whatever one's point of view, the Scots pine would cause problems.

After the glaciation of Britain, the Scots pine was one of the first trees to become abundant and it covered a large part of eastern England during the rather dry boreal period which followed, something like 7,000 years ago. At the same time, the forests of Scotland consisted almost entirely of birch. This is because birch is a pioneer. Its small winged seeds, produced in incredible quantities, found their way further and further north, following the receding ice. But birch is a short-lived tree and falls from the killing effects of wood-rotting fungi when it has been growing some 60 to 80 years. Thus, when the earth became dryer at about 2000 B.C., Scots pine increased its range to cover the whole of Scotland. Relics of these old pine forests still exist in Scotland and elsewhere, the remains of Scots pine being found in peat and 'drowned' or submerged forests. There must have been a time, however, when this species had disappeared from Britain, with the possible exception of the old forests of Scotland already mentioned.

Subsequently, probably about the time of James I, Scots pine reappeared, either through planting or from natural re-generation of isolated trees which still remained. Since that time it has grown well, especially in sandy areas of the south, and has been planted and regenerated (where sheep have been excluded), until today, it is the second most common tree in Britain! Oak is the most common tree. In Wyre we have a number of good examples which are rather scattered in distribution, and whilst some have obviously been planted during the last quarter of the last century, the origin of some others is not so certain.

No other pine has anything like its world distribution. Forests of Scots pine are to be found from Lapland in the north to the mountain slopes facing the Mediterranean in the south, and from northern Scotland to western Asia. It is one of the most economically important trees of the world and of great importance to Britain, having been imported from northern Europe for several centuries. Pepys in his diary refers to his purchase of 'swedish deals' for planking when he was Secretary to the Navy, but the timber is referred to by many names, the chief being yellow deal, red deal, redwood, northern redwood and Baltic redwood.

The Scots pine is fairly easy to identify. When young the tree is a symmetrical and graceful pyramid, but then it loses some of its lower branches and thereafter it begins to lose some near the top; after a time the tree becomes flat-topped with a few parallel

The long needles of Scots pine are produced in pairs. The young female cone is green, the scales tightly packed together with a fine red point in the middle of each. On the right, the cone has shed its seeds and now the scales are very loose.

and horizontal branches lower down. These older trees become individual and picturesque. A characteristic of these trees is the bark which is orange-red and shining. As I write, I am looking at a group of three Wyre Scots pine in the evening sun, and the trunks are almost luminescent. Looking at the bark closely, shows it to be papery and scaling, and in the young tree the branches are produced in regular whorls. The long thin needles or leaves may be anything from one to four inches in length and they are quite stiff usually greyish-green in colour, often twisted and margined with minute teeth.

The tightly clustered male flowers turn from red to golden yellow as they mature and the yellow pollen is produced in prodigious quantities. The young female cones are at first green but with a crimson tip to each scale, and in the centre of each 'boss' is a sharp point. They ripen to a light brown colour and vary much in size but in the first hot sunshine of spring the cones open almost explosively and the almost black and sharply-pointed seeds may carry half a mile in the strong breeze before they fall to earth.

The young trees first produce cones when they are about fifteen years old if they have had sufficient sun and thereafter they produce an annual crop, but some years are more prolific than others.

COMMISSION PLANTING

The considerable plantings of Douglas fir, European and Japanese larch, in Wyre have already been referred to but the largest acreage of planted tree species is the 700 or so acres of beech, *Fagus sylvatica*. This is the only broad-leaved tree which has been planted to any extent. Indeed, except for specimen trees of the Whitty pear, beech is the only planted broad-leaved species. The area of the New Parks is perhaps the best to see these new plantings, but some may be replaced where they are not growing well. Usually they have been under-planted to oak which they will eventually overtake. Although the beech is tolerant of the shade cast by the oak, the reverse is not the case.

There has been some controversy in the past as to whether beech is a truly native species. The general opinion seems to be held that there was a period in pre-Neolithic times when beech forests covered the South Downs, but for some reason a period intervened when the trees were no longer able to regenerate, possibly due to rabbits eating the young seedlings and they died out. However, beech must have been re-introduced in earliest historical times since many place names are said to be derived from it, such as Buckingham and, of course, our own Buckridge on the south-west side of the forest. There are many old beeches in Wyre, and beech woodland of considerable antiquity as at Seckley and Oxbind Coppice. When we think of Wyre as a whole, we must keep this tree species in mind.

COMMISSION OAK

Some 300 acres of Wyre held by the Forestry Commission are oak. These are mainly false standards, that is, standard trees which have grown from coppiced stumps. Such timber is not usually of high quality for several reasons. It is prone to various butt and heartrots passed onto it from the old decaying stump, and the root system is often too old to be adequate for the growing tree. A few acres, however, have been planted with new oak. This is a subject of profound importance for those who think of Wyre as a continuity far into the future. Should coppicing be preserved with its high demands on man-power and its low economic return, or should we turn our sights to the far distance and plant a new oak forest from the acorns of selected Wyre trees? Perhaps a compromise should be reached and both points of view implemented.

NORWAY SPRUCE, *Picea abies*

Next of importance as a plantation tree in Wyre is Norway spruce of which about 150 acres have been planted. It is otherwise known as common spruce and although the cones of this species have been found in English Tertiary deposits and it has been cultivated in Britain for at least 400 years, it is usually looked upon as an exotic, even though it is the well-known Christmas tree.

Today it grows naturally over a large part of Europe from the Urals and Lapland to the Pyrenees and the Alps, and reaches an altitude of 6,000-ft in Switzerland. The timber has been given a variety of names usually including the word 'white' such as whitewood, white deal, white fir and white pine.

A number of small stands and individual trees of a number of species of economic value are maintained by the Forestry Commission. It is of great value to have them at Wyre so that they can be seen side by side with the tree species selected to grow on a commercial rotation. In addition, of course, such trees are of value to the forester as they show how the species is likely to grow in the climate and soils of the district. If a change of tree species is desirable at any time in the future then information is already available on a number of factors including the all-important rate of growth.

It should be mentioned that a number of exotic tree species occur in Wyre outside the Forestry Commission's forest, notably in the grounds of Goodmoor Grange, and the avenue from Cooper's Mill on Dowles Brook to Uncles. What a catastrophe for the forest when the giant trees of several species that grew on the 'island' were felled as soon as the Forestry Commission took control! This was a grave mistake and Shropshire lost a

Norway spruce. About 150 acres of Wyre Forest are now planted with this species—the conventional Christmas tree.

glade of some of her most magnificent trees when this occurred. I was always under the impression that whoever planted the avenue of trees mentioned above, planted the island glade also. It was so dry under the spruce that when I camped out under them, as a boy well over fifty years ago, it could rain for several days on end before the water commenced to drip through. The sense of wilderness and of isolation was so intense that kettle and frying pan were hidden for a whole summer amongst the writhing roots of the old yew nearby, that still stands. Strangely, one could not hide a cup amongst its roots today.

The following notes and illustrations refer to these specimen stands and trees in the forest:

WESTERN RED CEDAR, *Thuja plicata*

In the western United States and Canada from Alaska to northern California, this species is an important timber tree. It grows to 200-ft in height in its native districts, but in Britain

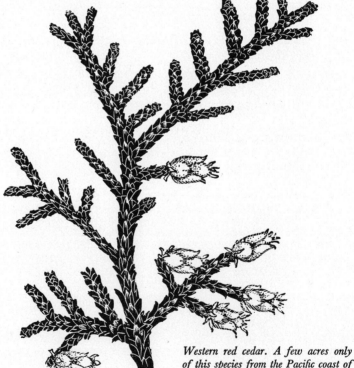

Western red cedar. A few acres only of this species from the Pacific coast of North America are to be found in Wyre.

where it was introduced by Lobb in 1853, a few trees just exceed 100-ft in height. Western red cedar grows much faster in Britain than it does in America which has the advantage of producing more timber of course, but the quality of the resulting product is not always comparable. The heartwood is pale, pinkish-brown to a rather deeper chocolate colour, and very distinct from the narrow pale coloured sapwood. The timber is very resistant to fungal attack and is being used to an increasing extent for exterior cladding of buildings.

The tree when grown singly is a fine ornamental pyramid. The foliage consists of flat, fern-like sprays, the branchlets being covered with overlapping scale-like leaves. This gives it a super-ficial resemblance to the species which follows, Lawson's cypress, but the foliage of *Thuja* when crushed, gives off a very distinctive scent which the cypress does not possess. In addition, the cones of *Thuja* are very small and terminal consisting only of a few scales of characteristic appearance.

LAWSON'S CYPRESS, *Chamaecyparis lawsoniana*

Without a doubt this is the commonest coniferous tree to be found in gardens in Britain where it serves a variety of purposes, the chief being as an evergreen hedge. Its popularity certainly derives from its indifference to soil type. It seems to thrive under almost all conditions. As a forest tree in Britain it is still some-what experimental although in S.W. Oregon and N.W. California it grows to 200-ft in height and may have a girth of 20-ft. It is an important timber being very durable out-of-doors, strongly scented and sometimes called Port Orford cedar. It was intro-duced in Britain in 1854 by Lawson's Nursery, Edinburgh,

Lawson's cypress. The most commonly planted coniferous tree in gardens in Britain.

Scotland. Like western red cedar, the branchlets are flattened and the leaves are scale-like, but they are in pairs and bear white streaks below. The cones are about one-third of an inch in diameter and are ripe in the first year. They regenerate easily.

THE UNDER-STOREY

It is one of the interesting phenomena of forests throughout the world that the foliage exhibits a stratification. Trees that are capable of growing to the greatest height in fierce competition with their neighbours contribute to the forest canopy. In this, the leaves are placed and orientated in such a precise way that the direct rays of the sun are intercepted before any other chlorophyll-containing living organism can reap a benefit. From the sky, and in our modern times through aeroplane travel, we are privileged to enjoy a heaven's eye view of the forest canopy, which resembles a billowy and tempestuous sea. If we look from beneath, say, lying on the ground, we look upwards through the just-opened leaves in a beech wood, and we see the intricate mosaic-placing of the leaves such that the sky can scarcely be seen.

But in our coppiced oakwoods an extensive shrub-layer occurs which is dominated by the hazel. One of the most delightful vistas of the forest is when the hazel leaves are opened almost to their greatest extent as a horizontal layer, just as the buds of the oak have burst into a froth of yellowish-brown, 40-ft above. It is at this moment that one is most appreciative of the under-storey, as the foliage layer of the shrubs is called.

In Wyre, although the hazel is such a common shrub it is by no means the only constituent species of the under-storey. In the rather damper parts of the forest the guelder rose and the alder buckthorn are to be found, the first named identifying itself by its large white inflorescence, although the non-botanist may only find the latter with some difficulty.

HAZEL, *Corylus avellana*

A shrub is a woody plant with a number of woody branches springing from a single rootstock or stool and not reaching a very large size. A tree is characterised by the presence of only a single branch or trunk, and although we look upon a tree as large in size, of course, we cultivate diminutive trees. The hazel

Hazel.

is one of our well-known shrubs. In Wyre, as in most other situations where it grows in woods, it is coppiced. This was carried out about every seven years, the resulting sticks being used extensively for sheep hurdles when 'folding' was practiced. In addition, they were used for a variety of purposes, chiefly for twisting along the top of a laid hedge, certain parts of large baskets (for carrying crockery), and for bean sticks. Of course, the hazelnut was, at one time, a good crop and well worth harvesting. Nowadays, the grey squirrels take the harvest. The entry in Amphlett and Rea is intriguing '. . . though so plentiful a plant, the mediaeval herbalist does not seem to have been able to find any virtue in it'.

The hazel is the earliest flower of spring. The long male catkins hang from the hazel twigs and open in January. The female catkins look like ordinary buds, but with blood-red filaments of the stigmas protruding from the tip. As an entomologist, however, I have to admit that I am reminded most of the hazel over the many square miles of our forest in early July when the oak leaves are at last fully expanded and smothering the under-storey, and I see the strange but very plentiful longhorn beetle, *Judolia cerambyciformis*, hovering over the flowers of hogweed in search of a mate. I know that their larvae spend one or more years burrowing into the old tortuous and knotty stools of the hazel, the main constituent of the Wyre under-storey.

ALDER BUCKTHORN, *Frangula alnus* (=*Rhamnus frangula*)

The alder buckthorn is a spindly, straggling, shrub in Wyre, common along the damp stream sides and boggy places. Perhaps it does not offer much contribution to the under-storey but, nevertheless, it seems to be scattered widely. The leaves are alder-like and the greenish-white flowers grow out of the young woody twigs. The berry-like fruits change colour from green to

The alder buckthorn, Rhamnus frangula.

red, then to a deep violet-black. Like the common buckthorn, it has been used as a purgative in medicine, and the wood as a yellow dye.

The larvae of the brimstone butterfly feed on the leaves of alder buckthorn and in the spring one can watch the light-coloured females fly along the paths and search out these shrubs and lay their eggs upon them.

GUELDER ROSE, *Viburnum opulus*

In striking contrast to the alder buckthorn, for most of the year the guelder rose can be distinguished from quite a distance. In

June and July the creamy-white flat clusters of flowers are conspicuous, the large-petalled ones being sterile. Then, in autumn, the rich ruby-red berries often weigh down the slender twigs and remain on the bushes long after the leaves have fallen. The maple-like leaves too turn crimson before they fall.

The guelder rose of the garden shrubberies is the self-same species, but is a variety in which all the flowers are sterile instead of the outer ones of the wild examples. It must, therefore, be propagated vegetatively, by cuttings or layers.

For Further Reading

ANON., 1941, *Handbook of Home Grown Timbers*, Forest Products Research, H.M.S.O., London.

BOULTON, E. H. B., 1937, *British Trees*, Black, London.

CARTWRIGHT, K. ST. G. and FINDLAY, W. P. K., 1946, *Decay of Timber and its Prevention*, H.M.S.O., London.

CLAPHAM, A. R., TUTIN, T. G. and WARBURG, E. F., 1958, *Flora of the British Isles*, Cambridge University Press.

DARLINGTON, A., 1968, *Pocket Encyclopaedia of Plant Galls in Colour*, Blandford Press, London.

EDLIN, H. L., 1944 (1st Edition), 1945 (2nd Edition), *British Woodland Trees*, Batsford, London.

EDLIN, H. L., 1958, *England's Forests*, Faber and Faber, London.

EDLIN, H. L., 1958, *The Living Forest*, Thames and Hudson, London.

GURNEY, R., 1958, *Trees of Britain*, Faber and Faber, London.

HADFIELD, M., 1957, *British Trees: A Guide for Everyman*, Dent, London.

POKORNY, J. and CHOC, V., 1967, *Trees of Parks and Gardens*, Spring Books, Hamlyn, Feltham, Middlesex.

SALISBURY, E. J., 1925, The Vegetation of the Forest of Wyre, *Journal of Ecology*, **13**:314–21.

STEP, E., N.D., *Wayside and Woodland Trees*, Warne, London.

TANSLEY, A. G., 1949 and 1968 (2nd Edition), *Britain's Green Mantle*, George Allen and Unwin, London.

THE FLOWERING PLANTS OF WYRE

THE EARLIEST FLOWERS OF SPRING

It is characteristic of the north temperate people that they are elated by the first natural signs of spring. After the succession of dull, cold, short days and long, dark, colder nights, the awakening life of the floral world spells a new hope of light and warmth. It is difficult to assign dates; indeed, to judge the throbbing pulse of nature by the calendar is to put oneself into serious error, at least, as far as judging when the flowering of our early plants occurs. Of course, geography, latitude and longitude are all of importance. In this regard, the forest is not well served. In the widespread pattern of deep clefts of the middle coal measures, it is late on winter mornings before the warming sun strikes, but such situations are sheltered from the searching, freezing, cold of the March winds. It cannot be said that the Forest of Wyre enjoys any amenities of climate. How often, on listening to the radio weather news, one hears statements of temperatures several degrees above what is actually being experienced and observed through the windows. 'The temperature will drop to as low as two degrees centigrade.' But all standing water at Wyre is observed to be frozen solid. When the cherry blossom whitens the orchards down the Vale of Severn, it still requires some ten days before those encircling Wyre return the compliment.

There are many plants associated with man's cultivation of the earth that are seldom to be found outside their flowering season. These are the ephemeral weeds, if we may speak in such terms! We shall not include them in our discussions—that is not to say that they are unworthy of our attentions. Indeed, such plants that man, by his own actions has, in a way, domesticated, have a charm and an economy on which I have often pondered. Why has man not 'improved' these ephemeral weeds and made them garden flowers, in flower all the year round?

I think, for our purpose, we should consider plants that flower before, or well before, the middle of April, and in the notes that follow of plants that can be found in Wyre, or around the fringing fields and lanes, common, well-known, and generally distributed species are included, as well as the rarer or more local plants.

SWEET VIOLET, *Viola odorata*

A species identified from the other wild violets, of which there are no less than nine native species, by the fleshy creeping stolon

Sweet violet.

which sends down roots at intervals, and, of course, by its delicate scent. The sweet violet also is characterised by the flower colour mostly being white. This species is not usually found in the woodlands but is most common along the hedge banks and the railway cuttings through the forest. It is often found blooming at the end of March and always during the first week of April.

Other species of violet known from Wyre are the marsh violet, *Viola palustris*, found in boggy situations in woodlands, usually. The flowers are much paler than those found in other violet species and the petals are marked with veins. Hairy violet, *Viola hirta*, resembles the sweet violet but possesses no scent, nor does it spring from a creeping stolon. The leaves and leaf-stalks are hairy. Pale wood violet, *Viola reichenbachiana* and common violet, *Viola riviniana*, do not come into flower until the sweet violet is going out of bloom from the middle of April and later. Dog violet or heath violet, *Viola canina*, also flowers rather later than the sweet violet.

MARSH MARIGOLD, *Caltha palustris*
The brilliant golden yellow flowers and the thick fleshy leaves and stems of the marsh marigold or kingcup are often in evidence as early as the end of March. Due to forestry drainage there are

The marsh marigold, Caltha palustris, *said by Amphlett and Rea to be one of the best-known flowers of the countryside and in the garlands carried about the villages on May Day, it was the one flower certain to be conspicuous. Times have changed, the human pressures have drained the marshes, ditches and village ponds, and now I only know one locality in the forest where I could be certain to find it!*

not now many boggy or marshy spots along the Dowles. I warrant it is much less common than it was when George Jorden trod the woods a hundred years ago! But as Amphlett and Rea truly say '. . . flowering at a time when everybody is ready to welcome the floral signs of coming Summer.' Strangely, the place where I always know I can find the kingcup in Wyre is where it grows cheek by jowl with the only remaining few plants of cottongrass, and is perhaps not far from a possible site of the Great Bog of Wyre.

The kingcup has great interest botanically in that it can be considered as a 'primitive' flower. The family RANUNCULACEAE to which it belongs shows a simple arrangement of the various floral parts and in all other families of flowering plants the flower is more complex, but must have been derived from these early origins seen in the RANUNCULACEAE.

WILD STRAWBERRY, *Fragaria vesca*

Along many of the pathside banks, especially the south-facing ones, and the old railway banks, the white flowers of the wild strawberry occur from early April. Soon afterwards the small sharp-tasting fruits can be picked. It is a member of the family

Wild strawberry, Ford Lane Crossing.

ROSACEAE. The cultivated varieties are not derived from this species but originate from North America. A cultivated variety, indeed, has become naturalised over a considerable part of a railway cutting and those who know of this make a good picking. The plants look tired and flagged at the end of the season.

LESSER CELANDINE, *Ranunculus ficaria*

This very abundant plant has been recorded as a Worcestershire plant as long ago as 1650. It is one of the many species of the family RANUNCULACEAE. It is to be found in almost every damp situation around Wyre, even in very shady situations. As a harbinger of Spring it 'stars the banks and meadows with gold before the winds of March have blown themselves away'. There are three sepals whilst the number of petals varies from eight to twelve. The fleshy dark green leaves are poisonous to cattle, but are generally avoided.

Lesser celandine (Goodmoor Cottage).

Wood anemone (The Newalls).

WOOD ANEMONE, *Anemone nemorosa*
This common and widely distributed plant is especially abundant throughout Wyre. It is a gregarious plant, and at flowering time, from March to May, it occurs in large snow-like drifts under the

oaks spilling out into the surrounding fields. The brown perennial rhizome sends up a flowering shoot in early spring consisting of a single flower and two or three leaves. The number of petals is variable, usually six or seven, but from five to nine is not uncommon and there is much variation also in the extent of a pinkish suffusion to the petals. Indeed, they are sometimes reddish purple, the leaves being tinged with this colour also.

It is a member of the family RANUNCULACEAE.

COLTSFOOT, *Tussilago farfara*

The bright yellow dandelion-like flowers of this perennial plant seem to push up overnight on every bit of waste-land after a warm day or two in March. This is long before the leaves appear as the solitary flowers terminate the special woolly and scaly shoots. There is considerable movement of the flowers. The buds are erect, then the flowers open by day and shut at night! The head droops after flowering, then when the fruits ripen it erects

Coltsfoot (Furnace Mill).

again. Coltsfoot is included in the 'daisy' family, the COMPOSITAE. It was and, indeed, still is in some quarters, thought to be a remedy for coughs and colds, and the dried leaves were smoked as an asthma cure.

JORDEN'S FLORAL GEMS

How fortunate for us now, that George Jorden, who spent some time of almost every day of his life in our forest, made a collection of the plants which he found there. He was a discerning botanist able to detect minute differences in structure, habit and taste, amongst the plants that came his way. But perhaps that is not unusual as he collected plants for medicinal purposes, prescribed by Dr. Fryer of Bewdley, for whom he worked. He it was who first realised that more than one species was to be found amongst our wild thyme which is to be found on the dry heathland around the forest. He first tasted them and found that one, *Thymus chamaedrys*, had a pungent biting taste and a powerful scent, whilst *Thymus serpyllum* had very little taste or smell. After fifty years of wandering in Wyre he published a paper in the first volume of the *Phytologist* and enumerated the plants that he had found. His collection of dried plants eventually made their way to the Hastings Museum at Worcester and two or three years ago, hunting around in dark cupboards, I found his forgotten *Flora Bella Locus*, as he called it, wrapped up in dusty brown paper. It deserves a better fate.

I am not a trained botanist, my professional training having been in entomology, the study of insects, so that I cannot claim to have the same degree of plant discernment as one who has spent his life looking at plants. I have not found a number of the plants that Jorden found. But that is not to say that they no longer grow in the forest, I may not have found them.

It has not been my good fortune to find the air heavy with the scent of the fragrant orchid, *Gymnadenia conopsea*, around the Great Bog as did Jorden in his time. I have never found the fragrant orchid, nor for that matter have I ever found the Great Bog! Some of the floral treasures found by Jorden in Wyre died out in his day. The 'summer lady's tresses', *Spiranthes aestivalis*, collected by Jorden in the Great Bog has never been found again. This appears to be the only specimen ever found outside the New Forest in Hampshire.

But it has been my good fortune to find a number of Jorden's floral treasures in the forest, often in the self-same places as where he saw them and many of his notes as to the situations favoured by these plants are just as true today. Of course, many plants which Jorden thought rare or uncommon, which he was so pleased to collect, are species often commonplace in other parts of the country. We have to understand that Jorden spent the whole of his long life within a radius of Bewdley to which he could walk. Apparently he never journeyed further than Ludlow Castle. Today, with our increasing mobility, the botanist is able to look at our country's floral wealth through eyes viewing wider horizons.

It is impossible, within a short space, to view the Wyre flora through Jorden's eyes. Three plants have, therefore, been chosen from amongst the rarities he found, for some descriptive notes. They are still in the Forest.

INTERMEDIATE WINTERGREEN, *Pyrola media*

All three British species of wintergreen have been recorded from Wyre, the intermediate and the lesser by George Jorden. Mrs. Quayle showed me where the intermediate wintergreen was still to be found in Rock Coppice. The bloom is very much like that of lily-of-the-valley, but the flowers are pinkish-tinged and in contrast to the very light green leaves of the latter plant, those

Intermediate wintergreen (Rock Coppice).

of the intermediate wintergreen are dark green and edged with minute spikes. The leaves spring from a rhizome which creeps through the forest litter at the base of the stringy bilberry.

BLOODY CRANESBILL, *Geranium sanguineum*

The colour of the petals of this rather bushy perennial cranesbill is a bright purplish-crimson and the name, both specific and popular, is derived from this. It is a plant of alkaline soils and, thus, it is local. It is also a plant of the north, being rare in the south-west and, indeed, absent from south-east England. It was first recorded in Wyre by W. G. Perry for the Shropshire side of Dowles Brook in 1841, and for the Worcestershire side by Gissing, in the first volume of the *Phytologist* in 1851, and George Jorden referred to it on a number of occasions. Its usual stations are on the Shropshire side of Dowles Brook where the little streamlets run into the brook from the north. Presumably, these are all streams that have traversed the relatively small beds of Spirorbis limestone, but it is probably significant also that all the plants occur on the south-facing side of the bank. Jorden remarked that 'scarcely a stray plant ever gets on the Worcestershire side of the brook', referring, of course, to the point that generally the plants are found on the Salop side. Wyre Forest is the only locality for Worcestershire for this plant but Amphlett and Rea

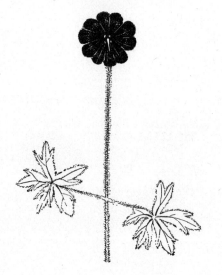

Bloody cranesbill.

Long-leaved helleborine.

remark 'this county (Worcestershire) has, therefore, hardly a colourable claim to the plant'.

One plant, I know, has grown in its present position for at least ten years. It is in a cleft in the south-facing bank where a small stream runs through. The plant is in shade yet flowers early, blooms being well advanced in mid-June, whereas Clapham, Tutin and Warburg give July and August as the flowering period. Within a few hundred yards the wood cranesbill, *Geranium sylvaticum*, is locally abundant, the masses of its blue-violet flowers being a feature of the area. This is now a young plantation of conifers which, as they grow, will, in a few years, blot them out of existence, but that is how nature acts. Then, when the trees are felled in the years to come, the same plant species will invade the new area. This is if the forest is then large enough, or on a sufficient scale, for the plants to exist within seed-throwing distance.

LONG-LEAVED HELLEBORINE, *Cephalanthera longifolia*

This plant, also called narrow-leaved helleborine and sword-bladed helleborine, was known in Wyre by Jorden and the other botanists who collected in the forest, just over a hundred years ago. But unlike a number of the rare and unusual plants that were to be found then, but have now apparently disappeared, this delicately beautiful white-flowered orchid is still to be found. To start a search for it during its flowering period of May to July would be embarking on a herculean task, without some clue as to its whereabouts. In 1963, making a thorough search, I found 34 flowering spikes, all under beech and all not very distant from old timber-hauling tracks.

The long-leaved helleborine is local and rare in Britain so that in Wyre it is to be treasured.

DANCING COLUMBINE, *Aquilegia vulgaris*

It is often difficult to put a name to a plant that one considers characteristic of a region in which one has special interest. Obviously everyone approaches the natural history of an area from different standpoints. The considerations of some would be coldly scientific related to the degree of dominance of the different members of the plant community. Others might regard rarity as the criterion. In my own case I am aware that plants appeal to me for a variety of reasons but particularly I believe when a plant fits its environment within narrow limits that is when a plant is

adapted to flourish only under certain restricted conditions. An
example of this is the occurrence in the mainly acid conditions
of Wyre of the lime-loving (and beautiful) bloody geranium,
Geranium sanguineum. But it is to be found only in the vicinity of
the small areas of Spirorbis limestone, or at the sides of streamlets which have passed through such areas. But why should the
Columbine play a part in my thoughts when I think of the

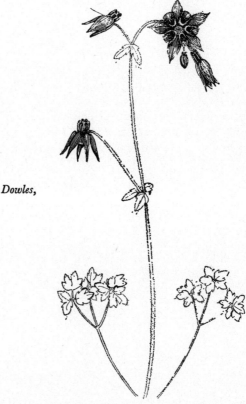

The wild columbine from Dowles,
Aquilegia vulgaris.

Wyre flora? *Aquilegia vulgaris,* for that is the name of the wild
Columbine, grows, often in profusion, as a truly wild and indigenous plant along Dowles and bordering a number of the paths
and damp rides that lead down to the brook. It has been known
there for well over a hundred years; indeed, it has been known
from Worcestershire as a wild plant since 1787. George Jorden,
the Bewdley botanist, of a hundred years ago, who knew the
forest and the trees and plants within it, like the back of his

hand, knew the columbine well and recorded it as from Furnace Coppice to Bewdley. Hickman also recorded it from Ribbesford Wood and Lickhill, Bewdley. The name *Aquilegia* is derived from the Latin *Aquila*, an eagle, but in what context I do not know. Amphlett states that this was from the form of the petals but I still cannot understand. The common name columbine, on the other hand, can be found in literature from the earliest times, although it has sometimes been assigned to species other than our *Aquilegia*. The inverted flowers have some similarity to a group of five pigeons clustered together.

It is a perennial plant which each spring marks its position by a tuft of delicately-coloured foliage of characteristic kidney-shaped leaflets before sending up a cluster of erect shoots up to about three feet high. The flowers usually open from late May to July and are dullish blue in colour, but sometimes reddish and white ones occur not infrequently. The long blunt-ended spurs contain nectaries and are visited by the bumble bees whose tongues are long enough for the purpose.

FLOWERS OF THE SHADE

In the forest and around its edges there is much shade. The trees have won the light by their habit of producing woody tissue and, thus, they are able to grow higher with every succeeding season. But many shrubs and herbaceous plants have become adapted to the varying shade conditions of growth near and under trees. One well-known, but interesting, feature of adaptation to shade is shown in the forest wherever the oak grows. Now, oak, and ash too, of course, do not produce their leaves until late in Spring and even when the buds have burst, the leaves are small and are remarkably slow to develop to their full size. But in the early spring the oak coppices possess a ground carpet of plants that have reached their zenith and are flowering whilst the oaks still appear much as they did in mid-winter. The green carpet of low-growing dog's mercury, *Mercurialis perennis*, with its inconspicuous yellowish-green flowers is one example of an early spring plant, but the bluebell, *Endymion nonscriptus*, is the plant which perhaps springs first to mind. But, whereas dog's mercury reaches dominance in the ground carpet on the calcareous soils in beech woods, the bluebell prefers light acid soils such as we have in Wyre.

Immediately following the flowering of these early herbs the shrub layer bursts into leaf. In our forest this is mainly the hazel, *Corylus avellana*, but the alder buckthorn, *Frangula alnus*, is also to be found with it.

Of the four herbs illustrated, two flower in the spring, usually around mid-May in Wyre, these are ramsons and cuckoo pint, whilst the third, enchanter's nightshade, blooms over a much longer period, usually from June to August. Lily-of-the-valley, the fourth, does not usually flower until the end of May and lasts for a few weeks only.

ENCHANTER'S NIGHTSHADE, *Circaea lutetiana*

Why this little plant should be called after Circe, the enchantress, is lost in antiquity, but the dense shady places around the forest

Enchanter's nightshade.

where this delicate, seemingly fragile, little plant extends its spike of tiny flowers, often give the feeling of magic. Unfortunately, it has often been given the status of a weed but we must express disagreement with Amphlett and Rea when they state that it has nothing in its appearance to recommend it. When one comes across it in little drifts in the dark corners of the woods, sometimes late in the year, one cannot help but exclaim 'enchanter's nightshade!' before passing on to where the sun is able to pierce the summer foliage.

This perennial herbaceous plant is one of the most successful in its adaption to the conditions of shade and although it thrives best in base-rich soils it can be found around the forest in damp ill-lit situations where, obviously, conditions are to its liking.

RAMSONS, *Allium ursinum*

From about the middle of May for a few short weeks all the valley bottoms of Dowles become spangled with the white star clusters of ramsons set on a thick lush carpet of its bright green broad leaves. Over long stretches of the five mile brook length, under the shade of oak and hazel, it is not only the dominant species of the carpet flora, but it occurs almost to the exclusion of all other species of flowering plants. The flower heads are borne on long stalks setting them high above their leaves and are a sight worthy of a visit to see them alone.

This member of the family LILIACEAE is a close relative of the onion, as its alternative common name of broad-leaved garlic implies. That is why it still grows in such profusion. It is seldom picked. As one walks through the leaves the bruises produce an overpoweringly repellent smell of garlic. It is quite impossible to picnic amongst it. Its name is said to be derived from an ancient word rams whose plural was ramsen. This had subsequently been given an additional plural ending and modified to ramsons.

Admire ramsons from a distance!

LILY-OF-THE-VALLEY, *Convallaria majalis*

The lily-of-the-valley is one of the forest gems and is to be found very commonly at a number of widely dispersed locations. At a few of these it gets picked rather heavily so that it is surprising

Ramsons or broad-leaved garlic.

Lily-of-the-valley (Unéless).

that it survives. The joy is that it does! It occurs mainly on
calcareous soils so that to find it growing together with the acid-
loving bilberry, *Vaccinium myrtillus*, in Wyre, is something out of
the ordinary. Lily-of-the-valley is one of the most widely-known
of plants and its scent is sweet and delicate. It flowers towards
the end of May and into June. The very day that I write this is
27th May, and I have been to visit one of its sites, to find the
slender one-sided racemes with the nodding buds not yet opened.

CUCKOO PINT, *Arum maculatum*
The family ARACEAE to which the cuckoo pint belongs is one of
the most exciting groups of plants in the world. I suppose when

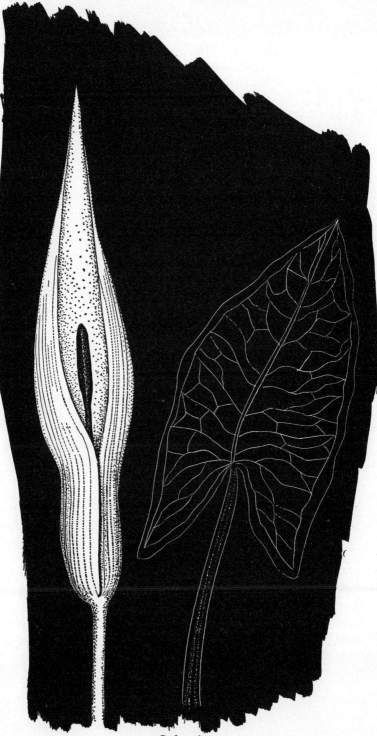

Cuckoo pint.

one has travelled down one of the great South American rivers, or gone inland into Central America, and seen the great mass of fleshy plants with arrow-shaped leaves, and with a great spathed inflorescence, trailing or climbing over the shrubs and trees, one looks at our cuckoo pint with more than usual interest. Like a large number of its tropical relatives it is very shade tolerant, but it is not so tolerant of lack of nutrients; so that it is in the forgotten places, in old dark orchard corners, where the cuckoo pint is to be found. Some points of special interest; the mono-cotyledons, to which the ARACEAE belong, have the special characteristics of having longitudinal veins on the leaves, but the ARACEAE have net-veined leaves, so are exceptional. Often, but not always, the leaves are splotched with black, hence *maculatum* of the specific name, meaning spotted. Cuckoo pint is more especially abundant in calcareous soils and in the forest it is not common, it is only around the bordering orchards where one comes across it. The starch from its tubers was used for stiffening the ruffs of the Elizabethan period and Gerarde in his 'Herbal' called it the starch-wort.

PLANTS OF DOWLES BANK

It seems strange that George Jorden found the willow-leaved spiraea (*Spiraea salicifolia*) along the banks of Dowles. He speaks of it as a very common plant in his day. As an indigenous plant it is found no further north in Europe than central France and yet it appears to naturalise itself very easily on wet river and stream banks, particularly in Wales, northern England and southern Scotland. However, 50 years or so later it had dis-appeared from Dowles except for gardens where today it still thrives, but only as a flowering shrub under some degree of cultivation. This latter amounts to a somewhat ruthless cutting down at least once a year. It had also disappeared by the turn of the century in other places in Worcestershire where it had once thrived, such as Welland Common. My illustration of the fluffy pink inflorescence is from the garden of Goodmoor Grange.

The meadow sweet of the same genus, *Spiraea ulmaria*, is one of the most common plants of the little wet meadows along Dowles and bordering the tributary streamlets. From high summer the strong and sweet perfume—sometimes sickly sweet—pervades the hot still days.

The willow-leaved spiraea (Goodmoor Grange).

Toothwort (*Lathraea squamaria*) is an anomaly. It is a green plant that is not green as, indeed, are all those plants we classify in the family OROBANCHACEAE. These are the two 'toothworts' and eleven 'broomrapes' now in the British list of plants, but the 'toothwort' or 'greater toothwort' is the only species found in Wyre and although all these root parasites, because that is how they make a living, are never common and most are rare, toothwort can be easily found in Wyre by all those who care to search. It is exceptionally common along the banks of Dowles, wherever the hazel bush grows and on the roots of which the underground rhizomes of this parasite attach themselves. What we see of the plant in early spring is a pale ivory

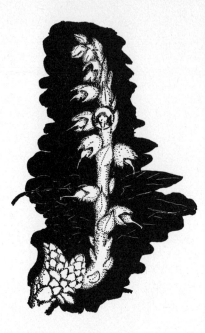

Toothwort (Taylor's Bridge).

coloured flower-spike with a purplish tinge pushing up in small groups around the bases of hazel bushes in 'moist places'. Along Dowles this means within 20-ft or so of the bank. I found that George Jorden of Bewdley had recorded the plant from Wyre over a hundred years ago. Although it does occur on the Worcestershire side of the brook it appears to be far more common on the Shropshire bank.

The long spikes of purple loosestrife (*Lythrum salicaria*) often enliven the banks of Dowles, at least where there are open meadows. It becomes more common as the Dowles approaches the Severn. Indeed, if one failed to find it in the forest then one should search the banks of the Severn from the site of old Dowles Church to Bewdley Town. This is not a hiding plant as it often grows to four feet tall and the dense colour of the flowers, although simply described as 'purple' in the modern flower books, appear reddish-purple to me.

Botanically it is an extraordinary flower in that it occurs in three distinct forms. In one the style is short and the stamens are long and medium in size. In the second, the style is medium whilst the stamens are long and short, and in the third the style is long and the stamens are short and medium in size. In addition,

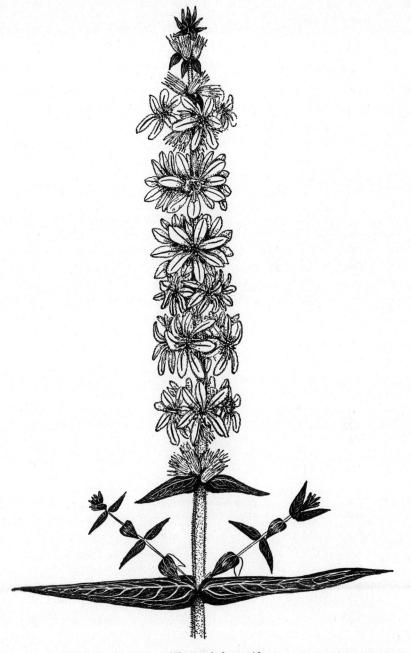

The purple loosestrife.

the pollen grains exist in three distinct sizes, according to the length of the stamens.

Technically purple loosestrife is known as a Helophyte or marsh plant but in Wyre we do not see it playing this role, only as a marginal water plant. Amphlett records it as 'one of the handsomest of our native plants', and I note that his eye is similar to my own and he refers to the colour as a deep purplish red.

TRAILING PLANTS OF WYRE

It comes as a surprise to many to find that the creeping jenny, *Lysimachia nummularia,* of our rockeries is a British native plant. Even so, it is thought that in many of its localities it exists only as an escape from cultivation. In damp, shady situations, it is a vigorous grower and the trailing stems with the root tuftlets must be trimmed ruthlessly. The trimmings are tipped away and from village tips in dark little stream valleys it often flourishes beyond expectations. Strangely, its fruits never ripen in Britain so that its entire distribution is occasioned by such vegetative reproduction. To see creeping jenny as a truly native plant growing wild, we must walk up the tributary streams of Dowles into the minute marshy flats. In high summer when the meadow sweet is blooming the vegetation is long, thick and lush but creeping and trailing in the shaded areas the creeping jenny is to be found, the pure yellow bells profusely produced alternately with the small shining circular leaves

At The Newalls I reversed the usual process and brought a

Creeping Jenny, a trailer in the damp valley bottoms and meadows with deep yellow cup-shaped flowers.

sprig of it back from Cook's Green and planted it in front of the house where it flourishes still.

Two species of periwinkle occur in Britain and both are to be found in Wyre in a wild state, although whether they originally came from a barrowload of garden refuse tipped in the hedge, it would be hard to give a firm opinion. The periwinkles are the sole representatives in Britain of a family of plants of great significance in tropical areas of the world.

The light-blue or bluish-mauve salver-shaped flowers of the periwinkle are some of the earliest flowers to be seen. As well as the foliage being evergreen they seem also to be ever-flowering. The shape of the petals is of great interest, there being a short and a long side to each petal giving the flower a propeller-shape. In habit we must look upon the periwinkles as shrubs

Lesser periwinkle, a trailer of the dry banks with light-blue-purple salver-shaped flowers.

because the long thin trailing stems do not die away, although ultimately the older parts lose their leaves. They never seem to set their seed in Britain in spite of flowering so profusely.

The lesser periwinkle, *Vinca minor*, is identified from the greater *Vinca major*, by the smaller flowers, which are only about an inch across, whereas in the greater they are almost twice this size; by the leaf stalks being very short whereas in the greater they are at least a quarter of an inch in length, and by the leaves being shiny and devoid of hair whilst in the greater the leaves are somewhat hairy. The long-tongued bees and the equally long-tongued hovering bee flies can be seen sucking the nectar, the latter in the very first warm days of spring. The flowers secrete a sticky material which gets transferred to the bee fly's tongue and when it is withdrawn the pollen grains stick to it and thus get carried to other periwinkle flowers and so fertilisation takes place.

The greater periwinkle was noted by Amphlett from Wyre but not the lesser; both now occur being especially abundant on drier banks around the old Wyre Forest Railway Station and the bridge over Dowles at Furnace Mill.

PLANTS THAT JUMP OVER THE HEDGE

Plants find themselves on the other side of the garden hedge for a variety of reasons. On the one hand, plants are cultivated in gardens that have originated in countries far away; they can, on occasions, be found outside gardens! This may be due to the seeds being distributed by natural means or trimmings and prunings which are carted away to a rubbish heap or waste patch outside the garden. Sometimes, of course, such plants may be naturalised deliberately. The plants or seeds may be transferred from the garden to woods, banks or pasture, to take their chance with England's native flora. There are a number of variants of these processes, but the reverse often takes place. Our native plants may be transferred from their natural places where they grow into gardens and these offered some degree of cultivation. This, unfortunately, often takes place today. Primroses are pulled up and planted in gardens, often with little chance of survival. It is certain, however, that this process has taken place on a very large scale in the past. A number of our rare native plants are commonly found in our country gardens. Examples can be given of native plants that have been taken

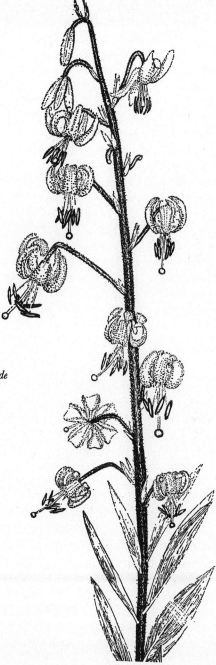

The martagon lily from a roadside verge.

into garden cultivation for some years then have become garden 'escapes' and naturalised themselves back into the countryside.

The two species of lily listed in the English Floras are of interest to us in Wyre. These are martagon lily, *Lilium martagon* and *Lilium pyrenaicum* whose common name appears to be lost in antiquity. They are both typical lilies with a bulb of loose fleshy scales without an outer skin, but they are easily distinguished at the flowering stage. The flowers of the martagon are purplish, whilst those of *pyrenaicum* are yellow. Both species are common inhabitants of the old cottage garden from whence they spill out to the adjacent road verges and woods. Neither plant appeared in the 'Flora' of Bentham and Hooker, but it seems a more tolerant view is now taken of the status of many of our plants. However, it seems possible that the martagon was once native, being found in Surrey and Gloucestershire. It is feasible that these plants disappeared from their natural haunts and found their way into country gardens and now, to some small extent, the process is reversed. Edwin Lees records one locality for *pyrenaicum* as 'the left bank of brook falling into Dowles Brook, Wyre Forest'. This seems a goodly distance from any habitation.

The illustration of a martagon is from a plant growing on a road verge just the other side of the fence from a clump growing in the garden of a dwelling near the old rail line.

STAR-OF-BETHLEHEM, *Ornithogalum umbellatum*

This liliaceous plant is doubtfully native to Britain. If it is an indigenous plant, then eastern England seems to have been its home. The long thin leaves are somewhat fleshy and are characterised by the midrib being grooved and white in colour. From 4 to 15 white flowers are borne on the flowering stem and the perianth segments, or, less accurately, the petals, each bears a dark green stripe on the back.

Star-of-Bethlehem was recorded for Wyre Forest by George Jorden whose list of rare plants to be found in Wyre Forest and the vicinity of Bewdley was given in the Botany of Worcestershire by Edwin Lees in 1867. It is of interest to note also that the drooping Star-of-Bethlehem, *Ornithogalum nutans*, also appears in this list. April to June is the period of blooming but, unfortunately, they soon get picked. This is a great pity because the plants are well distributed around the forest on hedgebanks, and if they could set seed then they could become an interesting and beautiful feature of the forest edge. Surprisingly there is one

Star-of-Bethlehem from a roadside verge.

steep roadside bank almost entirely isolated from human interference in Welch Gate where the Star-of-Bethlehem grows in
some profusion. It is protected by the constant thunder of traffic
which passes within a few feet. Picking there would be at the
risk of life or limb!

MUSK, *Mimulus moschatus*

Musk is a hairy little perennial with bright green leaves. The
flowers are purest yellow. This 'is the common musk of the
garden' as Amphlett and Rea wrote, and it hails from the Pacific
States of North America—British Columbia to California. This
is the species that once possessed the smell of musk, but which
no longer does. How this came about is a botanical or genetical
mystery.

It was reported from near Dowles Brook, Wyre Forest, many
years ago by a Mr. W. G. Perry, the record being published in
Leighton's Flora of Shropshire, as long ago as 1841. Now it is
not much grown in gardens, but this enlivening little plant still
stays with us. I have never found it in the forest but the plants
I know are not a foot high and they grow from between the
crevices in some old brickwork. For many years it has grown in
a small area in front of a shop, actually in the centre of Bewdley.
Conditions must be to its liking or it could not have survived for

Musk grows in Bewdley Town.

Green hellebore, only now in gardens.

perhaps half a century or more in this unlikely spot. But this is one of the joys of botanical exploration, even in our own well-trodden country. The most surprising plants occur in the most unusual places.

If either of the two indigenous British species of hellebore ever grew around Wyre it must have been before man recorded the plant life around him. But it was not until the middle of the nineteenth century that man took up his pen to do so. They are lime-loving plants so that perhaps they never did well in the predominantly acid conditions of our forest.

The two hellebores, *Helleborus viridis* and *Helleborus foetidus*, are both referred to as 'green' and also referred to by the common name of 'bear's foot', but the latter species is additionally known as 'stinking hellebore'. Both are recorded from the Clee Hills over a hundred years ago. The particular attribute of the hellebores is the contrasting greens of the foliage and the flowering stem. Indeed, they are of striking appearance as early as March.

But *Helleborus viridis* is to be found in old gardens around Wyre where it has held its place over many years.

Corydalis solida

Almost everyone must have noticed the yellow fumitory, *Corydalis lutea*, growing in fleshy clusters of ferny foliage from the crevices in old walls. The subject of this note is a closely related species with the same succulent and ferny habit of the leaves, but the blooms are much larger and of a dull reddish-purple colour. Behind each flower is a long straight spur in which bees thrust their long tongues for nectar. It is not a native plant but is indigenous to a large part of Europe from Finland to the Pyrenees and is found in Asia too.

Those who wish to see this most unusual plant growing naturalised along a hedge bank must look very early in the year. The purple spikes are visible with the first flush of greenness on the hedge bottom in April. An old forest cottage is nearby from which it originated, perhaps many years ago. Look for a hedge within a few yards of the old railway.

ORANGE HAWKWEED, *Hieracium aurantiacum*

The hawkweeds, the genus *Hieracium*, has never been a favourite group of mine. I can only think that, looking superficially rather like dandelions, I connected them, when I was a very small boy, with this latter plant and its common name of 'wet-the-bed'.

Corydalis solida (*near Wyre Forest Railway Station*).

The orange hawkweed growing in a forest rubbish tip.

Hieracium aurantiacum, however, is the only member of the genus which I could not only recognise, but with which I feel a bond of friendship. First of all it differs from all other species of the genus, as far as I am aware, in having brilliant brick-red to orange coloured flowers instead of the lemon or canary yellow of other species. It shares, however, the common character of having very hairy leaves and stalks; indeed, the hairs are often more than a quarter of an inch in length. I have seen it growing wild on the lower slopes of the Tatra Mountains near the Polish border of Czechoslovakia and also in the Goc Mountains of Yugoslavia, but I know a little patch of it in the forest, on the Salop side of Dowles. It is not far from a cottage front garden from which it was once obviously 'an escape', as it was at one time a common 'rock-garden' plant, but it has been in the forest for at least 30 years to my knowledge!

PLANTS OF THE FRINGING HEDGES

When George Jorden, the Bewdley Botanist, was persuaded to write a paper on the botany of Wyre Forest for the first volume of the *Phytologist*, he gave some account of the old trees in the hedgerows. This was some hundred years ago and Jorden pointed out the importance of the hedges as indicating which of our tree species are indigenous. He said 'they truthfully record the arboreal history of our primitive forests'. In this regard, Jorden records the occurrence of the small-leaved lime, *Tilia parvifolia*, in the old hedges (and also mentions one blown down at Dowles in 1846 that measured 17-ft 7-in in circumference when measured 7-ft from the ground). The old hedges were of great importance to our forebears for providing wood for burning, when wood was the only fuel for the hearth and the old trees of the hedge were pollarded and coppiced times without number.

The importance of our hedgerows today lies in different reasons, or really we can consider that it is an extension of the same reason which Jorden explained. Our hedges are natural harbourages for our wild life, not only for the shrubs and trees which can be laid, cut, and trimmed, but the banks and ditches, and the hedge bottoms, provide the only living space now available for a high proportion of our native plants and animals when the intensive economy of our fields has denied them of all else.

So that we look to the hedges, just as Jorden did a hundred years ago, in order that we may see today our own native flora and fauna still able to thrive, even if still vulnerable to population pressure of many different kinds.

MUSK MALLOW, *Malva moschata*

Closely related to the lime tree, just mentioned, but in a separate family are the mallows. In the hedges around Wyre we have a rather uncommon species of mallow, the musk mallow, *Malva moschata*, as well as the common mallow, *Malva sylvestris*. Indeed, we see the latter species here and there in quite spectacular abundance. But where the hedges divide the little forest fields, and rather more uncommonly along the lane-side, we see the musk mallow. This perennial plant is characterised by its large silver-rose flowers being bunched together at the end of the stem. The leaves also are deeply divided and whereas both

Musk mallow. *The silver-pink flowers shine out from the hedge. Smell them to see if you perceive the odour of musk (Sugar Lane).*

species have hairy stems and leaves, the musk mallow is much the hairier of the two. It is said that the flowers are slightly scented with musk, a scent which is rather more powerful in the evenings. A white variety is listed as occurring elsewhere in Worcestershire, but it has escaped my notice in Wyre.

FLEABANE, *Inula dysenterica*

Quite an uncommon plant in the Midlands is one of the numerous members of the family COMPOSITAE, fleabane, *Inula dysenterica* (sometimes the genus is given as *Pulicaria*). But on the Shropshire side

Fleabane. *The masses of golden-yellow daisy-like flowers have a special attraction for butterflies.*

of the forest the damp hedges are sometimes golden with the yellow daisy-like flowers of fleabane. Fletcher's Coppice can usually be relied upon to provide this thrilling floral sight. The leaves and stems are very woolly and the narrow leaves clasp the stem with a pair of ear-like projections which encircle it.

Where it does occur, fleabane is abundant, the whole damp ditch-side being covered with the plant. The mass of golden-yellow flowers in August and September is a great attraction to butterflies and other insects, which is something of a paradox as the dried flowers have been used in the past for insecticidal purposes, as the common name would suggest.

FIGWORT, *Scrophularia nodosa*
One of the most widely-distributed plants of the Wyre Forest hedgerows is the figwort, *Scrophularia nodosa*. Its long square-

Figwort. *The flowers are small and inconspicuous, but even so exert a powerful attraction for wasps which are also responsible for fertilising them.*

cross-sectioned stems rise to about three feet high and some of the small greenish red-brown flowers are to be seen throughout the summer. Whenever it is found, stand for a minute or two and watch for the wasps carefully hovering around the opened blossoms. The flowers are especially adapted to receive the wasp's mouthparts for lapping up the nectar, and fertilisation is effected almost exclusively by them.

PLANTS OF THE OLD RAIL LINE

The old railway ran from Bewdley northwards across Dowles Bridge, then through the forest to Tenbury Wells. The line through the forest roughly followed the course of Dowles Brook but gradually ascended. It was opened in 1861 and was closed to passenger traffic exactly one hundred years later to the day. A daily freight train ran for a year or two and then the track was taken up. Now a number of bridges have been 'blown' and as a 'natural' habitat for plants and animals change is bound to take place. This note concerns three plants of the old rail line, of interest to those who walk it. May a cautionary note be sounded —the ballast is hard and rough!

LONG-STALKED CRANESBILL, *Geranium columbinum*

The spreading tuft of reddish colour with purplish-pink flowers made an exhilarating sight on the line when I first beheld it, yet I must have passed it by a number of times just prior to its flowering. I had somehow mistaken it for meadow cranesbill, yet the leaves of *columbinum* are not nearly so finely and intricately divided as are those of the far more common *pratense*, the meadow cranesbill. But it is the length of the stalks of the individual flowers that gives us an easy positive identification. All the cranesbills possess two-flowered heads, except the bloody cranesbill, *Geranium sanguineum*, a forest prize for those who know the quiet places where it is still to be found. Herb robert, *Geranium robertianum*, of course, occurs along the line but it is altogether a much more erect plant than is our *columbinum*, and the individual flower stalks are very short, certainly less in length than the length of the flower. We are favoured also in the forest by the presence of the wood cranesbill, *Geranium sylvaticum*, right here in the south of its range in England, except for some Gloucestershire localities. It is also an erect-growing plant and prefers the woody shady places and is not, as far as I know, found along the line. To return to our long-stalked cranesbill, it is interesting to note that it is an annual whereas the forest *Geranium* species we have mentioned, except herb robert, are perennial. So many of the plants along the line are of annual habit, at least those that can survive from springing from the central large-sized ballast, and from the trodden ash path immediately on each side.

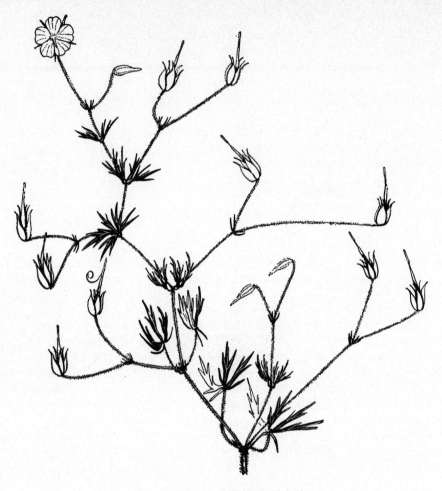

Long-stalked cranesbill (Railway line).

On the railway banks and cuttings, of course, there has been considerably less disturbance except for an annual cutting when the line was in use. With the removal of the rails, sleepers and poles, there has been much disturbance and it will be of interest to note the changing floral scene. Strangely, I think some of the line plants that have for years enriched our forest flora and the botanical history of Wyre, may find it difficult to compete as the forest gradually takes over, unless some element of management of this special environment is practised.

HARE'S-FOOT CLOVER, *Trifolium arvense*

This slender and delicately graceful plant is much more common in the south of England than in the midlands and the north. It is a plant of the sandy places and is more often to be found on the dunes and shingly areas around the coast, yet it was first recorded from Worcestershire as long ago as 1810, and that was near Kidderminster. Since then it has been found at the Devil's Spittleful near Bewdley but, as far as I know, it has not been recorded before this note as being found in Wyre. It was found growing on the line near the Blount Arms in 1967 in an area of tremendous floral exuberance. Alder, which one associates with low-lying ground and bordering rivers and streams as, indeed, it does along the whole length of Dowles, was springing up through the ash on the sides of a high embankment. These were well nourished and of vigorous growth and in the old trodden ash and clinkery way between, there was the hare's foot.

The flowers of hare's-foot are palish pink 'just peeping through the soft grey down which surrounds them', and the inflorescence is almost globular, but as the head ripens it elongates so that it

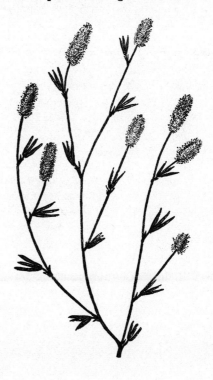

Hare's-foot clover (Blount Arms).

really simulates the fluffy foot of a hare although, of course, they are in miniature. It cannot be mistaken for any other species of clover or trefoil as it used to be called.

LESSER TOADFLAX, *Chaenorrhinum minus*

This small erect-growing plant only a few inches high has been called 'small toadflax' and 'least toadflax', and whilst talking of names, the genus was *Linaria* in Bentham & Hooker's Flora, on which most of us were nourished. Our little plant has quite an extraordinary history as far as Wyre Forest is concerned. But,

Lesser toadflax.

first of all, let us say something of the plant itself. It is to be found in Wyre only along the railway line. I certainly have never found it elsewhere, and my eye has often been glued to the little hot stony paths. It is exceedingly common on the old line and it must be noted that this is not a plant likely to burst upon one's perception. It always looks dusty and grey, 'glandular pubescent' as the botany books say, and the little flowers are pale purplish-violet borne on longish stalks and with blunt spurs behind. It is not an early plant by any means. It can be looked for in vain during May and early June, then it springs up suddenly and seems to be everywhere—along the line.

Now, for its history—it was first found in Worcestershire on the Broadway Hills in 1821 in the extreme south-east of the county, but when F. A. Lees found this diminutive plant at Wyre Forest Railway Station in 1883 he was under the impression that it was a species new to Britain, and he named and described it accordingly. It was subsequently found to be along the whole line of the Great Western Railway. This gave rise to the idea that it had been introduced in some commodity, carried in rail trucks from Mediterranean lands where it was native. Now it is believed to be a British native plant. Again, it is more common in the south, but it has been found sporadically as far as the north of Scotland. Abroad it is found as far as the Punjab.

PLANTS OF THE FOREST PATHS

Most of one's walking through the forest is by the paths, otherwise the going may be difficult and deviations and diversions from the accustomed paths are only for those heavily shod and strong of ankle. (Permission to do so must also, of course, be obtained from the land owner, whether Forestry Commission or private landlord.) Later in the year many bramble-entwined thickets are well-nigh impassable. It is not for nothing that such place-names in the forest as 'Breakneck Bank' exist! However, many of the old timber roads can easily be made out although dense thickets of young silver birch soon grow where the oak has been newly coppiced and the soil has been exposed by the churning of the wheels of wagon and tractor. But the ruts made by the old iron-shod wagon wheels were far deeper than those made by rubber cushion tyres.

The forest paths are of many sorts and, indeed, a path may change its nature several times in the course of a few hundred yards. It may wind along a swampy valley or piece of wet meadow, then climb over a ridge, where the bare rock is underfoot. But the plants to be mentioned here are those to be seen in abundance and sometimes profusion at the path edge that runs along Dowles, sometimes on one side and sometimes on the other.

WOOD SPURGE, *Euphorbia amygdaloides*

The wood spurge, *Euphorbia amygdaloides*, occurs throughout the forest, the plants appearing in small groups along the paths and, indeed, it is to be found along the roadside verges bordering the woods. The existence of this plant was first recorded for Worcestershire by William Pitt in 1810 in his *General View of the Agriculture of the County of Worcester* where he found it near Worcester 'along the Bewdley Road'.

The wood spurge. The lime-green inflorescence bursts from the cluster of reddish-green leaves in early May.

Twelve spurge species occur in Britain but some are garden weeds and seldom found in any other place. But in the family of spurges is included dog's mercury, the green carpeter of our dark spring woods and the box tree of our ornamental gardens. The box tree is probably indigenous to the southern English countries but almost certainly not to Worcestershire.

The flowers of the spurges, including our wood spurge are green in colour which causes them to be rather inconspicuous. They have a strange organisation. The inflorescence, consisting of a number of separate unisexual flowers, is called a cyathium and the embryo seeds hang down on a slender stalk into the encircling bracts.

It is a perennial plant, almost shrubby, and the dark leaves arise from the main reddish stalks, clustered near the apex. But by mid-April the pale lemon-green flowering spike bursts forth, first drooping then lifting upright. It is extremely attractive to the rare black longhorn beetle, *Strangalia nigra*, of which the Wyre Forest is one of its most northerly stations.

The wood sage lines the dry banks of the forest paths.

WOOD SAGE, *Teucrium scorodonia*

Along the drier parts of the brook path, one is never very far from the wood sage, *Teucrium scorodonia*. The leaves are much wrinkled and sage-like but are greener than those of the true sage, and the stem bases are tough and rather woody. The creamy, yellow-green flowers, beloved of bees and of hop-like perfume, are in bloom throughout May to September. It is a common enough plant throughout Great Britain wherever the soil is dry and on the acid side, at least not strongly calcareous, but to me it is a plant reminiscent always of Wyre.

Now called wood sage, it was once more commonly known as wood germander, and before that it was called ambrose. This was not from the name of the saint but a corruption of ambrosia, the food of the gods. The generic name *Teucrium* was said to be taken from Teucer, a King of Troy, who is supposed to have first used the plant for medicinal purposes.

The diminutive milkwort has deep blue flowers but sometimes they are white.

MILKWORT, *Polygala* sp.

The small but conspicuous gentian-blue flowers of the milkwort are to be seen in many of the dryer parts of the path where they peep up through the grasses, the bugle, and the ground ivy, the St. John's worts, the rock roses, and the myriads of other plants found on the path.

Its generic name *Polygala* is taken from the Greek, meaning 'much milk' on account of the beneficial effect on milk productions said to occur on pastures where the plants occur. But along the Dowles path nowadays a cow is seldom seen! The occasion would be confined to an animal breaking through a hedge at night then wandering down a lane into the woodland. But when I was a boy the Weavers had a few cows whose tinkling bells around their necks told of their location in the forest where they appeared to wander at will. No doubt they ate some milkwort but I would think that the 'pasture' to which they had unlimited access, although rich in species, was somewhat lacking in quantity—without a deal of searching for it.

Six species of milkwort are now recognised as found in Britain, but there are difficulties in their identification. Our species along the Dowles path is apparently *Polygala serpyllifolia*, but I stand to be corrected on this. Of the two species included in the name 'common milkwort', it is the species found in lime-free soils.

MARSH VALERIAN, *Valeriana dioica*

The marsh valerian, *Valeriana dioica*, does not actually grow on the path, at least not the relatively new, well-drained Forestry Commission road, but it grows so well in many of the boggy ditches bordering the path that it can be identified and examined without getting one's feet wet! The foot-high sharp-green spikes spring from a perennial, stolon-bearing root-stock and by halfway through May the pinky-white corymbs make themselves known. Where it occurs, it is found abundantly and then by the end of June the boggy patches are dotted with the heads of its feathery fruits. Amphlett and Rea, in 1909, said of it 'wild in all the bogs in Wyre Forest'. How pleasing it is, some sixty years later, to be able to say the same.

In Britain, the marsh valerian has a somewhat scattered distribution, but is found much less frequently in the south than the north.

A detailed examination will show that the small five-petalled flowers are unisexual and of two distinct sizes. The larger ones bear stamens only, whilst the small ones bear only pistils.

The marsh valerian is found in all the boggy ditches of Wyre.

The only other species of indigenous valerian, *Valeriana officinalis*, also borders the path in a few places. These latter appear to be where the trickles of water oozing through the bank cause the soil to be less acid. Common valerian, as it can be called, to distinguish it from the other species, is a much larger plant, growing in dense stands to a height of about four to five feet. Its large heads of bisexual flowers can be seen from June to August, and during July the silver-washed fritillary butterflies suck their nectar.

BUGLE, *Ajuga reptans*

The plant I remember most from my first 'expedition' along the Dowles path, when I was a small boy, is the bugle, *Ajuga reptans*. This is another widely-distributed plant, like the wood sage to which it is closely related, that I associate instinctively with the forest. It was particularly common along the wet sides of the

The short stout spikes of bugle are very attractive to bees and butterflies.

old stone road that ran along the brookside past the cottages as far as Weavers. Indeed, it still occurs there although the road is not now as wet as it was. But it occurs along all the forest paths where wet conditions prevail.

In early May the long, perennial, rooted stolons burst into short hairy spikes of reddish or bluish-green leaves, all tightly packed with campanula-like intense blue flowers. In the warm sunny days of June, the bees and the pearl-bordered fritillary butterflies jostle for position upon them.

GROUND IVY, *Glechoma hederacea*

This species, *Glechoma hederacea*, bears no relationship to ivy, but is a member of the family LABIATAE like the white dead-nettle and, indeed, several of the plants of the forest paths which have already been mentioned, the wood sage and the bugle. It is a delightful little plant, often forming a soft, hairy mat of foliage over the ground and across the path. The tiny violet-blue flowers bear purple spots on the lower lip and the leaves are edged with purple, but they are so near the ground that one gets only a general impression of a soft blue haze clothing the earth.

Associated with damp oak woods, ground ivy may locally become the dominant ground cover. This is particularly so when coppicing has taken place when the long trailing runners quickly smother the ground and stumps. Along the path it will scarcely ever be out of sight.

The ground ivy often gives complete ground cover especially after coppicing in the oak woods

Ground ivy tea was formerly a favourite spring medicine when our plants were much more used for this purpose than they are today.

Lousewort is an attractive plant with an unattractive name.

LOUSEWORT, *Pedicularis sylvatica*

The lousewort, *Pedicularis sylvatica,* is not a particularly attractive name to give this little cut-leaved, rosetted plant of the damp paths. Strangely, it often grows side by side with milkwort so that the derivation of its name seems singularly inappropriate. It was thought that cattle grazing meadowland in which the lousewort grew would not thrive and would become infested with lice! The reason for unthrifty cattle, of course, would be the generally damp conditions in which they grazed. I must say that I have a fondness for lousewort. It always appears to me to be a plant, not of the damp path, but of the high, sheep-grazed alpine pastures, as it is so closely pressed to the ground. Yet it certainly does well, often in the trodden centre of the Dowles path. Its pink hooded trumpets are large in relation to the size of the plant, a feature also of many alpine plants.

DISAPPEARING AND REAPPEARING PLANTS

If we survey the comparative abundance of the perennial herbaceous plants of Wyre over the period of our own recollection, and this is now approaching half a century, a number of changes are seen to have taken place. Those of us interested in the plant-life of Wyre are very fortunate in that it has been so well documented, due to the number of botanists who studied it extensively during the latter half of the last century. The observations and lists published in the Transactions of the Worcester Naturalists are now of far greater importance than ever their authors could have imagined. An examination of these lists shows that a number of plant species have disappeared, which is what one would expect with communications opening up around the forest, particularly with the advent of the motor-car. But what really is more remarkable is that so many species, some rare, others abundant, but no less attractive, remain to grace our forest. Examples of the latter being lily-of-the-valley and wild aquilegia. We must not forget that some plants have appeared in the forest that are novel immigrants and were unknown to the older botanists. We give below notes on a few species whose status appears to have changed over the last half century.

BROAD-LEAVED COTTON-GRASS, *Eriophorum latifolium*

Cotton-grass was first recorded from Worcestershire in 1851 when it was found by Gissing in 'Bewdley Forest'. Since then it has been reported from Wyre on a number of occasions, but unhappily it has been losing ground especially since the last war, with the draining of ground for afforestation. I know of no place now on the Worcestershire side of Dowles where it is to be found in Wyre. The one remaining site on the Shropshire side is dwindling so fast that in 1968 only about two dozen plants flowered. This bog was on a steep hill, a few yards from the brook, but when it was drained quite recently a carr of hazel, guelder rose, alder and buckthorn, quickly sprang up and is now choking it. Strangely, a plant of cotton-grass growing on the Dowles path actually flowered in 1968, although because of the situation it was a diminutive plant. This is a plant of the wet places on base-rich soils whilst the much more abundant common cotton-grass, *E. angustifolium*, is to be found on acid soils. The latter species was to be found in Wyre and was, indeed, also recorded by Gissing from his visit with George Jorden in 1851, but now I do not know where it is to be found. Dr. K. A. Kershaw of the Imperial College of Science kindly made my identification for me.

WALL-PEPPER, *Sedum acre*

Called wall-pepper on account of its hot peppery taste, this scaly evergreen succulent formerly covered many old walls around Wyre. In late June or early July it burst into a mass of star-

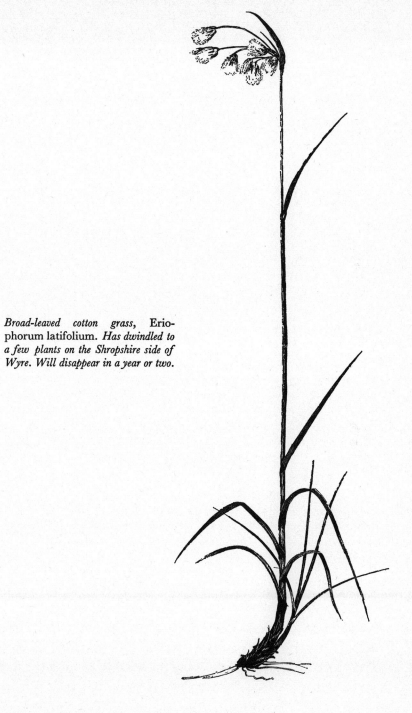

Broad-leaved cotton grass, Erio-
phorum latifolium. *Has dwindled to
a few plants on the Shropshire side of
Wyre. Will disappear in a year or two.*

shape bloom of the brightest golden yellow. In addition to the walls, here and there it is to be found on dry bare patches of rocky earth where a forest road has cut into a bank to round a corner. Wall-pepper is still to be found, but a great spate of wall removal for road widening and, indeed, the complete removal of old buildings within the last two years, means that, inevitably, wall-pepper has decreased.

Wall-pepper. Sedum acre. *Covers walls around Wyre with a golden mantle but the walls are disappearing on account of road widening and modernisation.*

When a piece of old wall is taken down see that the wall-pepper is put back on to the rebuilt wall, or collect the scaly and stringy stolons, and push them into another old wall with a piece of clay or old turf and push it tightly in.

AUTUMN CROCUS, *Colchicum autumnale*

Many living around Wyre must have seen their first autumn crocus in an old cherry orchard at the side of the road just as Cleobury Mortimer's crooked steeple came into view. Then the cherry trees were grubbed up and it is recollected that pigs were introduced. The piece of ground now seems to be more or less derelict—what a pity it was not left exactly as it was! That happened a few years ago. How fortunate that autumn crocus is still in the forest, spilling out from an old orchard on to the

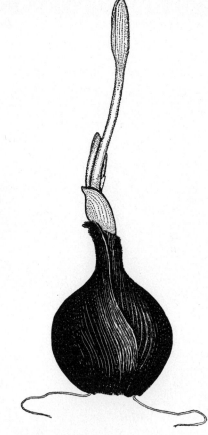

Autumn crocus, Colchicum autumnale. *Still lingers in very few forest localities but is being extinguished due to changing land use. A bulb with its emerging flower.*

railway embankment, sometimes reappearing for a few years and then becoming lost.

Other popular names for this attractive plant are meadow saffron and naked ladies, and botanically it is strange in that the flowers are produced in autumn when the leaves have died away. The bright green strap-shaped leaves are produced in spring which is when the seed-pod ripens.

TWAYBLADE, *Listera ovata*

Although this strange green plant is usually to be found on base-rich soils it is to be found around Wyre, not in the forest-land, but in the old paddocks and orchards all around the forest and along Dowles. We called our little field that traversed a steep

Twayblade, Listera ovata. *Disappears from some localities and appears in others.*

bank and which touched Dowles at a single point, the twayblade field. We used to find about half-a-dozen plants each year, but for the last three years they have disappeared from this field but happily have appeared in the anemone field during the last two years in slightly larger numbers. In old pasture, twayblade is not easy to find. The leaves give the impression of a plantain and the delicate green flower spike can easily be overlooked.

EARLY PURPLE ORCHID, *Orchis mascula*

In 1968, I did not see a single bloom of the early purple orchid; the year before I saw but one, in the anemone field at The Newalls, near Wyre Forest Station. Let this be contrasted with a year within my own experience. Forty-five years ago the meadows around Dowles Church on the side of Severn and running along Dowles as far as Dowles Manor, presented an extraordinary picture, the little fields were dazzling yellow with cowslips, rippled with drifts of bright mauve-purple of the early purples. Today, not a single specimen of either species can be found! This can only have been caused by what was apparently a harmless and attractive pastime of little girls picking flowers. With these two abundant species, also disappeared a rare one, the green-winged orchid, *Orchis morio*, which was to be found among the early purples. The purple helmet of the flowers were conspicuously veined with green, and it was recorded from Bewdley so many years ago. It was last known to me from this locality in 1931. Simple human pressure annihilated it.

GALLS AND THEIR CAUSERS

One of the most extraordinary aspects of our wild life concerns the plant galls. Everyone must have seen them because often they are so numerous, and of a bewildering range of shape, colour, and complexity. All of them are caused by other organisms, (they are termed 'causers') and, again, a wide range of groups of these parasites is represented. Galls, or cecidia as they are called, are defined as growth reactions by the host plant as a result of the parasite attack. A gall is formed either by a proliferation of cells of the plant, or by an enlargement of the existing plant cells, and is a direct result of a stimulation produced by the parasitic organism. The nature of this stimulation varies amongst the different causers and the only certain fact is that almost everything remains to be found out. This is certainly an enthralling subject for the researcher.

Two main groups of the plant kingdom are represented amongst the call causers. These are bacteria and fungi, an example of the former being the causers of the nodules on the roots of leguminous plants caused by the nitrogen-fixers, and of the latter the fungus *Synchitrium endobioticum*, which causes the potato disease known as black-wart.

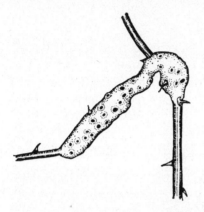

A galled stem of bramble caused by the gall wasp, Diastrophus rubi. *Up to 200 larvae may be present in one gall which is often hidden by herbaceous vegetation.*

In the animal kingdom three main groups of causers are involved. Firstly, there are the nematode worms, a remarkable feature of these being the period for which they can survive under adverse conditions. Secondly, the mites, most of which belong to a single family, the ERIOPHYIDAE of the ACARINA. They are always very small, generally cylindrical in shape, without eyes, circulatory system or respiratory system, and instead of eight legs possessed by most adult mites, two pairs only are present. The mouthparts are usually so small that they pierce and suck single cells. Males are often not much in evidence and parthenogenesis is commonly the rule. Lastly, there are five orders of the class Insecta. The plant bugs or HEMIPTERA, including the APHIDAE or greenflies, the PSYLLIDAE, or jumping plant lice, and the COCCIDAE, or scale insects. The aphids often produce galls of great complexity and, in addition, the life cycle is always complicated by asexual generations. The female coccid remains fixed in one place the whole of its adult life, sucking plant juice in that position, often causing a gall, whereas the male is mobile, more like a typical insect. The HYMENOPTERA is the major group containing the ants, bees and wasps, and a number of important gall causers are included as well as in-quilines or lodgers, parasites and predators of the primary gall causers. The cynipids, or gall wasps, possess legless larvae and usually produce galls on woody plants. They are remarkable also in showing an alternation of a sexually produced generation with an asexually produced one. The DIPTERA, or true two-winged flies also include an important gall-causing family, the gall-midges or CECIDOMYIDAE.

The observer of galls will find much to interest him in Wyre. So much indeed that it is possible to mention only a very few. Examination of the foliage of alder will show a number of leaves completely covered with the pustule-like galls caused by the mite *Eriophyes laevis inangulis*. A number of the yew trees show the so-called artichoke galls caused by the gall midge *Taxomyia taxi*. The robin's pin-cushion is familiar to everyone as a mossy

The marble gall of oak is familiar to almost everyone. The causer is the cynipid wasp Andricus kollari *and it is most abundant on coppiced oak and oak scrub. Generally on older trees it becomes less abundant.*

ball on the wild rose. The gall is caused by the gall-wasp *Diplolepis rosae*, but a whole range of inquilines, parasites and hyper-parasites—that is parasites parasitizing other parasites, is present.

The marble gall of oak is generally familiar to everyone who takes an interest in things around them and looks up at the oak foliage. Strangely, it is an introduced species having arrived from the Middle East about 1830 when large quantities were imported for dyeing woollens and for the making of ink. If you would like to make some ink, take a pound of galls and macerate them in a gallon of boiling water for 24 hours and then strain. Add 5½-oz of a solution of ferrous sulphate and 3-oz of a solution of gum arabic, together with a few spots of carbolic acid. You will then have about a gallon of ink, but you might find that that which you purchase from the stationers is of somewhat better quality.

The galls of the oak are most in evidence in Wyre and there are a number of different species. They would repay a lifetime's study. Alas, we only have one lifetime each.

For Further Reading:

AMPHLETT, J. and REA, C., 1909, *The Botany of Worcestershire*. An Account of the Flowering Plants, Ferns, Mosses, Hepatics, Lichens, Fungi and Fresh-water Algae, which grow or have grown spontaneously in the County of Worcester. Cornish Bros., Birmingham.

BENTHAM, G. and HOOKER, SIR J. D., 1954, *Handbook of the British Flora*, Seventh Edition, Reeve, Ashford, Kent.

CLAPHAM, A. R., TUTIN, T. G. and WARBURG, E. F., 1958, *Flora of the British Isles*, University Press, Cambridge.

LEES, E., 1867, *The Botany of Worcestershire or the Distribution of the Indigenous and Naturalised Plants of that County*, Worcestershire Naturalists Club, Worcester.

LEIGHTON, W. A., 1861, *A Flora of Shropshire*, Davis, Shrewbury and Van Voorst, London.

STEP, E., 1941 and various other editions, *Wayside and Woodland Blossoms*, 3 vols., Series I, II and III, Warne, London.

THE FERNS, FUNGI AND STONEWORTS OF WYRE

THE FOREST'S FERNY FLOOR

The ferns of Britain number about 37 species if we except the club mosses, horsetails, and other related groups which are sometimes lumped in with them. Ferns are often dominant in the ground layer; we have only to have bracken in mind to realise this. In some of the flood-meadows of Dowles not far from Furnace Mill, bracken grows so luxuriantly as to be seven or eight feet in height. Even so, the coal seams lying only a few feet below the surface of Wyre bear witness to an age when the ferns and horsetails were not only dominant in the ground layer but were, in addition, the forest forms.

The life cycle of a fern is very unlike that of a flowering plant. Perhaps the most important respect lies in the presence of two distinct phases in ferns. This is what is known as the alternation of generations. When the spores are shed from the spore-capsules, often in extremely large numbers, those that fall on damp situations protected from sun and wind, germinate and by cell division form a small, green, shield-shaped body, called a prothallus. After a time this organism produces an egg cell in a special organ called an archegonium and at the same time motile male cells are formed, one of which passes down the tube-like entrance to the archegonium, and fuses with the egg-cell. It is from this fusion body that the young fern develops. Thus, two forms of the fern plant occur, the prothallus and the fern with which we are familiar, but the sexual process of reproduction takes place in the inconspicuous prothallus.

COMMON SPLEENWORT, *Asplenium trichomanes*

Sometimes called maidenhair spleenwort, *Asplenium trichomanes* is to be found on a wet north-facing wall in the forest where human pressure is slight. The bright green fronds with shining black stalks grow in delicately out-curving tufts and are about four or five inches in length. The sori containing the sporangia are in small groups, usually four, on the back of the small pinnae and when the sporangia burst, releasing the dust-like spores, they are revealed by the flap-like indusium as being black and polished.

Gerarde in his 'Herball' called this wiry little fern 'waterwort' as well as 'maidenhair'. Surprisingly, Amphlett and Rea in the *Botany of Worcestershire* do not mention its occurrence specifically in Wyre, although they do refer to it as being general in the Severn district of the county.

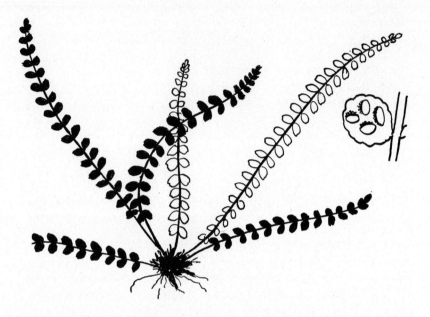

The common spleenwort. Now not so common, but to be found on wet walls that do not get much sun. Enlarged segment of frond shows the arrangement of the sori.

HART'S-TONGUE, *Scolopendrium vulgare*

A species which occurs commonly in a number of deep shady dells to the north of the forest and rather less commonly elsewhere. This is a fern which has suffered at the hands of the fern-grubber, but the rough nature of the ground and extensive bramble thickets have, almost miraculously, saved it. The long, narrow, leathery fronds are about a foot long and curled, and from about one and a half to two inches in width. The fronds have a foot-stalk of a few inches in length and brownish-green in colour. The young fronds are tightly curled. The sori are long and narrow and run in two diverging parallel rows. The indusium bursts along the centre for the sporangia to evert their spores. The old Latin name *Lingua cervina*, literally meant hart's-tongue and the present generic name referred to the sori on the back of the fronds looking like a centipede—*Scolopendra*.

The uncurling fronds of the hart's-tongue fern. Still common in the Shropshire side of Wyre.

WALL RUE, *Asplenium ruta-muraria*

There are ten native British species of spleenwort of which wall rue, also known as rue-leaved spleenwort, is not only one of the smallest but is the smallest of all British ferns, and certainly one of the least conspicuous. Around Wyre it seldom grows more than a couple of inches in height and is often only a single inch. Originally a rock-dwelling species it is now more easily found growing on old walls and bridges where it clings tenaciously by its fibrous roots to the crevices in the old mortar. The irregular wedge-shaped leaves are dull green in colour and usually rather dusty in appearance. Indeed, Gerarde called this little

The dusty little wall rue is common on the old walls and bridges in Wyre. Enlarged segment of frond shows the spore capsules emerging from the indusium.

fern 'white maidenhair' on this account. There is no distinct midrib to the pinnules and there are from two to five flap-like indusia covering the sporangia on each.

It has been called 'wall rue' for over 400 years! Turner referred to it as such in his *Names of Herbs* published in 1548.

OAK FERN, *Thelypteris dryopteris*

This has recently been re-discovered in the forest by M. C. Clark and S. W. Greene (1962) after a lapse of nearly a hundred years when it was noted in the *Worcester Naturalists Club Transactions* (1:88) 1864. E. Step took objection to the name of oak fern as he considered that this name was used for common polypody, *Polypodium vulgare*, by the old herbalists who preferred to collect this fern when it was growing on oak trees. Step calls it three-branched polypody, which at least is descriptive, as the fronds are divided into three stalked segments before being further subdivided. It has a creeping, slender, rootstock. It is certainly refreshing to find this fern re-established, even if in a small location, after Amphlett and Rea, in 1909, stated that it had 'to a great extent disappeared from the county.'

NORTHERN HARD FERN, *Blechnum spicant*

In the writer's view, this is the characteristic fern of Wyre Forest found almost everywhere on the forest floor except in the dense coniferous plantations. Called 'hard fern' on account of the harsh nature of the fronds when they are grasped but this term does not appear to go back far in time. Parkinson (1640) is said to refer to this species as foxes fern and other common names given to it are snake fern (in the New Forest) and rough spleenwort. It is sometimes placed in the genus *Lomaria*.

The long, simple, pinnate fronds are of two distinct types. The outer barren ones spread and generally lie curved over the ground whilst the inner fertile fronds spring erectly from the centre of the tuft, and the segments of the frond are narrow. The sori occupy the whole area of the underside of the segment. The barren fronds grow from six inches to nearly a foot in length, but the fertile fronds usually grow to something in excess of a foot.

Other ferns of Wyre listed by Amphlett and Rea are bracken, *Pteris aquilina*, of course; common ceterach, *Ceterach officinarum* at Dowles Bridge; heath shield fern, *Lastraea montana*; the male fern, *Lastraea filix-mas*; prickly-toothed shield fern, *Lastraea spinulosa*; broad shield fern, *Lastraea aristata*; common polypody, *Polypodium vulgare*, generally distributed; adder's tongue, *Ophioglossum vulgatum* near Bewdley; common moonwort, *Botrychium lunaria*, Bewdley.

THE FOREST FUNGI

Fungi are plants, members of the vegetable kingdom, but they are very special and unusual plants, because they do not possess the photosynthetic pigment, chlorophyll. Thus, they are not able

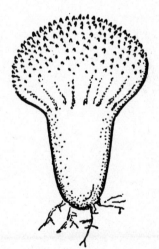

The common puff-ball, Lycoperdon perlatum (*Lycoperdon literally means wolf-dung*), *are first of all white and rather solidly fleshy and covered with short spines. When mature the outer skin is dry and papery and spores are released like puffs of smoke when ruptured.*

to build up their own carbohydrate food material from the carbon-dioxide in the atmosphere, water from the earth, and not forgetting the energy requirement which is derived from sunlight. Fungi, therefore, must derive their nutrients from other organic matter, either living or dead. A large number of plant diseases are caused by pathogenic fungi but a far greater number subsist on dead plant tissue. Fungi are, therefore, the scavengers of the plant world and with their aid the over-mature trees of the forest are decayed and broken up to re-form the 'earth-mould of mother nature', enabling the forests to regenerate anew.

The structure of a fungus is unusual. The vegetative part usually escapes our observation. This is no small wonder as it consists of an interlacing complex of thread-like cells usually invisible in the ground litter. That part of the fungus plant with which we are familiar, however, is the fruiting body, examples being the common mushroom, and the bracket fungus, so common on our birch trees. The fruiting body produces the spores, the dust-like sexual elements which are so small and produced in such a large quantity that distribution is effected far and wide.

It is, therefore, the fungus fruiting body which excites our interest both from the appreciation of its beauty of colour and form, and from the point of view of its edibility. In Britain, it is only the common mushroom which is generally considered to be edible although on the continent many dozens of species are consumed. What frightens most people away from fungal cookery is the knowledge that quite a number of species are poisonous, and a small number are dangerously so. An exact identification of the species is important. In Wyre we have a number of delicious species, but also we have some dangerous ones! Luckily, however, we have a number of good textbooks on the edibility of our native fungi with coloured illustrations and really one cannot go far wrong with the shaggy inkcap and the parasol!

It is due, in the main, to Carleton Rea that a very full list of the species of fungi in Wyre Forest can be given. His paper on this subject appears in Volume 8 of the Worcestershire Naturalists Club Transactions (1923–1931). It is of interest to examine what this very competent naturalist considered to be the limits of the forest. He said that it extends from Fastings Coppice, Coppice-gate, on the north to the Ribbesford Woods on the south, bounded on the east by the River Severn at Seckley Wood, and on the west by the River Rea at Mawley Hall Park near Cleobury Mortimer. This area is roughly estimated to include some six thousand acres.

His list of fungi gives the remarkable total of 1391 species, comparing favourably with the 909 species given by Rayner in

The oak daedalea, Trametes quercina. *The thick grey brackets of this fungus are to be found on old oak stumps and fallen logs of oak. They are extremely tough and cannot be broken away with the hand. They are growing serially in the illustration. Common throughout Wyre.*

1917 for the New Forest. The acreage of the latter is about 92,000. The Wyre Forest list contains over twice the 600 species listed in 1906 for Epping Forest, which extends to about 5,500 acres, roughly the same acreage as Wyre Forest.

Rea gives notes on a number of the more remarkable species in his list.

Glischroderma cinctum is known in Britain only from Wyre Forest, and in addition is very rare in Europe. Rea collected it with his friend W. B. Allen on a charcoal heap at Button Oak in 1909, and he subsequently found it at a number of other sites in the forest.

Lepiota citrophylla. This uncommon species was collected by John Ramsbottom, a well-known Keeper of Botany at the British Museum, in 1922.

Cortinarius (Myxacium) epiplius. First found in Britain in Wyre Forest by Rea in 1896.

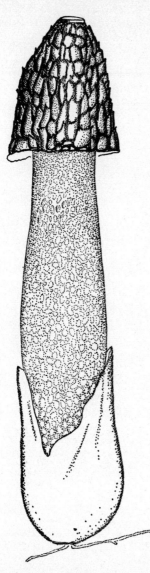

The stinkhorn, Phallus impudicus, is unmistakable. The fruit-body is first like an hen's egg in size and shape before the stalk and evil-smelling cap bursts through. The cap is covered with a jelly-like substance and covers the spores, which are distributed by flies that are attracted to it. Found in a number of Wyre localities.

Cortinarius (Inoloma) argutus. First recorded as British in 1899 in Hampshire and subsequently found in Wyre by Rea in 1902.

Astrosporina fulvella. The first British specimens were collected in Coach Road Coppice, Wyre Forest in 1903.

Flammula rubicundula. This species was described by Rea from specimens collected in Wyre in 1892. It has since been found in the Lake District.

The parasol mushroom, Lepiota pro-
cera, occurs in great abundance when
August and September are damp. It
is one of the most succulent of fungi.
Occurs with regularity on the Worcester-
shire side of the forest.

Boletus nigrescens. This species was first found in Britain near the
Great Bog of Wyre in 1911.

Stereum insignitum. This rare species was found by Rea on beech
stumps in Seckley Wood, Wyre, in 1922.

Clavaria luteo-alba. This species was first described by Rea from
specimens collected from the 'flats' bordering Dowles Brook in
1902 and 1904.

The panther, Amanita pantherina,
possesses an olive-brown cap with
numerous white warts on the top
surface. It is dangerously poisonous.
Occurs in a number of situations in
Wyre.

Clavaria greletus. First found in Britain by Miss Violet Rea in 1922
at Breakneck Bank, Wyre.

Pustularia rosea. This species was first found by Rea at Virginia
Water and he described it subsequently, finding further
specimens at Golden Valley, Wyre.

With such a wealth of species in the Wyre fungus flora it is
difficult to make a selection for further discussion so that I hope
the captions to the illustrations will speak for themselves.

THE DELICATE STONEWORT, *Chara delicatula*

The stoneworts are something of a mystery. At least those who
have studied them have been undecided as to their ancestry and
to their relationship with other plants. They are also strange in
that they are completely aquatic, spending the whole of their life
cycle completely under water. That is what the books relate,
but we shall have something to say about this later.

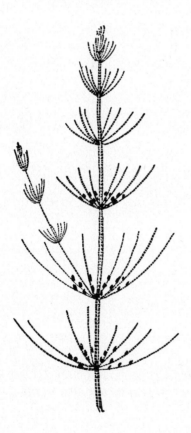

A frond of the stonewort, Chara
delicatula, *from Wyre. The oogonia
are shown on the branchlets.*

The stoneworts are grouped together as the CHAROPHYTA and are found usually in ponds and pools, but also occasionally in slowly moving water; often found in brackish water. They are filamentous and whorled in shape and a translucent green in colour, or greyish green. This leads to one peculiarity of the group, and that is their ability to absorb a large quantity of lime which often gives them a rough, harsh, texture. Sometimes they are very brittle and, of course, it is this characteristic which gives them their name of 'stoneworts'.

Another point of great interest concerns the very simple form of their fruiting organs and it is this that sets the nearest relatives of the stoneworts amongst the green algae, so that they are primitive plants of great simplicity. But, unfortunately, this also means that the microscope is absolutely necessary, and is the reason why this fascinating group of lowly plants has received little study. We have, however, had two scholarly publications dealing with them. In 1924 *The British Charophyta* by J. Groves and G. R. Bullock-Webster was published by the Ray Society in two volumes, and in 1950 *The British Stoneworts (Charophyta)* by G. O. Allen was published by the Haslemere Natural History Society.

An oogonium of the stonewort showing the spiral cells encircling the fertilised egg cell. Much enlarged.

There appear to be about 33 species of stoneworts to be found in Britain but they are pretty well world-wide in their distribution, and throughout the world there are about 250 species.

The fruiting organ of a stonewort is known as an 'oogonium' and is quite unlike anything else found in plants, but as a structure is of great antiquity. The fertilised egg cell, known as the 'oospore', is enclosed by five cells which, although straight out first, begin to twist. As they elongate so they become spirally wound around the oospore. The tips of these cells become cut off and form a circlet called the 'coronula'. Beneath the coronula are slits through which the male elements, called 'antherozoids', swim and penetrate the egg cell. After fertilisation the spiral enveloping cells break down and release the dark-coloured, almost black, oogonium. The organs which produce the male elements are known as 'antheridia' and are globular and orange coloured, easily seen with the naked eye, and of great beauty when viewed under the microscope.

Caddis larvae sometimes make their cases from the oogonia of stoneworts.

It was a delight to find a stonewort in the forest. For a year or two I had been intrigued by a grey, harsh, filamentous growth in a shallow ditch alongside a track on the Shropshire side of Dowles. A seepage of water trickles down the hill and the water standing is no more than an inch or so in depth, but the presence there of bloody geranium shows that the water is lime-charged. The grey-green, dense and brittle, tufts were mostly growing out of water! Indeed, in the middle of summer there is hardly any water present, just damp mud. The plants, when unravelled, were about three inches in length and having decided that they were stoneworts, they were sent to Kew Gardens for identification. They were determined as *Chara delicatula*, one of the commonest British species and particularly abundant in Scotland and Ireland.

The Wyre stonewort is confined to a few yards only of the ditch, but has now been growing in its almost amphibious state for many years. May the delicate stonewort flourish for many years in our forest!

For Further Reading

AMPHLETT, J. A. and REA, C., 1909, *The Botany of Worcestershire*, Cornish Bros., Birmingham.

ANON., 1950, *Edible and Poisonous Fungi, Bulletin* 32, Min. of Agric. and Fisheries, H.M.S.O., London.

CLARK, M. C. and GREENE, S. W., 1963, *Thelypteris dryopteris* (L) Slosson and *Lycopodium clavatum* L. in Wyre Forest, *Proc. Birmingham nat. Hist. Soc.*, **20**(2): 38.

FINDLAY, W. P. K., 1967, *Wayside and Woodland Fungi*, Warne, London.

RAMSBOTTOM, J., 1943, *Edible Fungi*, Penguin, London.

RAMSBOTTOM, J., 1945, *Poisonous Fungi*, Penguin, London.

STEP, E., 1922 (and other editions), *Wayside and Woodland Ferns*, Warne, London.

THE INVERTEBRATES OF WYRE

THE FOREST SHELLS

The MOLLUSCA constitutes one of the most important of the backboneless, or invertebrate, groups of animals. They are certainly very numerous although the great majority of the 100,000 differently described world species are only found in the sea. Perhaps most of us would recognise a mollusc as either a snail-like creature with a single, more or less whorled, hard shell, or a two-shelled animal like an oyster or mussel. In addition, there are the seemingly naked slugs in which the shell is not very apparent. One hundred and eighty species of mollusc are found on land or in freshwater in Britain. Of these, 85 species are land snails and 23 are land slugs. They are usually much more abundant in limestone or chalk areas. Indeed, in peaty acid districts they are virtually absent. Aquatic species are more often found in weedy pools; very few are to be collected from fast streams such as Dowles where there is little vegetation, but there are usually a number of species to be found in slow rivers such as our river Severn. Although ponds are not a common feature of the forest, yet there are a number of small pools from which water-snails can be collected.

Shell collecting was, at one time, extremely popular but a list of the species found in Wyre has not been traced. However, as Nora McMillan's book, full of illustrations in colour and black and white, has now been published, the reader is exhorted to look for shells and try and name them. Collecting land shells has a number of advantages to commend it. An important one is that collectors are so few that the numbers of snails are not likely to be much depleted by restrained collecting. One might even obtain some commendation if a few slugs are picked up from some forest gardens.

Snails and slugs show strangely diverse habits. About half the species are to be found only in undisturbed stable situations away from the close proximity of man such as in woodland, deep hedge bottoms or cliffs. Some species are to be found in excessively damp situations, although not exactly aquatic, yet on the other hand a number of species have adapted themselves to dry conditions such as on sandy heaths and downland. Other species inhabit old walls and rocky areas. Old neglected areas are also good collecting places but well tended gardens are avoided by these animals. It has already been mentioned that the presence of lime in the soil or general environment is of great importance, but although in Wyre, over the major part of the area conditions are generally acid, observations show that snails and slugs, whilst not being abundant, are certainly present.

The writer must confess to being a compulsive stone turner. Indeed, my own family have often remarked that 'no stone is left unturned'. In old gardens, if edging stones are removed the very large *Limax maximus* is commonly found. The ground colour is grey, but is spotted overall with black making it a very handsome creature. Commonly, it is four inches in length and may grow up to as much as six inches. They are known to find their way into the kitchen at The Newalls! *Milax budapestensis* is a medium-sized slug found in forest gardens. It grows to about two inches in length, and in colour is a dull-brown speckled with black, but the sharp keel running the length of the back is yellow.

When it is raining, the wall in front of the Hop Pole Inn is the place to find the common garden species, *Helix aspersa*. It occurs

Clausilia rolphi is a many-whorled snail usually found in limestone areas but found in Wyre.

there in hundreds. The very variable snails, *Helix nemoralis* and *Helix hortensis*, are also to be found in many forest situations. The ground colour is yellow or yellowish-brown and five black bands, to a greater or lesser degree of intensity, follow the whorl of the shell around. These are the species which the song thrush is so fond of and whose broken pieces of shell are to be found around the thrush's 'anvil'.

A small snail with a shell of 9–11 whorls, *Clausilia rolphi*, is to be found in the litter under oak trees and in the tunnels around old grass roots made by the woodmouse. It is stated that it is to be found on calcareous ground. So much for acid Wyre!

COLLECTING

To make a collection of shells it must be said, first of all, that there is no need to collect more than two or three examples of each species. This is with the exception of the three variable species which are also very common, *Helix aspersa*, *Helix nemoralis* and *Helix hortensis*. Snails are killed by dropping them into boiling hot water. Do not let them die a lingering death in a closed container without any attention. When dead, the soft parts are pulled out of the shell with a piece of bent wire and the shells are washed. Do not remove the horny coating which is often present on the shell, just remove extraneous dirt and other particles, When dry they can be stored in almost any small container, but it is absolutely essential that full data of collection accompanies them. This consists of the date of collection, place of collection, such as the parish and county, or a map reference, and, finally, the name of the collector. The specimens then, and only then, are of scientific interest and may be referred to in any type of publication.

It is almost impossible to make a satisfactory collection of slugs. When collected they should be kept alive for a day or two whilst a positive identification is made, and notes made of size, colour, and other features, and then they should be released. But, if anyone, as a result of reading this note, should make a set of coloured illustrations or take a set of colour photographs of our snails and slugs of Wyre, then the writer would feel that his own work was well worth while.

THE CRAYFISH OF DOWLES

The largest member of the Crustacea found in freshwater in Britain is called the crayfish, a lobster-like creature three or four inches in length. As every schoolboy and girl knows, who has done zoology to 'A' level, its scientific name is *Astacus fluviatilis*, as it has been a 'type' animal specially to be studied and dissected. This is because in 1879 T. H. Huxley wrote *The Crayfish— An Introduction to Zoology*. All 371 pages are devoted to the study of this one animal as an example of all animals. This, of course, was Thomas Huxley, whose picture we may remember with his bushy side whiskers and holding a human skull. In his preface to the book he makes, to my mind a memorable statement— 'I have desired . . . to show how the careful study of one of the commonest and most insignificant of animals, leads us, step by step, from everyday knowledge to the widest generalisations and the most difficult problems of zoology; and, indeed, of biological science in general.'

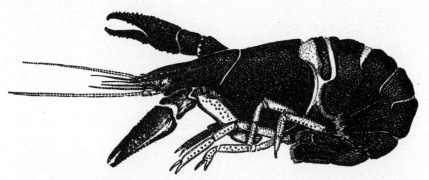

The freshwater crayfish drawn from a specimen taken near Ford Lane Crossing. Abundant throughout the Dowles and its tributary streams.

Huxley was well aware of the existence of at least two forms of the European crayfish and he says that in our own rivers where the crayfish occur we should find the red-clawed and the white-clawed varieties. Coming up-to-date, I believe, it is now accepted that the single indigenous British species is the white-clawed form, not *Astacus fluviatilis* at all, but more correctly named *Potamobius pallipes*—so every schoolboy is wrong. But the red-clawed ones have been introduced from France where they are reared in large numbers for the table. A number of attempts to 'farm' them in Britain have not proved successful but that is why the red-clawed species now occur here and there in this country.

It was my recollection that many of the crayfish of the brook and streams of Wyre had red-streaked claws, so before writing this a visit was made to Dowles and a crayfish was soon found under a stone. It showed just a tiny point of red at the tip of each claw. Perhaps the influence of some content of French ancestry has now been much diminished! Incidentally, Huxley wrote that the crayfish was absent from Severn and in this context he doubtless meant the Severn Valley, but he was in error here.

In Wyre Forest the crayfish is abundant, occurring under almost every likely stone in mid-stream where the flow of oxygenated water is fastest and clearest. This is not only in Dowles but also in every little tributary stream. That is in summer, in winter they bury themselves deep in the rock crevices under the banks. It is remarkable that even in such a predominantly acid region there is enough lime leached out of the sparse bands of spirorbis limestone for this tough calcium-impregnated crustacean to exist.

The derivation of the 'crayfish' is interesting. It is derived from the French 'ecrevisse' and, indeed, the old English form of the word was 'crevis' or 'crevice'. So that it has nothing to do with the word 'fish'!

THE SHIELD BUGS

The word 'bug' has acquired a very much wider significance in our language than the purely entomological connotation. 'Getting the bugs out' of some piece of equipment now has the meaning of finding and removing some badly functioning component. If a room has been 'bugged', we understand that it is wired with listening devices. In a biological sense the term 'bug' is often used to described almost any small organism, even bacteria, but we intend here to use the word in its exact sense.

Members of the insect suborder HETEROPTERA are the land and water bugs and they form part of the order HEMIPTERA. All these insects have mouthparts especially adapted for piercing and sucking. The mandibles are modified into stylets which are enclosed within the especially lengthened labium and this special structure is generally bent backwards and held underneath the body. Often members of the Hemiptera bear a superficial resemblance to other insect orders such as beetles or flies. A quick look at the structure of the mouthparts soon settles whether or not it is a member of the Hemiptera.

The division into the two suborders is principally made on the characters afforded by the wings. In nearly all the Heteroptera the wings are divided into two distinct areas, a basal area which

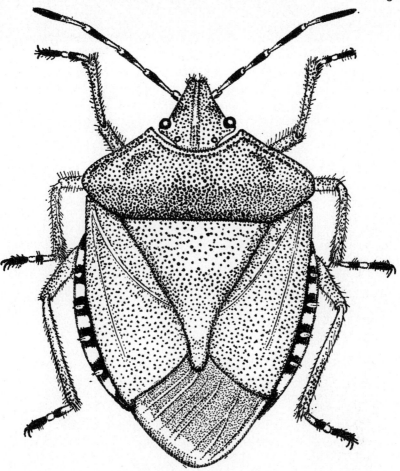

The sloe-bug, common along the old railway track.

is hard and leathery and an apical soft membraneous area. When the insect is at rest the wings are folded flat across the usually flattened body and the apical membraneous portions of the wings overlap. In the other suborder, the HOMOPTERA, which includes the froghoppers, leafhoppers, cicadas and aphids, the wings are of the same texture throughout their area and they are held tent-wise over the body which is not generally flattened.

An important point concerning the biology of the bugs is that they do not undergo a complete metamorphosis during their life cycle as do, say, the butterflies and beetles. There are only three stages, not four; the egg, the larva and the adult.

The shield bugs comprise an important element of the Heteroptera there being 40 British species; a total of just over 500 species of the Heteroptera, as a whole, are found in Britain. A number are moderately large and handsome insects. They are divided into four families of which the PENTATOMIDAE, with 21 species, is the best known.

Shield bugs is an appropriate name as they are almost all flat, broad, and shield-shaped. The transversely barred abdomen projects from the wings on each side.

I have not been able to find any records of shield bugs from Wyre Forest and it would appear that this group, indeed the Hemiptera as a whole, would be worthwhile work for anyone wishing to make a specialised study of these interesting insects and their occurrence in Wyre Forest. Their identification does not present many difficulties and an excellent illustrated book is available in the Wayside and Woodland Series.

The sloe bug is easily found on the dead seed heads of mullein in Wyre.

My illustration is of the sloe bug, *Dolycoris baccarum*, a shield bug found throughout the British Isles. It is usually found around the flowery margins of woodland. It is nearly half-an-inch in length and yellowish or reddish-brown in colour, sometimes with a purplish tinge. The projecting edges of the abdomen are conspicuously banded with dark brown and a light yellowish brown. They are somewhat hairy. In spite of its name it sucks the juices of a wide range of host plants.

Towards the end of August it can be found easily, swarming on the dried seed heads of mullein along the old railway track through the forest.

ALDER FLY AND SNAKE FLY

There are only six species of the order MEGALOPTERA found in Britain; indeed, there are only 200 species found throughout the world. This order consists of the alder flies of which there are two British species, and the snake flies of which we have four species. One alder fly, the species *Sialis lutaria* is common along the banks of Dowles Brook and, no doubt, is also to be found along the smaller tributary streams. May and June are the months given for its emergence, but in Wyre, halfway through June is the most likely time to see it.

The alder fly is a robust insect, about three-quarters of an inch from the front of the head to the tip of the wings in the resting position. The general colour of the insect is very dark, the head and body being black and the wings smoky-brown

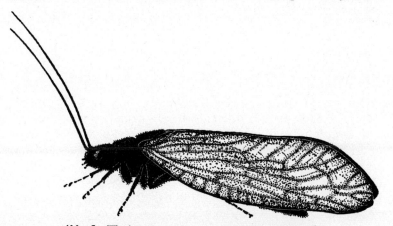

Alder fly. The immature stages are aquatic (Dowles Brook).

with prominent black veins. The black antennae are thread-like. They can be found resting on vegetation near to the water. The eggs are laid in large batches and are quite commonly observed very close to water at the end of June. When they hatch, the young larvae drop into the water below. The larval stage is spent entirely in the water in mud at the bottom of the brook and lasts for nearly a year. It is elongated with the last segment produced into a long filamentous spine. As well as the six thoracic legs, the alder fly larva is quite exceptional in possessing seven pairs of jointed appendages which serve not only as additional legs for swimming and holding onto the stream bottom, but for respiration too as they are well endowed with minute vessels able to absorb oxygen from the water.

Making up the six species of the British MEGALOPTERA are four snake flies or *Raphidia*. They are quite unmistakable, and although amongst the easiest insects to name as snake flies, they are amongst the most difficult to separate out as individual species. A snake fly is characterised by its extraordinary long neck and its clear net-veined wings. The latter are rather like those of a lace-wing fly in shape and are quite clear.

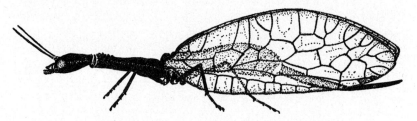

Snake fly. The immature stages are spent in rotten wood.

The female snake fly possesses a long sharp egg-laying tube and she inserts this in rotting wood where beetle larvae are living. The separate species of snake fly appear to show some preference for different tree species. The young snake fly larvae are predaceous and prey upon the beetle larvae and other insects which they find in the decaying wood. When they are fully-fed the larvae leave the wood and make a pupal chamber, either in the bark or at the base of the tree in the debris or soil. When they emerge in summer they fly well and live on small insects. They are very pugnacious. Of the four species, two are common and two rare, and the only species which I have found in Wyre is

Raphidia xanthostigma, which is said to be solely confined to willows.

DRAGONFLIES

Members of the order ODONATA or Dragonflies are predaceous insects, medium to large in size with aquatic nymphal (larval) stage. The head of the adult is of characteristic shape with very large prominent compound eyes and with short threadlike antennae. The two pairs of wings are very similar in shape being slender and covered with a net-like reticulation of veins. The abdomen is long and slender, in some cases exceedingly so. The lower lip (labium) of the nymphs (larvae) is modified into a highly successful catching organ and respiration is carried out by means of rectal or caudal gills which are often prominent. Dragonflies are most abundant in the neotropical region and throughout the world there are upwards of 4,500 species.

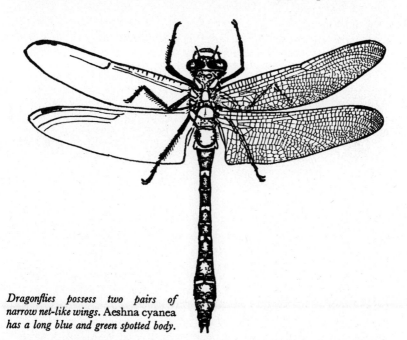

Dragonflies possess two pairs of narrow net-like wings. Aeshna cyanea has a long blue and green spotted body.

The dragonflies are, perhaps, most noted for the brilliant beauty of the body colouration which is often almost jewel-like. Often they exhibit, especially the males, a bloom-like deposition which may wear off. Although most dragonflies possess colourless membraneous wings some possess a brilliant metallic colouration.

Forty-three species are known from the British Isles if we except what we may call 'rare vagrants'. Although this number is small, seen against the hundred times greater number of world species, it may be considered a good representative sample as it contains species in eight of the eleven large and widely distributed families.

So far, a list of the dragonflies of Wyre Forest has not been traced and I have never met an odonatist collecting along the Dowles Valley. When I saw *Aeshna cyanea* hawking and settling on an outstretched finger-like twig, I was always after other quarry. But, at a very early age, I had read about the dragonflies of the Upper Carboniferous whose outstretched wings measured roughly two feet across so that I could easily imagine myself back to when time was young. But I always paused in my ploys and watched.

R. J. Tillyard the great odonatist wrote in his *Biology of Dragonflies* in 1917 '. . . We find in the Odonata a singularly isolated group, marked by very high specialisations of structure, superimposed upon an exceedingly archaic foundation.' This is oft quoted but had a remarkable effect upon me.

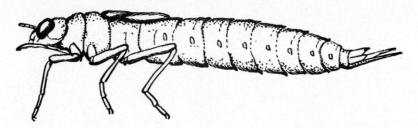

The immature stage of a dragonfly is spent in water where it feeds on insects and tadpoles. The catching organ or "mask" is normally held underneath the head. Side view.

Mr. F. Fincher's list of six Wyre Forest dragonflies which he communicated to me and to which I have added a few notes, is as follows:

Aeshna cyanea (Müller). This large species possesses a blue and green spotted abdomen. It is common and has a wide distribution in England but is absent from Scotland and Ireland.

Agrion splendens (Harris). Said to breed in streams with muddy bottoms in more open areas than where *A. virgo* is found.

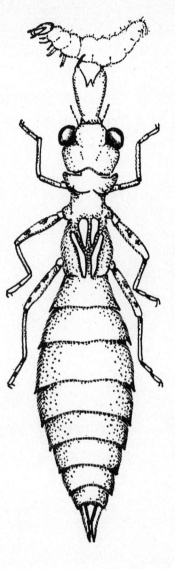

The mask is hinged and can be shot forward to grasp its prey with sharp pincers.

Agrion virgo (L.). The immature stages are found in streams with clean gravelly bottoms in woodland areas.

Coenagrion puella (L.). Said to fly over ponds and ditches, or damp meadows.

Gomphus vulgatissimus (L.). This species is locally rare and is usually confined to England south of the Thames. It has the habit of settling on the gravelly shores of the streams in which it breeds.

The females fly in woodland only coming to Dowles Brook to
oviposit.

Pyrrhosoma nymphula (Sulzer). Said to breed in still water such as
ponds but will also breed in small bog-holes.

GIANT LACEWING

The largest British lacewing fly is *Osmylus fulvicephalus* (Scopoli)
and it measures up to 50 mm or two inches across the wings. I
have called it the giant lacewing; certainly the intricate patterning of the veins well merits the name of lacewing. The head is
orange-coloured, hence its specific name. In the forest it occurs
along shady streams in deep valleys where the stones at the
edge are wet and mossy. When it is disturbed the flight is feeble,
but even so, in the dense shade of its haunts, it is sometimes
difficult to follow. It cannot be mistaken for any other species
of lacewing fly.

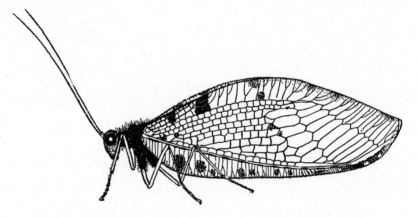

The giant lacewing of the deep shady valleys of Wyre (Osmylus fulvicephalus).

The old Linnaean order NEUROPTERA contained the 'nerve-
winged' insects. It has, however, since been divided into the
MECOPTERA consisting of the scorpion-flies, the MEGALOPTERA
consisting of the alder-flies and snake-flies, with the Neuroptera,
in the narrow sense, being retained for the lacewing flies.

Although 250 species of scorpion-flies are known from the
whole world, only four are found in Britain. Somewhat comparable figures are shown by the alder flies and snake flies, there
being 200 world species, but only six species found in Britain.

However, there are 54 lacewing species in the British list. Many
are to be found in Wyre, but I know of no one who has specifically
made a study of them in this locality. The more common species
of the genus *Perla* are bright green or bluish-green and hibernate
on the ceiling of our bedroom at Wyre. The wings become brownish or reddish-brown during the winter, but transform to green
again in spring, and their eyes are of lustrous copper.

The giant lacewing is on the wing from May to July and the
eggs are laid in rows of from two to twelve. The sluggish larvae
are amphibious in habit and live along the wet stream margins.
Their long curved, scythe-shaped jaws are most effective weapons,
and when the lacewing larva senses movement in the moss
through which it is leisurely making its way, it makes a number
of stabbing movements and when its prey is pierced, a poisonous
material is pumped into its body. When movement ceases,

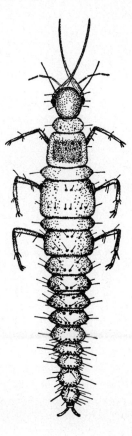

*The larva of the giant lacewing with
its scythe-shaped jaws for seizing,
poisoning, then sucking its prey.*

which is shortly afterwards, the prey's liquid contents are sucked out. Their main food appears to be the aquatic larvae of certain flies (Diptera).

A remarkable courtship is displayed by the giant lacewing. The male attracts the female by everting special scent glands and at pairing the female extracts a large white spermatophore or bag-like process containing the spermatozoa from the body of the male and transfers it to her abdomen. She partially devours it.

GREY SEDGE

In silver-grey forceful flight comes one of Dowles handsome caddis flies, the grey sedge of the trout fisherman, or *Odontocerum albicorne* of the entomologist. It is over an inch across the wings and its long antennae are held out before it as it flies over the water or through the alder foliage. The antennae hold the clue to its rather easy identification, the separate segments are toothed, hence the generic name of this insect and, indeed, its family name ODONTOCERIDAE.

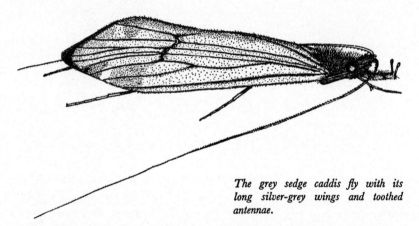

The grey sedge caddis fly with its long silver-grey wings and toothed antennae.

The caddis flies, or TRICHOPTERA represent a separate order of insects closely related to the butterflies and moths, the LEPI-DOPTERA. Instead of the wings being covered with scales as in this latter order, however, the wings of caddis flies are hairy. The name Trichoptera literally means hairy-winged whilst Lepidoptera means scaly-winged. Nearly two hundred species are known from Britain but it is a controversial point whether

The caddis worm of the grey sedge in its case of sand grains.

the caddis flies were evolved before the butterflies, or the other way about. I am inclined to the former view. Nearly two hundred different species of caddis are known from Britain. Although the adult caddis flies are terrestrial, the immature stages are aquatic, being found in various sorts of freshwater, rocky streams, slow-moving rivers, ponds, or lakes, according to species. There is, however, one exception, one species lives on land throughout the whole of its life cycle and it is a strange insect in other respects, and it is of the greatest interest to us in that it is known in Britain only from Wyre Forest, but we shall return to this species in a later note.

It is usual to think of caddis larvae or caddis 'worms' as they are often called, as making for themselves a case of various materials with which to protect their bodies as they crawl about in the water. In fact, a large number of species do this but a substantial number do not. Many of the latter spin webs of a silk-like material with which to trap small organisms, plant and animal, on which they subsist. A smaller number construct a long bag-like tube on the surface of a stone or piece of sunken wood and catch bits of vegetable debris as they pass by.

Our grey sedge caddis worm is found in fairly fast-flowing water of streams or rivers and it makes a case of sand grains and small pieces of stone. This is larger at one end than the other and it is arched; the head and legs of the larva can be seen partially poking out from the larger end, whilst its rear end is protected by a small stone partially blocking the small orifice and kept in position by radiating strands of a silk-like substance. The larva and its case was first described and illustrated from specimens collected in Dowles. Caddis flies are exceptional amongst insects in regard to the chrysalis. In most insects this is a quiescent resting stage and movement is generally severely restricted but in the caddis, although at first it rests within the old caddis case it made during the larval stage, when it is ready to change to the adult phase it cuts the top off the case with its strong toothed mandibles and swims to the surface with oar-like hair-fringed legs. It then crawls out of the water on to a stone or an emergent stem and there assumes the final stage.

CADDIS FLIES OF WATER AND LAND

The caddis fauna is a not inconsiderable component of the fauna of almost every freshwater habitat, and often the immature stages of Trichoptera are present in extraordinary numbers. The various species have widely different feeding habits. Some, (the HYDROPTILIDAE) are very small and pierce the individual cell walls of algal filaments and suck out the contents. Several species occur in Dowles but have not been identified. Others, (the PHILOPOTAMIDAE and HYDROPSYCHIDAE) do not construct cases but spin webs and feed on the various organisms which become entangled. These, also, can be found in Dowles. Species of the family RHYACOPHILIDAE are free-living and wander slowly around over mossy stones and are generally carnivorous. One species is abundant in Dowles. The popular conception of a caddis worm, however, pictures a larva inhabiting a case constructed of a number of pieces of vegetable or mineral debris cemented together. This is true for a number of families, including the LIMNEPHILIDAE, containing 56 species (over a quarter of the species found in Britain).

No list of caddis flies of the Wyre Forest area appears to have been published as such. However, some records are available from the larval description work carried out by the present writer, first published in the Proceedings of the Royal Entomological Society under the general heading 'Larvae of the British Trichoptera', and later published in a monograph entitled *Caddis Larvae*. Material of six species in four families are recorded from Dowles Brook, Wye Forest.

THE LAND CADDIS ONLY IN WYRE

This is only a small fraction of the total number of species probably occurring in Dowles, the smaller feed streams and the pools in the forest. With the exception of *Enoicyla pusilla*, the species recorded are generally common insects, but the distribution of this latter species is extraordinary. In Britain, it is known only from the fringes of a coppice extending southwards from Dowles Brook in the vicinity of Wyre Forest railway station. Between

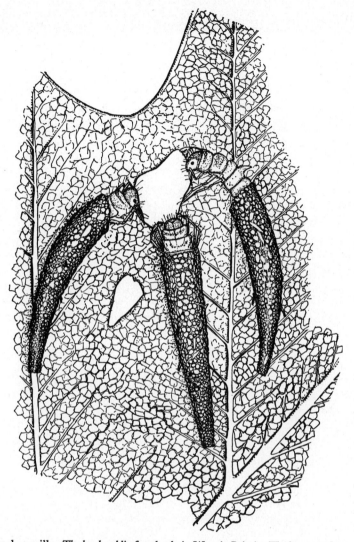

Enoicyla pusilla. *The land caddis found only in Wyre in Britain. The larvae make cases of sand grains and feed on dead oak leaves.*

1868 and 1879 it was collected by two eminent entomologists, Fletcher and McLachlan, the name of the locality being given as 'near Worcester'. R. McLachlan, in 1874, published the great work on this group of insects entitled *A Monographic Revision and Synopsis of the Trichoptera of the European Fauna*. The exact locality of the capture of *E. pusilla* remains a mystery unless it was a guarded reference to Wyre Forest; the Victorian entomologists often resorted to this in order to put their collecting rivals off the track. Be that as it may, it was not rediscovered in Britain until 1957 when, with my daughter Sari, we actually camped on ground from which the larvae crawled and wandered on to our clothes!

In addition to the unusual character of the locality of this species in Britain it is, indeed, an extraordinary insect. The genus *Enoicyla* is unique in the Trichoptera, in that the larvae are terrestrial. Instead of spending the larval and pupal period in freshwater it is found around the fringes of oakwoods where it consumes the dead leaves, reducing them to a skeletal condition.

The adults emerge very late in the year, usually during October and November, and the females are wingless.

This species then is of special interest and its biology is being studied in several countries on the European mainland. It has, so far, not received special attention in Britain.

OTHER CADDIS SPECIES IN WYRE

Oligotricha ruficrus is a rare caddis, large in size with smoky black
    wings and black veins, but with a bright yellow neck. In
    Worcestershire it is also known only from Broadmoor Wood
    Pool at Rubery. A single specimen was found near the Whitty
    pear tree so that it probably breeds in the small pool nearby.
    It usually favours deep weedy pools in woods.

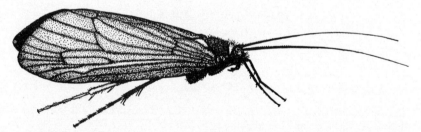

Oligotricha ruficrus. *A rare caddis fly found in the heart of Wyre. The larvae make cases of small pieces of waterweed arranged spirally.*

Rhyacophila dorsalis. The green naked larva of this species crawls
    slowly over mossy stones in Dowles, then catches and con-
    sumes any small creature it comes across. The speckled adult
    caddis are often to be found in abundance.
Plectrocnemia conspersa. The larvae of this species spin nets in order

to trap small organisms brought down by the current. Usually to be found where the water flows fastest. The nets are constructed under or at the sides of stones.

Anabolia nervosa. The large larva of this species constructs a case of sand grains to which is attached one or two large sticks. They are found crawling over sandy stretches on the brook bottom.

Potamophylax latipennis. The larva of this large species makes a case of small stones and they hide during the day under large stones where considerable numbers may congregate.

Odontocerum albicorne. This species, known as the grey sedge, is found along the length of Dowles.

Limnephilus sparsus. A few specimens reach the lit windows of The Newalls from a small stream about 200 yards distant.

Halesus digitatus. Almost every evening throughout the Autumn two or three specimens of this large species are to be found attracted to the lit windows of The Newalls.

Many more species of Caddis Flies are to be found around Wyre by the diligent observer. Not the least reward would be the gathering of information concerning the habits of this fascinating group of insects.

THE YELLOW BRIMSTONE—HARBINGER OF SPRING

The first butterflies of spring appearing on those warm afternoons of late March and early April when the blackthorn hedges turn white and the dandelions suddenly open their saffron heads, enrich the spirit and elevate the soul. The bright yellow butterfly of purposeful flight delighting the beholder so early in the year is the brimstone butterfly, *Gonepteryx rhamni*. Yet usually when it is first observed it has assumed the butterfly state for about eight months, having emerged the previous August or during the last few days of July. Indeed, the butterfly state often lasts for a whole year and sometimes the adults of two generations may be found flying together. For a brief period, after emergence from the chrysalis, it flies along the woody rides and flowering hedges seeking nectar and then disappears into hibernation. 'Disappears' is the correct expression as, seeking a thick ivy-covered tree or dense holly bush, it settles under a leaf and the shape and colouration of the undersides of the wings are so like the leaves that it is virtually impossible to search it out, at least by day. However, if at night a search is made by torchlight then they

shine out more or less conspicuously. When hibernating amongst
the ivy leaves it has been said that; 'The wonderful similarity
between the butterfly and the leaves is so perfect that it is one
of the most remarkable instances of protective resemblance that
occurs in nature.'

*The brimstone butterfly on ivy-
buds. Within the dense foliage
of the ivy it hibernates from
August to March.*

Each wing possesses a prominent angle; indeed, a literal translation of the brimstone's scientific name is the 'angle-winged of the buckthorn'. The veins are especially prominent and the very slight folding of the wings contributes to this. In addition, there are a few rusty-red spots and marks that look more like imperfections on a leaf than the pattern on a butterfly's wing.

The wing colouration of the sexes is markedly different. That of the male is a brilliant sulphur yellow, paler underneath with a pronounced greenish tinge. That of the female is only the palest yellowish green on top and a pale lime-green beneath.

Fertilisation does not take place until the spring and then the eggs are laid singly on the two species of buckthorn, the common buckthorn, *Rhamnus catharticus*, and the alder buckthorn, *Frangula alnus*. Both species occur in Wyre although the alder buckthorn appears to the writer to be by far the commoner of the two, being found along all the banks of Dowles and its tributaries, even if many of the bushes are sparsely leaved and spindly.

The long bluish-green larva with a pale stripe along the side is difficult to find on the buckthorn leaves, as it always assumes a position that makes it look so much like the leaf itself.

The distribution of the brimstone butterfly is thus the distribution of the two species of buckthorn and at Wyre it is near the northern limit of both. With the disappearance of many of our hedges a forest habitat assumes a much greater importance for the continued existence of such species as the brimstone butterfly—the harbinger of spring.

WHITE BUTTERFLIES OF THE FOREST GARDENS

Representatives of eight different families of butterflies are resident in, or frequently or infrequently migrate to, Britain. Altogether these comprise 68 different species. Ten of these are classified in the family PIERIDAE in which the wing colouration is normally in white, yellows and orange.

The black-veined white, *Aporia crataegi*, has been extinct in Britain since 1925, although in the nineteenth century it was widely distributed in southern England. Its last remaining foothold was in Kent, but there are entomologists who believe it still holds out in that county. It is of academic interest to note that this species occurs in the list of rarer lepidopterous insects found in Worcestershire in Hasting's *Illustrations of the Natural*

History of Worcestershire of 1834, as being found in woods near Worcester.

The wood white, *Leptidea sinapis*, of delicate appearance and flight is now no longer found in Wyre, but probably it is still to be found within Worcestershire.

The Bath white, *Pontia daplidice*, is a very rare migrant from France. It has occasionally arrived in Britain in large numbers, but collectors and parasites have soon wiped them out.

The two clouded yellows, *Colias hyale* and *Colias croceus*, are migrants too, but fly the Channel most years, and in spite of breeding well in our southern counties during the summer, feeding on lucerne and clover, they never survive the winter in any stage. Occasionally, however, they are very abundant and have been collected in Wyre.

The brimstone butterfly, *Gonepteryx rhamni*, is a common insect of Wyre. I believe this species is much more common today than it was, say, 40 years ago. Then, to see a couple during a day's walk through the forest, was an event. This spring of 1968, I have seen as many as a dozen during a day!

It might be said that our common garden whites bear little relation to an account of the wild life of our forest. But this is not the case. Our forest gardens, lanes, and little waste patches, offer living room not only for forest plants, insects, and other creatures, but also for insects from the broader world around which constitutes, in a sense, a buffer region. Here, the creatures dependent on forestry and on horticulture mingle. It would be a sadder world without our garden whites.

ORANGE TIP, *Euchloe cardamines*

The underside of both sexes of this butterfly is generally similar to that of the other 'whites', members of the family Pieridae. The irregular greenish patches on the hindwing cause the insect to merge into the colouration of the white and green umbels of the hedge parsley in Spring. This is when the adults of this single brooded species are on the wing. The male, however, is distinguished by a brilliant orange patch on each forewing. This gives the popular name to the species and also enables a very easy identification to be made, at least as far as the male is concerned.

The eggs are laid at the bottom of the flower stalks of a number of species of cruciferous plants, but rarely the cabbage. Usually it is hedge garlic, cuckoo flower (ladysmock), and on honesty of

Orange tip butterfly on tuberous pea, Lathyrus montanus (*Far Forest*).

the cottage gardens. The long bluish-green caterpillar is often attended by ants who relish a secretion which exudes from a series of hollow spines. Indeed, the larvae of all the whites possess this glandular secretion but the caterpillars of the orange tip appear to be most favoured by the attentions of ants. The chrysalis is long, thin and pointed, and attached by the tail-hooks or cremaster, and a girdle of silk.

The orange tip has become very abundant around Wyre Forest these last few years. I never remember seeing it so plentiful as in 1970.

SMALL WHITE, *Pieris rapae*

This species is one of our most common butterflies and certainly its milk-white colouration makes it conspicuous as it flutters

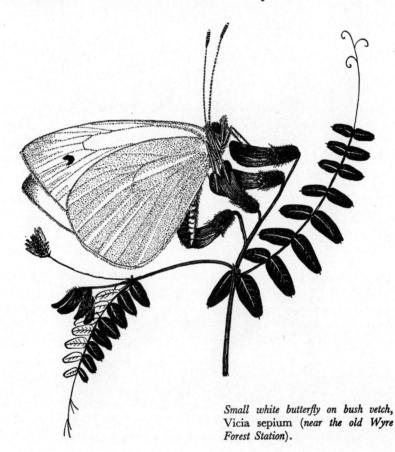

Small white butterfly on bush vetch, Vicia sepium (*near the old Wyre Forest Station*).

along the lanes and in the forest gardens. Its two broods in the year, and sometimes three, mean that on sunny days it is seldom absent during spring and summer through. The caterpillars feed on various species of the cabbage family, the CRUCIFERAE and, unfortunately, it is the cabbage itself that is most attractive. Thus, this beautiful butterfly has become a pest and has, indeed, acquired a cosmopolitan status, having been accidentally carried as far as New Zealand and the United States. It was indigenous across Asia to China and Japan. Often there has been a price put upon its head. But we would be the poorer without it. Suddenly we were saying two or three years ago, 'Where have all the butterflies gone?' This was because the growers of cabbages could at last prevent their crop from being spoiled. Whilst it has become relatively uncommon in the vegetable-growing area, around our forest it is as abundant as ever it was, and it enlivens the summer day.

The angular chrysalids are secured by a silken girdle and are toned to fit in with their background.

LARGE WHITE BUTTERFLY, *Pieris brassicae*

The large white is much larger than the small white and green-veined white, so that it can be distinguished from size alone, even on the wing! The female measures nearly two and a half inches across the wings, and the male just slightly less. Both sexes possess a black tip to the forewings but the female, in addition, bears a pair of black spots and a bar on each forewing. There are two broods annually, the spring brood being distinguished by the black wing tips which are powdered with white scales. Like the small white, the present species has earned an unenviable reputation as a pest. Again, the food plants of the caterpillars are confined to the CRUCIFERAE, the cabbage and brussels sprout plants being especially attractive. Unlike the other species, however, the eggs are laid in fairly large batches so that often the cabbage plant is reduced to a sad series of leaf ribs.

Although generally distributed throughout Britain, there is a very wide variation in abundance from year to year. This is due to two main reasons. Firstly, it is a migrant, coming to us in some years from France in exceedingly large numbers. They have been likened, on occasions, to white clouds coming in from the sea. But, and secondly, when the resulting caterpillars appear in plague proportions, they are attacked by a small braconid wasp

Large white butterfly on common vetch, Vicia sativa (*Rudds Bridge*).

called *Apanteles glomeratus*, and sometimes they are practically wiped out. Immigration and parasitisation, thus, are responsible for the wide fluctuation in numbers.

One would think that the caterpillars would be an easy prey for birds, sitting about in large batches as they do, but they are seldom taken by birds as they are unpalatable. Even to human beings they have a distinctly unpleasant smell. The adults too, although they are so conspicuous, are not often eaten by birds. The adult butterfly is attracted to purple flowers of lilac (the spring brood) and buddleia (the autumn brood).

GREEN-VEINED WHITE, *Pieris napi*

This white is not so easy to distinguish on the wing, but the moment it settles its identity is declared. The wings on the underside are heavily scaled with grey and black which gives them a greenish hue. There are two broods in the year. The first fly in late April, May and June, and from eggs laid by these individuals another brood flies in July and August. The green-veins of the second brood are not so heavily marked as those of the first, although the black spotting on the upper wings is more distinct.

The eggs are laid on various species in the CRUCIFERAE, especially hedge garlic, otherwise Jack-by-the-hedge, *Alliaria petiolata*, but many other species may be selected. The caterpillar is greenish above but whitish grey beneath.

The green-veined white butterfly is generally distributed throughout Britain, but usually keeps to its favoured places. These are the leafy copse fringes and marshy spots.

BUTTERFLIES OF THE NETTLES

It is something of a paradox that two of our most brilliantly coloured and generously hued butterflies are associated with one of the meanest of our flowering plants—the stinging nettle. Perhaps, if we except the cabbage whites, they are our most commonly occurring butterflies, which is much to our delight. These are the small tortoiseshell, *Aglais urticae*, and the peacock butterflies, aptly and richly named, *Nymphalis io*. One must confess that when a small or large garden white flies on to the aubretia of the forest cottages, one does not have the same conscience about them and one cannot prevent visions of holed and tattered cabbages from clouding the otherwise pleasant and

Green-veined white butterfly on wood vetch, Vicia sylvatica (*Blount Arms*).

The small tortoiseshell butterfly on watermint. Note only four functional legs.

wholly satisfying sight. On the other hand, it can never be
thought that the spiny gregarious caterpillars of the small
tortoiseshell and peacock ever make the slightest difference to
the evergrowing banks of stinging nettles. But what a delightful
method of biological control to contemplate!

The two butterflies are closely related to each other and are
classified in the vanessid section of the family NYMPHALIDAE.
Formerly they were placed in a separate family VANESSIDAE,
but this is now thought of as only part of the first-named family.

Both the small tortoiseshell and the peacock go through an
annual life cycle and pass the winter hibernating as the adult
butterfly. Both species are commonly met with during the winter
months in barns, roof voids, outhouses and also indoors where
they often cling in the folds of curtains in unheated rooms. Unfortunately, if they happen to select a centrally heated room they
will soon become active when they should be sleeping the winter
through. It would be best to transfer them to an unheated room
or attic, remembering to give them access to the out-of-doors at
the end of March or beginning of April.

The uppersides of the wings of the small tortoiseshell are rich
tawny with yellow and black markings, further ornamented
with a row of crescent-shaped spots of deepest blue. The undersides of the wings, as indeed in the case of the peacock butterfly
also, are in the sharpest contrast. They are dull black, grey black
and a dull creamish colour in the pattern shown in the illustration. On each wing of the peacock there is a brilliant peacock
eye on a background of dull carmine, but the underside is glossy
black with a fine and delicate patterning.

The peacock butterfly. A delicate
patterning of dull and glossy blacks.

In both species the eggs are laid in fairly large batches and the young larvae keep together under webs only leaving the web to feed, but they scatter when nearly full-fed in order to pupate. The chrysalis stage lasts less than a fortnight then the final glory of a beautiful butterfly is released.

The stinging nettle is not a truly forest plant but it is a very common plant in the fringing farmland around the forest from Button Oak to Far Forest. We are admonished by Mr. Peter Scott not to so tidy up our lanes and farmlands that the stinging nettle disappears, thus to deny sustenance to our peacock and small tortoiseshell butterflies. I somehow cannot foresee this happening around Wyre.

THE RAGGED COMMA

The comma butterfly, *Polygonia c-album*, is an indigenous species of Wyre. By that I mean that with all the fluctuations in distribution which have occurred with this ragged little butterfly, since records have been kept, it has remained an insect inseparable from the Forest of Wyre. When I first saw it, its vivid orange-brown with tattered outline was spread on the lower branches of an oak on the path from Dowles to Ford Lane crossing. I was very small and the distribution of the comma was restricted to the counties of Worcestershire, Herefordshire and Monmouthshire. In the years following, it became widespread almost over the whole of the country although nowhere common. It was found to be attracted to the long purple spikes of the buddleia bushes throughout England. Now its distribution seems to have contracted again to what it formerly was. It is called the comma because of the silvery white mark in the middle of the underside of the hind wings, but it really is more like a 'C', as in its specific name. It is a strange wayward insect with a number of characters peculiar to itself. There are two cycles in the year, but like the majority of the species in the vanessid section of the family NYMPHALIDAE the winter is passed in the adult stage. But although most species seek out some sheltered spot in which to overwinter, such as dense ivy, a hollow tree, or an old barn, the comma clings to the bark of a high tree branch exposed to all the winds of heaven. The extraordinary thing is that it survives. Another unusual feature, in fact unique, as far as the British butterflies are concerned, is that in the summer brood two distinct forms of the butterfly are easily distinguished. What

The ragged comma with its "c" mark on the hind wings.

may be called the typical form is inseparable from the over-wintering form, but this exists together with a much lighter coloured form with a rather more rounded and less ragged margin to the wings. This variety is called *hutchinsoni* and for a long time its significance was obscure. Petiver, 150 years ago thought it was a separate species and he called it the 'pale comma'. It never occurs in the overwintering brood.

It was a Miss E. Hutchinson who recorded the 'pale summer variety' of the comma as she called it in 1887, and now it is named after her. Frohawk, who gave us the magnificent two-volume butterfly book, reared a large batch of commas in 1894. From 275 eggs, laid between 17th April and 1st June, he was succesful in getting 200 butterflies to emerge from 30th June to 2nd August. Of these, 41 were of the pale *hutchinsoni* form, the remainder were typical. All the *hutchinsoni* appeared in early July before the typical form, with but few exceptions.

The eggs are laid on the food plant in small chains of three or four and are green with ten white vertical ribs or ridges. They become yellowish before the young caterpillars hatch out. The full-grown caterpillar is blackish 'netted with greyish' and the back, from segment six to segment ten, is white. It is covered with large projecting spines and from the top of the head emerge a pair of club-like processes. The food plants are nettle, hop, currant, and it has been reported as also feeding on gooseberry and elm. Of these, I have found the comma caterpillars in the forest on all three of the former species, although hop does not occur at all commonly and red-currant occurs in some hedges by cottages along Dowles. Nettle and hop are closely related botanically and actually so is the elm, but currant and gooseberry are not so close.

In marked contrast with the small tortoiseshell and peacock butterflies, whose caterpillars are found living gregariously together in webs, the caterpillar of the comma is a solitary individual, and although the eggs are laid a few together as previously mentioned, I never found more than one on a bush. The chrysalis hangs downwards and is brownish-pink and there are some silvery or golden spots.

Chrysalis of comma butterfly hangs downwards from a knob of tiny hooks (a cremaster) which catch in a silken pad woven by the caterpillar.

The comma is an extremely rapid flyer but if a fulvous coloured butterfly of swift approach glides and flutters around, keep perfectly still, it will often oblige by resting for a short space on some sunny foliage.

THE FRITILLARIES

Of the three large fritillary butterflies found in Britain, how delightful that two are found in Wyre, and occasionally the third wanders in from the north-west, I believe. In years gone by they were excitingly abundant, but even now there seem to be many more about than a few years ago. In 1969, standing entranced, I saw four silver-washed and two high brown fluttering and cavorting around the same bank of bramble-blossom sprays. In 1970 twelve silver-washed were seen together.

Fritillary butterflies possess a number of things in common. Firstly, in the colouration of their wings—the upper sides are of a uniform golden fuscous brown, if those are the words that can describe it, but superimposed is a reticulated pattern or chequering of brownish black. This latter is the colouring of the veins and all the cross veins. Of course, we have another meaning of the word fritillary—the genus of liliaceous plants to which the snake's head fritillary belongs, found in the damp meadows of Oxfordshire and, alas, not native to Wyre. But here the box-like flowers are chequered with a darker colour. Is this the real similarity of word meaning? Perhaps some etymologist will expound to this entomologist?

With our fritillary butterflies, however, it is the colouration of the undersides of the wings which excites our aesthetic admiration. All fritillary butterflies appear to have the underside of the hindwings variously spangled and splashed with a metallic sheen-like silver colour. The high brown fritillary, *Argynnis cydippe*, with rounded tips to the forewings shows its silver

High brown fritillary butterfly. The larvae feed on the leaves of the violet.

spangled into discreet patches. I have not been able to find a satisfactory explanation for its name 'high brown', for me a quite inadequate name for this thrilling and beautiful insect. I like to refer to it as 'silver spangles'. The silver-washed fritillary,

Argynnis paphia, is a somewhat larger butterfly and always gives the impression of possessing even greater mastery of the air as it glides down from the tops of the oaks, flits along the ride with fluttering wings, then beats up to the tree tops with little show of haste, yet with such rapidity that it would be useless for some

Silver-washed fritillary butterfly. After years of rarity it is to be found in numbers.

mortal to endeavour to follow except with one's sharpened and straining eyesight. The silver of our silver-washed is not spangled but is washed in streaks of green, rose and copper 'in sheer loveliness' as Beaufoy remarks.

Over a period of well over forty years looking at the butterflies of Wyre, the dark green fritillary has been found on several occasions but although the spikey and spiney caterpillars of all the three species feed on the leaves of the violet, the dark green seems to prefer countryside of a much more open character, the bare hillsides of downs and the cliff-tops of our coast are more to its liking. The biology of the silver-washed fritillary, however, has a special interest for us. The larger but rather duller and browner female lays her eggs on the lichen covered bark of mature oak trees. It is at the end of July and beginning of August when the eggs are laid and within a fortnight, the young cater- pillars hatch out and start off life by making a meal of their egg shells. There must be some reason for this partaking of a seem- ingly indigestible first meal—a practice of so many species of butterflies and moths. My own view of this, which is just a guess, as I have not seen any experimental evidence to support it, is that the highly patterned egg of ridges and pits picks up micro- organisms from special glands in the ovipositor of the female, and by eating the eggshell these are taken into the gut of the newly hatched caterpillars. These micro-organisms then help to digest the cellulose and related substances taken into the gut by the caterpillar when it eats a leaf. After the egg shell breakfast the tiny caterpillar then hibernates in the crevices of the bark for several months until spring when it crawls down to the ground and wanders about until a violet plant is found. This must be quite a task for such a small creature. Then it commences to consume the leaves.

I hope the reader will have seen that an essential part of the environment for the continuation of the presence of the silver- washed fritillary amongst us in Wyre is not only the presence of the violet plant in profusion but also the conservation of mature oak trees in substantial stands for the over-wintering of the almost microscopic newly hatched caterpillars.

Since writing the above I have found that Gerarde in his *Herball* of 1597 refers to the name 'fritillary' as being derived from the old name *fritillus* which was the name for a chessboard. It was also the name for a general chequered pattern with which dice boxes were decorated.

THE EYES OF THE FOREST

The night hath a thousand eyes and between mid-April to the end of October, so has the forest. These are the eyes of the satyrs, if that is what we may call the butterflies of the family SATYRIDAE. Most would consider a satyr to be a woodland god, partly of human and partly of bestial shape, a companion of Bacchus. But our forest satyrs are not of shaggy form, nor have I seen them sip as much as the fermenting juice of an over-ripe plum as would a red admiral butterfly. One cannot describe as bacchanalian the nectar of bramble, wood sage and heather, which it is their usual habit to suck through their long coiled proboscis.

The eyes of the satyrs to which I refer are on the wings and are not seeing eyes, although, of course, they do possess compound eyes of great complexity and of exceptional sensitivity. Those who have stalked a wall butterfly in the bright hot sun as it flits a few feet from your step along the stoney path, will know this. The satyrs eyes look out at you even when they are asleep on a curving slender grass in the uncertain light of a June dusk, or in an afternoon cold May drizzle.

Eleven species in the family Satyridae are given in the British list of butterflies. Of these, six are common throughout Wyre and of the remaining five, two are distributed no further south in our island than the Lake District; one comes down as far south as the Staffordshire 'mosses', another is confined to regions of chalk. The last can be considered a coastal species, only being found locally in the inland counties, although Hastings in his *Illustrations of the Natural History of Worcester* in 1834 mentions the grayling as occurring in 'Bewdley Forest', but it has not been found there within living memory. But our own six are a delight, and in the days of despair and gloomy forebodings concerning the future of our butterflies, it is pleasing to report that our forest satyrs are just as numerous in Wyre as they were 40 years or so ago. Indeed, one now common species did not occur here at that time. It seems appropriate to write my notes on this latter species first.

SPECKLED WOOD, *Pararge aegeria*

Along the grassy paths and shady lanes this chocolate-brown butterfly, spattered with creamy patches, abounds. It flits around just a few feet in front of your step, circles above your head, and

The speckled wood butterfly resting on wood melick (Melica uniflora). *To be found from early spring to late autumn.*

then resumes its beat. This is where the sun filters through the leaves of the oak dappling the path like its own wing pattern. It may rest with wings outspread on a leaf, then four pairs of eyes, as on the wings of our satyr, may be counted, three on the hindwings and one in the apex of the forewings. When sitting with wings close pressed, showing the cream dappled browns of the underside, then the eyes of the forewings show like a viper's eye, but those of the hindwing peep through only as smokey-circled pale spots. The earliest English name for the speckled wood was the 'enfield eye' which was given to this species by Petiver, and this was early in the eighteenth century. Somewhat later it was referred to as the wood argus. Of all the British butterflies, the speckled wood appears amongst the first with the first sunny days of spring, and is one of the last to brave the weak sun of late autumn—not the selfsame butterfly, as there may be as many as four successive broods during the year, but usually it is three. The bright green caterpillar with its long stripes of yellow and dark green feeds on couch, cock's-foot and some other grasses. The dumpy chrysalis hangs suspended by a hooky cremaster entangled on a silken pad. I first saw the speckled wood in Borth Woods near Aberystwyth, but now they flutter into the barn room at my cottage in Wyre, seeking the shade as I write and draw.

WALL BUTTERFLY, *Pararge megera*

I would describe the colour of the upperside of this sun basking butterfly as golden fulvous brown. As it flirts with you along a sun-baked wall or sandy path the colour seems almost to possess luminescent qualities. Glowing, not with fire, but like some living metal. How different from so many satyrs that prefer the northern cloudy skies!

As it spreads its wings to soak in the full warmth of the sun one discerns the fine reticulation of dark chocolate brown of the veins and cross bars. It shifts position restlessly as you approach, then it is off again only seeking the hot stone, brick or dust. I cannot remember when I first saw the wall butterfly to recognise it from the pictures in Richard South's book, but this must have been before my eighth birthday because I had caught a grayling butterfly soon afterwards, and in my immature exuberance and ignorance I thought I had found a hybrid between a speckled wood (forewings) and a wall butterfly (hindwings)!

The wall butterfly. Sun-drenched walls and rocky banks are its favourite haunts.

I should say something of the underside of the wings of this satyr. But how can I describe the eye set in the golden ring in the forewing? It stands from its background watching and protecting. Set on the hindwings are six and sometimes seven eyes, each with a bright white pupil, and surrounded by a fine oscillographic pattern.

The caterpillars which are whitish green dotted with white and with three long whitish stripes having dark green edges, feed on a number of grasses including cock's-foot and annual poa grass. There are two broods in the year and sometimes three, and this butterfly is just as common today around the forest as I recall it was so many years ago.

MEADOW BROWN, *Maniola jurtina*

This satyr has only one pair of eyes set in golden fuscous spots which are small in the male but large and showy in the female.

The meadow brown butterfly. Now everywhere abundant but was not to be found in Wyre fifty years ago.

Elsewhere the forewings are smokey brown and sometimes almost bleached in appearance.

Careful approach down the hayfield's side or along the flowery ride by the wood's edge show the underside of the meadow brown to be suffused with paler tones, but the eyes are always open as in some wide-eyed predaceous bird.

I first met this species on the steep grassy slopes of the Lickey Hills behind the Rose and Crown gardens, but they were, this last year, more numerous about The Newalls and along the Dowles path with all its tiny meadows, than I ever remember.

The caterpillar has the usual characters of the Satyridae, green with longitudinal stripes, and its food-plants comprise various common grass species. It is said to be the commonest butterfly in the English countryside.

GATEKEEPER, *Maniola tithonus*

The woodland lanes of Trimpley, rising from the Severn valley was where I first met with the gatekeeper butterflies as they flew backwards and forwards in front of a five-barred gate. They kept to the roadside of the gate—this was where the mauve-purple heads of the knapweed stood out from the long grass.

This is another satyr that appears to be more widespread about the forest than was formerly the case. Now it appears along the grassy rides quite deep within the forest and where there are no gates to keep! But this is where the long creamy green spikes of the wood sage grow and that is the attraction for our 'hedge eye' as Petiver called it, who named it thus a century and a half ago. The flowers of the bramble rambling over the woody edges are also sought. The double pupilled eyes of the 'hedge eye' are set in triangles of fulvous orange and there are borders to all the wings of smokey brown. The male has an additional wide bar on the forewings making sex identification in this species the easiest task of all the Satyrs except, perhaps, the meadow brown.

This insect is single brooded in the year, appearing on the wing in July and August, and the caterpillar, like all our satyrs, is a night grass-feeder. The species preferred are cock's-foot and couch.

RINGLET, *Aphantopus hyperantus*

One cannot perceive the eyes of this sooty-brown satyr when it flits along the forest edge amongst the clumps of stump-springing

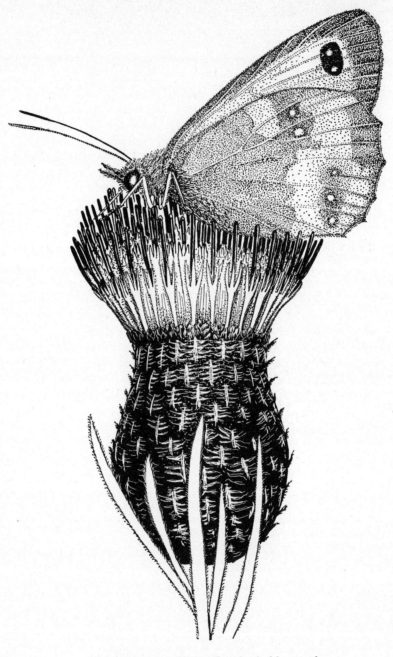

The gatekeeper butterfly on a flowerhead of knapweed.

The ringlet butterfly.

oak shoots, or amongst the meadow-sweet laden flowery edge of Dowles in July and August. But, strangely, when it has left its chrysalis only a few hours before, the thin white wings' edge can be clearly made out.

It is when at rest on grassy stem, leaf of oak, or nectar sipping at bramble, that all eight pairs of eyes are there to startle. Three pairs straddle the forewing apex and five on the hindwing, and all are white pupilled on a yellow-ringed black ground. There is much variation in the prominence of eyes or rings, as the books call them, but they are more than rings and sometimes they are absent.

There is only a single brood of this species each year yet it never appears to vary in abundance. The caterpillar is greyish brown with long stripes, and feeds on the cock's-foot and other grasses, preferring the damper places.

SMALL HEATH, *Coenonympha pamphilus*

When I was a boy and showed my small collection of butterflies to friends and relations, much to my discomfiture, it always raised a laugh when I referred to the small pale tawny-winged butterfly with greyish brown edged wings as the small heath. As I then lived in Birmingham this was like referring to the insect as an Acock's green or a Handsworth; small heath was the name of a suburb. In the past it was known as the 'selvedged heath eye' and the female as the 'golden heath eye' (she is paler than her consort), but it was also referred to as the 'gatekeeper' just as the previous species. I must admit to a liking for the name of 'heath eye' for this most diminutive of our satyrs which I came upon at Sutton Park, to the north of Birmingham, and to which I walked with my haversack and butterfly net from Handsworth, where I then lived. I much admired the little eye on the underside looking from the forewing, although in this most variably coloured insect the eye was often reduced to a mere dot, but the downy, almost sage-coloured underside of the hindwings appealed to my sense of nature.

The small heath butterfly.

This small butterfly is to be found almost throughout the summer months on many of the small, and even minute, patches of heathland with which the forest is edged and dotted. This type of habitat includes quite long stretches of the old railway line where drainage is good and the heaths and heather grow, and on whose purple flowers the heath eye loves to sit. The heath eye is the butterfly I associate with summer walks in the rain and cold August evenings, when dusk has not quite fallen. The heath eye selects slender grass stems on which to sleep through inclemency, or the darkness of the night. So one sees them weighing down a grass-head with their own weight and the weight of the dew, and with a beady cobweb or two. Sometimes they have company in the shape and hue of blue butterflies; in the hot sun they love to sport together with rapid twisting flight.

There are our six satyrs of Wyre to be seen and enjoyed by all who will walk a few hundred yards. This account of them, however, cannot be closed without mention of a single specimen of the Scotch argus, *Erebia aethiops*, found flying in Wyre some 80 miles south of its most southerly locality in Lancashire. This was in 1947, but this satyr with the red-ringed eyes has never been found there again.

THE GREEN AND PURPLE HAIRSTREAKS

Two species of hairstreak butterfly abound in and around the forest but can be enjoyed only by the sharp-eyed. The upperside of the wings of the green hairstreak, *Callophrys rubi* is of a rich nut-brown colour sparsely dusted with gold, but the underside is of apple-green velvet. When the Weaver family left Dowles, their minute brookside meadows were invaded by silver birch and broom, and it was then that the green hairstreaks could be seen in May and June flirting with the waving tips of the fresh bright birch foliage.

The purple hairstreak, *Thecla quercus* is a butterfly of the high oak and in July and August small groups can be seen circling around the branch tips so high above the grassy path that they are visible only in flight. The purple blue suffused wings of the male or the rather brighter patched female are not for human eyes during aerial flight, but the silvery dove-grey of the underside shines in the sun.

Walking through Woodward's Coppice towards Pound Bank, under the oaks, a butterfly suddenly fell from the sunny branches

The green hairstreak (above) *and the purple hairstreak* (below).

above into the stringy heather lining the path. It was the first purple hairstreak butterfly that I had seen, and its delicate scaling and hues of shining purple and subtle greys exhilarated me. But that was nearly 50 years ago!

The dumpy rather slug-shaped caterpillars of the green hairstreak feed during June and July on broom and bilberry, as well as on the berries of buckthorn and buds of bramble and dogwood. Elsewhere than in the forest they are said to eat dyer's greenweed and needle furze. These two latter plants are too rare around Wyre to offer much sustenance to them. In colour they are palish green with a dark central line down the back with yellowish triangular patches on the sides of most of the segments. The black-speckled purplish brown chrysalis is covered with minute hairs and lies slung to the ground with a few silken strands amongst vegetable debris with but little protection during the winter months.

The purple hairstreak caterpillar is reddish brown and clothed in fine hair. There is a black line down the centre of the back which is whitish at the edges. In addition there are pale oblique stripes edged with black and the breathing pores are blackish encircled with a lightish hue. Also present, but absent in the green hairstreak caterpillar, is a grey somewhat shield-like mark on the second segment behind the head. It feeds on the leaves of oak, then turns to a reddish brown and dark-spotted chrysalis on the earth beneath the tree on which it has been feeding, only but loosely fixed by a strand or two of silk and its old cast caterpillar skin.

Of the other species of hairstreak found in Britain little can be said as far as Wyre Forest is concerned. I have seen none of them there but perhaps some careful observer may be lucky. The brown hairstreak, *Thecla betulae*, with its orange bands, flies in August and September and although a high flyer, sometimes comes down to feed on the nectar of the bramble blossom. The eggs overwinter and do not hatch until May when the young caterpillars feed on the leaves of the blackthorn. The eggs of the rarer and local species, the white letter hairstreak, *Strymon w-album*, also overwinter and the caterpillars feed on the leaves of the wych elm, but may also feed on the common elm. Again, they may be looked for on the bramble blossoms where they may be identified, if approached with extreme caution, by the w-shaped mark on the hindwings. But it is on the flowers of privet and the wayfaring tree, during June and July, that the black hairstreak, *Strymon pruni*, the rarest of the British hairstreaks, should be sought. These are its favourite sunning and sipping places, but the caterpillars feed on the leaves of the blackthorn. Wait for its wings to open. They are brownish black with a row of orange patches along the edges.

SKIPPERS AND BLUES

The small butterflies of the forest are mainly for the quick-eyed, at least when the sun shines. A point of colour flashes and they are gone. A competent naturalist should be able to identify all our butterflies on the wing. But we have not all such expertise. On dull days our butterflies are at rest and should be searched for on long grass stems and flowers. The underside of their wings are then displayed and are usually intricately-patterned.

The skipper butterflies, or butterflies of the family HESPERIDAE, are strangely transitional; although true butterflies, they show many characteristics of moths. They are all rather dumpy in shape with large furry heads, but their wing shape, pattern, and colouration, show wide variation. Of the eight species on the British list four occur in Wyre and, indeed, all are abundant.

The family LYCAENIDAE contains the 'blues', 'coppers', and 'hairstreaks', and of the 11 species in the blues, the common blue and the holly blue, are found in Wyre.

GRIZZLED SKIPPER, *Pyrgus malvae*

The grizzled skipper is one of our smallest butterflies and certainly one of our most active. When it flies in the sun at the end of April and in May, it can be followed only with the greatest difficulty. It is a wary butterfly, darting off at the slightest disturbance. The larval food plant is wild strawberry and sometimes bramble, but the caterpillars do not become visible unless the rolled-up leaves in which they live are unrolled.

The grizzled skipper butterfly. Everywhere the wild strawberry grows.

The ground colour of the upper wings of the grizzled skipper is greyish-black streaked with longer grey hairs, but on this there extends a pattern of rather squarish white marks. The wings are lighter underneath, the white patches being placed on a greenish grey or tawny grey background. The male possesses a long streak-like fold along the front edge of the forewing in which scent glands are situated. This is another common butterfly of the forest's sunny paths and still as common now as it was many years ago.

LARGE SKIPPER, *Ochlodes venata*

It is always pleasurable to see this bright fulvous orange butterfly in such numbers every year in Wyre. It flies in May and June with an extremely rapid motion but never seems to fly so far that one does not see its next resting-place. The male possesses a conspicuous oblique black raised streak in the central area of the forewings. The undersides of the wings are greenish tawny and some pale spots on the upper surface show through as pale yellow blotches. When at rest the large skipper either holds its wings vertically, flat over its back, or at an angle. The caterpillars feed on a number of grass species.

The large skipper butterfly.

SMALL SKIPPER, *Thymelicus sylvestris*

This skipper flies rather later than the large skipper, appearing in July and August. The wings are not quite so bright as in the previous species but the male possesses a similar black oblique streak on the forewing. The caterpillars also feed on a number of species of grass. It is common throughout Wyre, especially so in a number of open but sheltered spots.

DINGY SKIPPER, *Erynnis tages*

Along many of the forest paths, especially perhaps the Dowles Path, the old railway line and the aqueduct path, the bird's-foot trefoil grows. The yellow clustered pea-like flowers are to be seen where the sun can reach the earth. The caterpillars of the dingy skipper feed upon the plant exclusively. This small brown quick-flying butterfly emerges in May and is seen through to June, and when it perches it does so with wings outstretched.

When resting at night the wings are folded tent-wise like those
of a moth. In this respect it is unique amongst the British butterflies. Over many years now the dingy skipper has been a common
spring butterfly in Wyre and is still as abundant as ever it was.

HOLLY BLUE, *Celastrina argiolus*

The flower buds and developing berries of the holly and the ivy
are the food plants of the holly blue butterfly so that this beautiful little lilac and silver-blue butterfly could just as well have
been called the 'ivy blue'. There are two broods each year
although the second may not, every year, be complete. One of
the earliest butterflies of spring, a warm March day will often
bring them out. The female lays her eggs at the base, or on the
stalk, of holly flower buds and she can be identified by the
black border to her forewings. When the young caterpillar has
devoured its way out of the eggshell it feeds on the young buds.

Caterpillar of holly blue butterfly.

It is peculiarly slug-like in shape, eats halfway into the bud, and when not eating, its small head is withdrawn, out of sight, into the front part of the body. The second brood occurs in July and eggs are laid on the young buds of ivy and the resulting chrysalids are attached to a stalk or leaf. They pass the winter in the chrysalis stage. The holly blue occurs over much of southern England but becomes much rarer to the north and is absent from Scotland. It is common, and in some years abundant, all around the forest, perhaps more especially in the Far Forest area where the holly is allowed to grow into standards for the Christmas berry crop.

COMMON BLUE BUTTERFLY, *Polyommatus icarus*

Perhaps the most abundant of the family LYCAENIDAE, the blue butterflies, in Britain as a whole, is the common blue but it is nowhere in such numbers as are a number of the other blue butterfly species. This is because some of the other species, the chalk-loving ones, are often present in their locality in extraordinary abundance but may not be found for many miles around. The common blue is with us everywhere, if only very sparsely. I shall always remember my first encounter with this species, when I was a very young boy, on a railway embankment within the city of Birmingham. In and around Wyre there are a

Common blue butterfly.

number of sunny paths and heathy patches where the bird's-foot trefoil grows and it is on these plants, as is the case with the dingy skipper butterfly also, that the caterpillars feed. Two broods occur, one in spring and early summer, mid-May and most of June, and the other in August and September. The sexes are quite

distinct, the males being of a brilliant light violet-blue, almost an
azure blue, whilst the females are brown with but a variable
dusting of blue scales and a series of orange-red spots around the
outer margins of the wings. This species overwinters as young
caterpillars which secrete themselves around the base of the food
plants.

Although in the sun we see these most attractive butterflies
with their wings open, on wet or cold summer days we are only
likely to see their undersides as they hang on the long grass
heads, often in company with other species such as the small
copper, *Lycaena phlaeas*, and the small heath, *Coenonympha pam-
philus*.

MOTHS OF THE SUMMER NIGHT

One of the important and special features of the Forest of Wyre
is the extraordinary variety and abundance of moth species.
Many rare and strange sorts are to be found amongst the oak,
birch and alder, and amongst the shrubs and herbs of the woodland borders. The old orchard fringes also harbour species not
found, except in regions far away. The moths of the summer
night are part of our childhood memories. They flew encircling
the lamps and came bumbling in through the windows. One
reads that those days are gone, and that such insect profusion
has vanished with the new farming techniques. We are fortunate
then that in Wyre, buffered to some extent from modernity, we
can still enjoy the sight of many small creatures that are said to
have disappeared from many parts of the country.

Here are three moths of the many species found today in Wyre.
A certain amount of mystery and uncertainty concerning its
distribution and scarcity surrounds the alder moth. The moth-
hunters have always considered it a prize—with unfortunate
results for the moth.

The alder moth. A rare moth throughout Britain, but found in Wyre.

The alder moth, *Acronycta alni*, is of medium size and the forewings are dark silver-grey in colour clouded and suffused with black. There is a large heart-shaped mark in the lightish coloured area near the apex of each wing, and the hindwings are light silver-grey, almost white.

Strangely, the caterpillar advertises its presence by sitting in the middle of a leaf with its bizarre colouration of black and yellow transverse bands and its long club-shaped hairs which are quite unlike anything found on other moth caterpillars in Britain. But it appears to be solitary; perhaps one sees a single larva and no more in a season. On the other hand, the adult moth is shy and retiring, occasional specimens turning up in the mercury vapour light moth traps of the entomologists, and single examples have been caught on the moth-hunters' treacle patches.

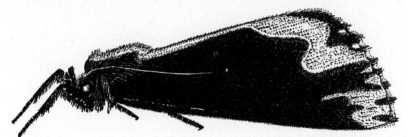

The bird's wing moth. A moth of the southern and eastern counties of England, but found in Wyre.

Although odd specimens have turned up in various parts of Britain, it is usually thought to favour the wooded areas of Hampshire (The New Forest) and Sussex (Ashdown Forest), but it can be found each year in Wyre Forest. The caterpillar is mostly found in July and August, mainly on alder but on other trees and shrubs too, and the moth is out in May and June.

The bird's wing moth, *Dypterygia scabriuscula*, is another medium-sized moth and its darkish almost black forewings are marked in a pattern of reddish buff said to be like a bird's wing. Its reddish brown caterpillar is striped with lines of yellow and black dots and the head is glossy brown marked with black. It feeds on plants of the genus *Polygonum*, and the docks and sorrels, so that it is mostly to be found around the fringing fields of rough grazing around Wyre. Like the alder moth, the moth flies in May and June. The point of interest concerning the bird's wing is that in Wyre it is right on the edge or, indeed, just outside its normal range of distribution. It is a moth of the southern and eastern counties of England.

The figure of eighty moth, *Tethea octogesima*, is so called because the pair of whitish marks bear some resemblance to the numerals,

The figure of eighty moth. A moth of the eastern counties, but common around Wyre.

although the base of the 'o' tails away somewhat. The caterpillar feeds at night during the months of July and August on the leaves of poplar and the moth is on the wing during May and June. It occurs mostly in the eastern countries, but it is stated in Richard South's book to be 'locally not uncommon in Worcestershire and Herefordshire.'

I have not found the poplar trees on which the caterpillars feed, near The Newalls, but it is exceptionally common here, coming to light and settling on the white cottage wall.

THE HERALD AND THE ANGLE SHADES

Two moths of beauty and interest found around the forest are called the herald and the angle shades. They are both somewhat larger than medium-size and although both are generally distributed throughout Britain they are worthy of the reader's attention, so that they can be identified and some appreciation of their different life cycles can be gained.

The herald, *Scoliopteryx libatrix*, was so called by Moses Harris in 1782, but another English name was given to it by Haworth in 1802—this was the 'furbelow'. It cannot possibly be mistaken for any other species. The outer edge of the forewings are scalloped and on a background of light greyish or rusty brown of somewhat frosted appearance, a double whitish line crosses the wing and between the lines and the body there is a bright orange suffusion.

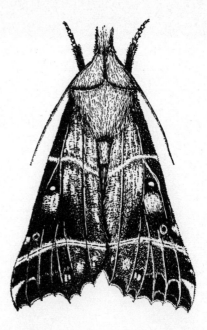

The herald moth.

The long thin green caterpillar feeds on the leaves of various species of willow and probably poplar during the months of June, July and August. The moth first appears in this latter month and thereafter until October when it can be seen sipping nectar from ivy blossom, and it then hibernates. For this purpose it seeks out sheltered situations in barns, outhouses, roof voids, and is often found also hanging tightly to folds of curtains in our homes. Here it rests inanimately during the winter months, but becomes active again in spring.

The angle shades, *Phlogophora meticulosa*, is rather similar in size to the herald but there the similarity ends. It is of a delicate mixture of pinks and browns with the forewings crossed with a broad silver-grey band. There is also a large olive-green triangular area. The whole effect is of exceptional beauty. The wings are folded around the body giving them a somewhat crumpled appearance. When the newly emerged moth is seen, delicately rosy and hanging poised but motionless, it is difficult to believe that such a leaf-like object is indeed a moth.

It will be seen that all the drawings of moths and butterflies illustrating this work show the insects in their natural postures. Thus, in the moths, when they are at rest one observes the top side of the forewings only, both wings if the view is from above,

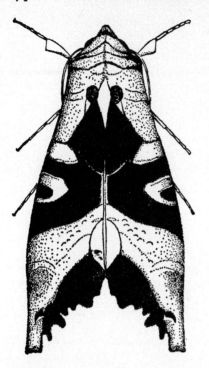

The angle shades moth.

but only one wing if observed from the side. The hind wings are generally invisible.

THE OAK, BRINDLED AND BORDERED BEAUTIES

All the British moths have been given common or popular names, that is with the exception of the very small ones, the micro-lepidoptera. How quaint, strange, apt, descriptive, or pretty, many of them are! The brindled white-spot, the brown silver-lined, the light emerald, the latticed heath, the maiden's blush, Haworth's pug, the beech-green carpet, and the rusty wave, are but a few names taken at random. Eight names begin with 'beautiful' for example, the beautiful brocade, and quite a number are known as 'beauties', with some suitable adjective preceding it. Three of the common and characteristic moths of Wyre are among them, the oak, brindled and bordered beauties. In addition, the great oak beauty, a rare moth in Britain but common in Wyre, will be discussed.

Among the several hundred moth species known from Wyre, (and for well over a hundred years the moth collectors have been busy), the family known as the GEOMETRIDAE is well represented.

All three mothy 'beauties' which are described below and illustrated are classified in this family. They are called 'geometers' for short. The word means 'earth measurer' and refers to the caterpillar stage. This is stick-like in appearance with six true legs at the fore end and with only four false legs at the hind end; most moth caterpillars possess ten of these latter clasper-like legs. When they walk, progression is made by making a series of loops (thus they are often called 'loopers'), as though they were measuring out the surface on which they travelled.

OAK BEAUTY, *Biston strataria*

A species closely related to the brindled beauty, and like it very variable. Usually the forewings are whitish with a smaller inner bar of brown edged with black and a larger similarly coloured bar near the apex of the wings. The whitish areas of the wings are variously speckled with black scales. Again it is a robust and hairy moth, rather larger than medium

The oak beauty.

size. Similarly also, the moths appear at the same time, during March and April, and the males are attracted to lit windows around Wyre. The caterpillar most generally feeds on oak, birch and elm, but has also been found on sloe, plum and rose. It is not generally thought to be a common moth, although it is generally distributed over England and Wales.

BRINDLED BEAUTY, *Lycia hirtaria*

This medium-sized moth is robust and hairy, and 'brindled' is an apt description of its colour. It is barred and speckled with yellows and brown of different intensities, and the individual specimens vary enormously. The moth appears very early in the year, March and April being the period when it is found resting on tree trunks. But the male is attracted to light and is perhaps more often seen sitting on the lit windows of our dwellings. Although, South, in his *Moths of the British Isles*, states that

The brindled beauty.

this species is commonest around the London parks, it is certain that this is not so today. Around, Wyre, however, it is still a very common insect. The caterpillar is to be found on a number of tree species, although the leaves of plum and pear appear to be its preferred diet.

BORDERED BEAUTY, *Epione repandaria*

A much smaller moth which is of more fragile and delicate appearance than the two preceding species, although still in the family GEOMETRIDAE. It is orange-yellow in colour with an outer band of purplish grey. This band occurs on both fore and hind wings which at first sight makes the moth appear smaller than it actually is. The two previous species are cryptically coloured,

The bordered beauty.

blending into their usual background of tree bark. The bordered beauty on the other hand is brightly and eye-catchingly coloured. Somehow it does not need to evade its enemies.

The caterpillar feeds on the leaves of alder and willow, the former being its customary food in Wyre, and the adult moths emerge in July and August, more commonly towards the end of this period.

MOTHS THAT SHOW RED FOR DANGER

A subject of ever-increasing importance to professional zoologists, entomologists, biologists, and to the amateur naturalist, is that of warning colouration, (and, to some extent, warning behaviour), of animals at the confrontation by a predator.

This needs something of an explanation. It is possible, or perhaps more accurately, probable, that the process of evolution of many important groups of animals, especially insects, has been modified by this natural phenomenon. In a way, it is strange that it was from collections of butterflies made in the great Amazon forests that the first laws of insect colouration were elucidated. Certain butterflies were obviously poisonous, or at least unpalatable to predaceous reptiles, amphibians, birds and mammals. To the extent that palatable butterflies varied towards a resemblance to these unpalatable insects, it conferred some advantage upon them in the great struggle to remain alive until reproduction had been effected. What extraordinary matters of interest these were to those great Victorians, Bates of the Amazon, and Wallace of the Malayan Archipelago! It was, for instance, clear that those butterflies that mimicked the poisonous ones were in very much of a minority. Of course, if one thinks about it, it would pay the predator to taste every one to see whether or not it was eatable!

The female was the vulnerable sex. It did not matter a great deal if a substantial percentage of the male sex was caught and eaten. Thus, it came about that in some butterfly species only the female sex showed a resemblance to the poisonous species thus conferring an advantage upon it when predation appeared inevitable. As one delves further into this subject of the mimicry of one insect by another, so it becomes even more fascinating, and a number of natural laws become evident. As has just been mentioned the species mimicking is always much less numerous than the species being mimicked. Again, many species in widely-separated groups adopt a common pattern when mimicking a noxious model. In Britain, indeed, in Europe and elsewhere, the wasp advertises its presence and its possession of a painful sting, by the pattern of yellow and black transverse bands. This same pattern is seen to be adopted by a number of harmless and palatable species such as various species of dipterous flies of several groups, a species of longhorn beetle, *Clytus arietis*, common in the forest, several species of moths in the 'clearwings' family, and a number of others. There is a statistical advantage to the individual species in being like the others.

Another type of colouration is referred to as crypsis. This is the well-known wing and body patterning to simulate the background on which the insect usually rests, such as the bark of a tree. Or the insect could look very much like a leaf, a bird dropping, or some other natural object. It is not proposed, however, to deal further with 'background colouration' at this point but rather to deal with some special points of great interest shown by the poisonous insects themselves.

It is now becoming well-known that insects which subsist on poisonous plants, that is, poisonous to other animals including mammals, and, indeed, man himself, contain the poisonous substances in their bodies. These chemicals change but little in the insect's digestive system but, of course, protect the insect from being eaten. In the first place the protection derives from

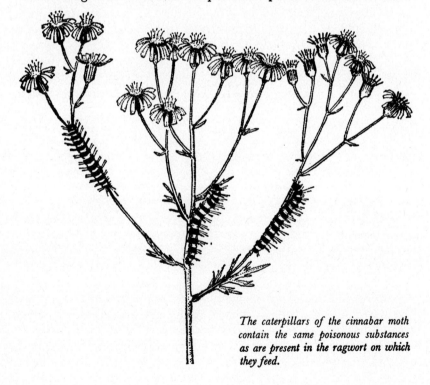

The caterpillars of the cinnabar moth contain the same poisonous substances as are present in the ragwort on which they feed.

the insect living on the noxious plant, and thus being avoided by grazing animals. Now, in the second place, insects that contain chemical substances poisonous to other animals would derive a great advantage if they were coloured in some easily recognised vivid patternings. Otherwise, they would be caught by a predator, probably killed or damaged, then spat out or rejected in some other way. This is precisely what has come about by natural selection.

Let us first take the example of the cinnabar moth, *Hypocrita jacobaeae*. This is a medium-sized moth whose wings are brown and pinkish vermilion, and its flight is very weak. It has no need

Above. *The garden tiger moth at rest shows two colours only, creamy white and chocolate brown.*
Below. *When the garden tiger moth is disturbed it shows its red underwings and it also makes a rattling noise.*

for great activity in order to avoid a predator. The hindwings are almost entirely red in colour—red for danger! The moths contain a complex of poisonous substances derived from the equally poisonous ragwort on which the larvae feed. The caterpillars are of interest too because they have adopted the wasp pattern; they are brightly and distinctly ringed throughout the whole of their length in black and yellow. They have no need to hide as do so many moth larvae which feed only at night and conceal themselves amongst the plant debris on the ground during the day. The larvae of the cinnabar rest and feed quite boldly on the ragwort plants during the bright day. Only the cuckoo appears to feed on them. The cuckoo seems particularly adapted to digesting caterpillars containing toxic substances because it also eats the woolly caterpillars of the tiger moth.

The garden tiger, *Arctia caja*, is a large fat-bodied moth which when at rest shows the distinctive patterning of its wings

The five-spot burnet moth found in a few colonies around the forest has red spots on its forewings and has red hindwings. It contains the very poisonous substance hydrocyanic acid. Shown emerging from its cocoon.

which consists of a chocolate-brown reticulation on a creamy white background. But if disturbed the forewings are held forwards to reveal the bright crimson hindwings spotted with a metallic blue. In addition, the moth can make a rattling noise known as stridulation although, so far, the means of making the noise has defied observation. The caterpillars of the garden tiger feed on a variety of leafy plants, a number of which are poisonous.

Both the cinnabar and the garden tiger are to be found around the forest, the adult moth of the former putting in its appearance in May and the garden tiger in July.

There is yet another moth species found in a few colonies around the forest which advertises its poisonous nature by warning colouration. This is the five-spot burnet, *Zygaena trifolii*, and in recent years an extraordinary story has been unfolded about this and other species of burnet moth.

It has been known by moth collectors that these metallic blue-green moths with red spots on their forewings and red hindwings were very difficult to kill in the entomologists' killing bottle containing the extremely poisonous potassium cyanide. It has now been found that the burnet moths actually contain hydrocyanic acid in their fluids which causes them to tolerate this gas when it is given off by the action of carbon-dioxide in the air on the potassium cyanide of the killing bottle. The burnet moths then are very poisonous and they show red for danger!

HELPING MOTHS TO SURVIVE

Old forest land which has remained extensive over several hundred years is characterized by a wealth of insect species. This is because a large number of different habitats are available for colonization and also because the whole of the habitat, at least in the past, has never been completely changed. The forest has been felled by rotation, some part of it being cut each year so that all the forest was at different stages of growth. Oak coppicing took place on an 18 year rotation. One of the first principles then in conserving the wide spectrum of insect species which we are fortunate to still have in Wyre is to have the compartments of the forest at various levels of maturity, from the sprouting oak stumps, or even the freshly-cut stump, to high forest.

Another important principle to follow is to ensure the continuity of the wide variety of tree species found in Wyre. If we

look at the two lists of moths compiled within the last few years
we find that L. J. Evans' list contains 263 species whilst that of
C. Betts, made up mainly from mercury vapour light collecting,
consists of 154 species. The former list was made from sallow
collecting and sugaring as well as from mercury vapour light
trapping. On examination of these lists of species one is immediately struck by the extraordinary variety of food-plant species
which they represent. The oak and the silver birch, whilst
important in this respect, must not be allowed to dominate the
situation when thinking of a situation which will conserve the
rather remarkable moth fauna of Wyre.

The alder is an important tree of Wyre in terms of the insect
fauna. It grows well not only along the banks of Dowles but
many of the small tributary streams produce good trees. When the
young stems shoot up and are just upwards of an inch in diameter
the rare and beautiful white-barred clearwing lays her eggs on
the bark and the resulting caterpillars feed on the wood, boring

The white-barred clearwing, Aegeria
spheciformis, *lays its eggs on the
young stems of the alder and the larva
tunnels down the centre of the stem.
The Wyre alders should be so cut as
to ensure a supply of young stems every
year.*

a tunnel down the centre of the shoot. A number of other species
of moths have larvae which subsist on the leaves of alder. The
alder moth, *Apatele alni* with its strange larva with clubbed
hairs is common in Wyre, although local and rare elsewhere in
the country. The alder kitten, *Cerura bicuspis,* again with a strange
larva, is presumably called a kitten because it is closely related
to, but smaller than, the puss moth. Others, including the iron
prominent, *Notodonta dromedarius* will feed on several other tree
species as well as alder.

At a late stage in the life of an alder tree when the trunk falls
due to its roots being undermined by floods, which is usually the
case, the alder wood wasp, *Xiphydria camelus* inserts its eggs deep
into the bark. The larvae then tunnel into the dying or dead
wood. This insect species supports a complex of parasitic species
which stimulated Gerald Thompson to make his BBC award-

winning film about its complicated life history. They are common along the streams of Wyre wherever a falling alder provides the special habitat. In conserving the insects of Wyre the alder tree plays an important role in all stages of its growth.

KENTISH GLORY, *Endromis versicolora*

There is one large and very beautiful white and chestnut banded and speckled moth which is now thought to be confined to Wyre Forest as an English species, although it is found in Aviemore in Scotland. That is the Kentish glory moth, *Endromis versicolora* which is on the wing early in the year when it makes its appearance during the first warm days of April. The larvae feed exclusively on the leaves of the silver birch and usually are to be seen in small groups feeding near the tip of a branch. The trees selected are usually in a somewhat isolated position or at least at the edge of a copse or along a woodland ride. The locality seems to shift about from year to year, and the old railway line was once a favourite.

The Kentish glory moth, now found in England only in Wyre. The large fat green caterpillars feed on the leaves on the terminal twigs of the silver birch. The selected trees are usually along sunny paths and banks.

One of the most successful methods of collecting the males of the Kentish glory was by 'assembling'. This consisted of rearing a few moths to maturity in order to obtain a virgin female. In practise a female pupa was purchased from a dealer and when the young female moth hatched out it was taken to Wyre, placed in a muslin bag and hung on the branch of a convenient tree. Then she 'called' a scent, or more correctly a chemical male stimulant or attractant was emitted from special glands and the males would come flocking in. Several dozen males were sometimes attracted by this means.

The large orange-banded cranefly, Tipula atrata, *can be seen laying its eggs in rotting stumps of oaks.*

If we wish to conserve the Kentish glory moth so that our descendants may experience the beauty of this lovely insect, there is no doubt in the mind of the writer that *all collecting of it should cease forthwith.*

THE FOREST WOOD-WASPS

The 'ants, bees and wasps' group of insects, known as the HYMENOPTERA, is a vast assemblage of insects. There are not only more than 60,000 species already described, but many more are thought to await discovery. The insects in this order possess a number of important characteristics in common. First of all, they have two pairs of membraneous wings which interlock with each other by means of a row of minute horny hooks. In addition, the abdomen, in the majority of the order, is usually constricted with the first segment of the abdomen fused with the last segment of the thorax. An ovipositor, or egg-laying tube, is always present and it may be specially modified for sawing, piercing, or stinging. Usually the larvae are legless. A remarkable feature of the Hymenoptera concerns the social structure of the colonies shown by the ants as well as certain families of wasps and of bees.

This account, however, is of the wood-wasps which, together with the sawflies, make up the most primitive, that is, the least developed, of the ants, bees and wasps. The wood-wasps and sawflies together are called the SYMPHYTA and they differ from the rest of the Hymenoptera, the more highly developed section, by not showing the constriction of the abdomen, the wasp-waist. In addition, the larvae bear legs. The wood-wasps themselves are grouped together into a single family, the SIRICIDAE. They are large insects, conspicuously coloured, sometimes black and yellow or metallic, and the abdomen terminates in a spine. In

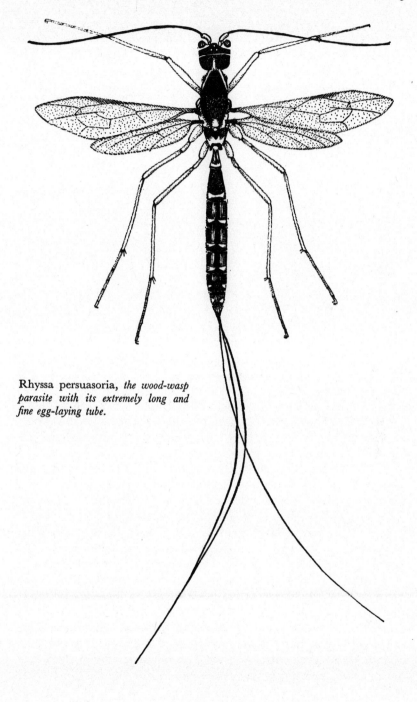

Rhyssa persuasoria, *the wood-wasp parasite with its extremely long and fine egg-laying tube.*

the female there is also a stout ovipositor used for drilling holes through tree bark. This is where the eggs are laid and the larvae spend the whole of their existence boring into wood. The wood-wasps are divided into two groups, the first of which attack coniferous trees and are great forest pests in many parts of the world. The second group attack only broadleaved trees and they are of much less importance as tree pests. The wood-boring habit,

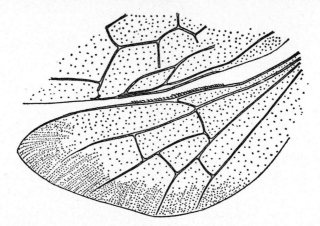

The wing-locking mechanism common to the ants, bees and wasps. Note row of small hooks on front edge of hind wing. Sirex cyaneus.

however, has resulted in their distribution almost throughout the world on account of the larvae being carried about in timber. In Britain it is difficult to give a precise ruling as to which species are truly indigenous.

Urocerus gigas is a very large hornet-like species which, although I have not personally seen it, certainly occurs in Wyre. This is known because several times the extraordinary parasite *Rhyssa persuasoria* of this species has been observed deep in the forest. A tree infested with the large fat larvae is usually already sickly having been attacked by the fungus *Stereum sanguinolentum*, but it is a remarkable fact that there are special glands in the thorax of the larvae in which the fungus is maintained. Presumably, the larva can reinfect the wood with the fungus if, for some reason it dies off.

Perhaps the most remarkable feature concerning the biology of the wood-wasps is the phenomenon of parasitism. One parasite, named *Rhyssa persuasoria*, is a large, but slender, member of the highly developed group, the ICHNEUMONIDAE. The female, having

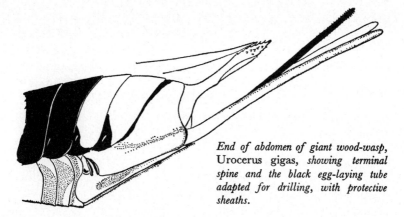

End of abdomen of giant wood-wasp, Urocerus gigas, *showing terminal spine and the black egg-laying tube adapted for drilling, with protective sheaths.*

found a tree which she has decided is infested with *Sirex* larvae, thoroughly explores it with her antennae. These are continually palpated and held against the tree bark with their dorsal surfaces in contact with it. When she decides to bore, the insect lifts herself up to the fullest possible extent, almost appearing to stand on her head, whilst the ovipositor is held downwards and guided between the back legs. When the drilling action of the ovipositor has cut a shaft near to its fullest extent, an egg is passed down it. The canal is so fine that a human hair cannot be passed down. The accuracy with which the female *Rhyssa* finds the larva of the *Sirex* has often been remarked upon

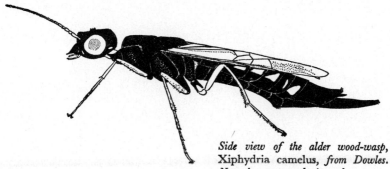

Side view of the alder wood-wasp, Xiphydria camelus, *from Dowles. Note the stout egg laying tube.*

but oddly enough, in a high percentage of cases, the borings are abortive in that holes are cut nowhere near the host larva, so that the young *Rhyssa* larva must inevitably perish. But surely the degree of success is remarkable, in that it is sufficient to ensure the continuation of the species. Only well-developed larvae of *Sirex* are parasitized by *Rhyssa*. Not only are they nearer the outer surface of the timber, but small larvae do not contain sufficient nutrient for the complete development of the parasite although this takes only about five weeks.

One of the earliest records of another member of the Siricidae, *Sirex juvencus*, is given by the great entomologist Westwood in his *Introduction to the Modern Classification of Insects*. This concerned a specimen taken sometime before 1836 (the date of publication of this work) in Wyre Forest. This is puzzling, as this species is usually considered to have been introduced, and a more unlikely place to find an introduced insect 130 years ago, in the middle of a forest, is hard to envisage.

But with all the conjecture concerning the origin of the larger species of our Wyre wood-wasps, at least there is one species in the genus *Xiphydria*, which must be native to our forest. This is the alder wood-wasp, *Xiphydria camelus*, the subject of the biology

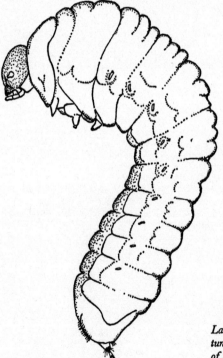

Larva of the alder wood-wasp. They tunnel into sickly trunks and branches of silver birch and alder.

of which species, with its extraordinary group of parasites, was the subject of the film made by Gerald Thompson already mentioned.

The alder wood-wasp is black in colour with a row of white spots along the sides of the abdomen. Taking Britain as a whole, it is a rare and local insect but it is fairly common along Dowles where the females lay their eggs in holes cut into the bark of a recently-dead branch or tree of alder or birch. The larva tunnels in the wood for about ten months and after a short pupal stage, the adults bite their way out of the wood making circular flight holes. This species is parasitized by four different hymenopterous insects, perhaps the most remarkable being *Aulacus striatus*. The female of this species finds the egg shafts made by the wood-wasp female and then passes her own ovipositor down and deposits an egg on those eggs which it can reach. This rare parasitic insect occurs along Dowles as a number have been reared from birch branches attacked by *camelus*.

Another strange parasite is *Rhyssella curvipes* whose behaviour is similar to the closely related *Rhyssa persuasoria*, already mentioned as parasitizing *Sirex*, but it is not known whether it occurs along Dowles for, as far as I know, it has not been collected.

The alder wood-wasp, and its associated parasitic fauna, is one of the more remarkable entomological treasures of the Forest of Wyre.

THE FOREST ANTS

The ants constitute a very small well defined family of the order HYMENOPTERA, the FORMICIDAE. Ants, like some of the bee species, are social insects living in colonies which may consist of a relatively small number of individuals or, on the other hand, may contain a very large number. Actual counts made in mound nests of *Formica rufa*, the wood ant, varied between nearly 20,000 and nearly 100,000 individuals!

Most people are able to recognise ants. The three well-defined regions of the usually wingless body, the head, thorax and abdomen, together with the dark and shining colour aid identification by the non-specialist. The naming of our 38 British ant species is, however, a task for the specialist.

He would be very unobservant who set foot within the forest during spring and summer who failed to see the wood ant,

Formica rufa. Their large mound-like nests of leaf and twig fragments, pine needles, and other vegetable debris are strewn
through the forest in every direction. In 1965 I counted 35 of
such nests along about three quarters of a mile of the path along
Dowles Brook; each of these nests was actually on the path edge
and with a south-facing aspect. At frequent intervals columns of
wood ants traverse the path, many carrying vegetable debris for
the nest, or insects such as caterpillars for food. It is difficult to
sit down for a picnic in the forest without finding a few ants
running over one's clothes. Sometimes the first signal of their
presence is a painful nip on the ankle.

The life history of this ant, briefly, is as follows:

Winged females and males are produced in small swarms at
some time during June. After fertilisation the female returns to
her old colony or one of its numerous offshoots, where she is
hospitably received and she then commences to lay eggs. The
legless larvae are tended by sterile females known as workers and,
indeed, all the tasks of the colony are carried out by the workers.
The wood ant is unable to start a colony on her own as she is
not capable of tending the young larvae herself as can other
species. The larvae spin thin papery cocoons before pupating.
These are known popularly, but erroneously, as 'ants eggs', and
are used for feeding fish in aquaria. The ant colony is perpetual
unless it terminates by accident, such as fire.

A list of some of the species recorded for Wyre Forest is given
below, with additional notes:

Formica rufa, the wood ant. This is a large ant, workers being
from one sixth to one third of an inch in length with the males
and females somewhat larger. The head, antennae, legs and
abdomen are dull dark brown, whilst the thorax, node and bases
of the legs are reddish, to give it its specific name. Very common
in Wyre Forest where the nests are commonly sited on old tree
stumps of oak. This species has disappeared from many localities
in England where it was formerly abundant. Collingwood states
'The overall picture is one of decline and extinction in the
smaller woodlands of the region (The South Midlands), whilst
the species continues in great abundance in parts of the larger
woodlands.'

Formica exsecta. This is known as the narrow-headed ant and is
somewhat like the wood ant in general appearance, but is rather
more yellowish and the head and thorax are blotched with
brown. New branch colonies are produced by the community

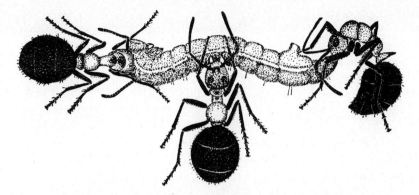

Three wood ant workers carrying off a caterpillar of the speckled yellow moth.

sending out groups of workers with a young female who establish themselves at a little distance from the main colony. Young females will sometimes start a colony by laying in the nest of the negro ant, *Formica fusca*, who then tend the young larvae. This species was recorded by Blatch for Wyre Forest in 1901 in the *Victoria County History, Worcestershire*, but has not been recorded since that time.

Formica sanguinea. This is called the blood-red ant and is similar in size or may be even larger than the wood ant. It is extremely fierce and does not build a mound of vegetable debris over its nest, although it will sometimes construct a screen of leaves, etc. in very hot weather, probably to conserve moisture. The female is more distinctly red in colour than *F. rufa*, but the male is more nearly black with reddish legs. The workers of this species do not tend and nurture their own larvae, but having raided another nest, as of *F. fusca*, carry off pupae and those which they do not eat hatch out and subsequently look after their captors' larvae. It is thus known as a 'slavemaker'. Most nests of *F. sanguinea* contain a number of *F. fusca* workers. The blood-red ant is abundant in Wyre Forest.

Formica cunicularia. This species was collected in Wyre Forest by Donisthorpe in 1908–1909, but it has not been collected since 1916. It is a local insect usually found on stony banks in Southern England and South Wales.

Lasius fuliginosus. Common in Worcestershire.

Lasius niger and *Lasius flavus* are both very abundant.

Lasius mixtus and *Lasius umbratus* are both widely distributed.

Formicoxenus nitidulus. This is known as the shining guest ant because of its polished appearance. It has reddish yellow head and thorax, the legs being paler and the abdomen is dark brown. It is small, being only about 3 mm in length and it is found in the nests of *Formica rufa.* It is recorded for Wyre Forest.

Myrmica rubra, the red ant, *M. laevinodis, M. scabrinodis,* and *M. sabuleti,* are all common and widely distributed according to Collingwood.

Myrmica lobicornis. This species is usually found in isolated colonies and is recorded from both the Worcestershire and Shropshire parts of Wyre.

Myrmica schencki. A single worker of this species was found in 1946 by W. E. Hammond and K. G. V. Smith in Chamberline Wood, Wyre Forest. A wide search has failed to reveal further specimens. *This is a very rare species and this is the only English record.*

Myrmica sulcinodis. This species was found in Wyre Forest in 1908 by G. W. Ellis and A. H. Martineau, but has not been seen in recent years.

Leptothorax acervorum, the slender ant, is abundant. Its peaceful disposition is well-known. Often uses the abandoned borings of beetles or narrow spaces under loose bark fairly near the ground.

Leptothorax nylanderi. As its recorded distribution closely follows the river Severn it is probable that it will be found on the edge of Wyre, but no specific records have, so far, been found.

Stenamma westwoodii, Westwood's ant, has been recorded from two localities in Wyre Forest.

The ants of Wyre are abundant in numbers and in species, and there are great rarities to be found. They would well repay a study.

THE UBIQUITOUS BEETLES

Of all the groups of animals on earth, the beetles are the most numerous. Twenty years ago there were estimated to be 220,000 described species and 3,700 of these are to be found within the British Isles. No group within the animal kingdom, and certainly no order of the class of Insects, shows such a wide diversity of habitat. They are to be found in almost every situation. It has been said that their adaptability and the structural modifications which they exhibit have evidently contributed much to their dominance, for the imagines of no other order of insects have invaded the land, air and water, to the same proportional degree. Although species of 12 separate beetle families are truly aquatic insects living in freshwater, the great majority of beetles are dwellers in the ground or are closely associated with it.

Various reasons have been given to account for the successful exploitation of the earth by beetles, but what seems certain is that the solidity of the integument shown in the majority of species has been an important factor in protecting them not only against enemies of various kinds, but also against adverse physical conditions. 'The various sclerites are fitted together with a precision that marks them out as truly marvellous pieces of natural mechanism,' as stated by Imms.

The beetles or Coleoptera are characterised by the forewings being modified into horny or leathery wing cases or elytra as they are called. In almost all cases these meet to form a straight line down the centre of the back. The hindwings are membraneous and when at rest they lie folded under the elytra, but often they are much reduced or sometimes absent altogether. They have biting mouthparts and the prothorax, the first division of the thorax bearing the first pair of legs is large and mobile, the middle division, the mesothorax bearing the second pair of legs and the elytra, is generally much reduced. The metamorphosis is complete, there being four distinct stages in the life cycle, egg, larva, pupa and adult.

The forest offers many habitats for beetles especially as the range of timber species is moderately large for those species with wood-eating larvae, or are associated with decaying wood and its associated flora such as the fungi. The introduction of exotic species of trees in connection with forestry is bound to increase the number of beetle species to be found in the forest, provided the old, traditional habitats related to coppicing oak, do not entirely disappear.

As far as is known to the writer no comprehensive collection, or list, of beetles of Wyre Forest exists in spite of the fact that the forest has been a popular collecting site for the Lepidoptera, the butterflies and moths, and for other orders of insects and, in addition, there are known to be present a number of uncommon and indeed, very rare, species. We certainly need to know which species occur and in a number of cases there is scope for original work on their biology and their relationship with other plants and animals.

Accordingly, here are some notes on a few beetle species which have been noted in the forest over a number of years, although they have not been systematically collected.

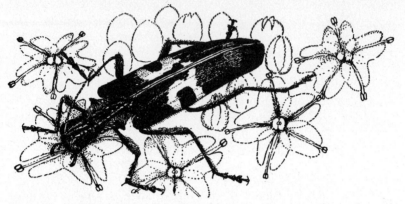

Rhagium mordax feeding on the pollen of hogweed. Note the eye-like marks on the elytra. About ¾ inch in length.

In a forest it is not surprising that a substantial number of species in the longhorn group or CERAMBYCIDAE are to be found. The larvae of this family are predominantly wood-feeders, some species boring into relatively sound wood whilst others require it to be in an advanced stage of fungal decay. The largest species,

Oecoptoma thoracica is one of the carrion beetles in the family Silphidae, common in the forest. The thorax is reddish-yellow which makes the insect very distinctive when it is found by rolling over the carcass of a dead animal. The specimen illustrated was found under a dead woodcock. The larvae feed on the decaying flesh.

and one that always gives the writer a thrill when it is observed, is *Stenocorus meridianus* whose larvae feed mainly on the timber of the cherry tree in Wyre, but it is a strong flyer in the hot sun and has been seen a mile or so away from the nearest cherry tree. The insect exists in two colour phases with occasionally something of a mixture. The colouration of this handsome beetle is given as 'head and thorax black, elytra entirely black, or reddish-yellow, or with apex and suture black, or base only yellow, antennae black or yellow.' Fairly closely related to the above species is *Rhagium mordax*, which I first met along Dowles when

I was a boy. They are strongly attracted to a white colour and a number flew on to my white woollen sweater. Athough feeding on the rotting stumps of a variety of tree species, oak is the most favoured. Another handsome longhorn beetle is the black and yellow and very variable *Strangalia maculata*. The larvae of this species also feed in old tree stumps, both of oak and birch. The adult beetle can be searched for on the large white inflorescences

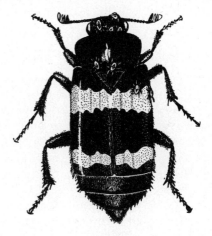

Necrophorus investigator *is one of the burying beetles found in the forest under dead animals. This species is black with bright orange bands. It is a local insect in Britain. The adult beetles burrow under the dead body of a small animal such as a mole until the body sinks into it. Eggs are laid and the larvae feed on the decaying flesh.*

of hogweed and other members of the Compositae. These flowers are particularly attractive to many longhorn species including another quite common species *Judolia cerambyciformis*. This latter insect is more often found in the southern counties. It feeds on the exposed roots of oak and birch trees and the larvae tunnel through the earth in search of tree roots. It has a peculiar hovering flight when searching for a mate on the hogweed. Without a doubt, however, the most interesting of the forest's longhorn

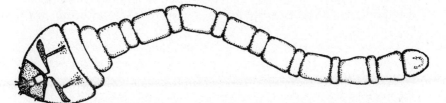

Melasis buprestoides *has an extraordinary larva with a much enlarged head quite unlike any other beetle larva. It bores into the felled trunks of alder and other tree species, where it cuts strange disc-like galleries which are characteristic and quite easily found where trunks have been lying for some length of time.*

beetles is *Strangalia nigra*. This slender black and fast-flying beetle is rare in Britain and Wyre is the most northerly part of its range. Indeed, it is now said to have disappeared from many of its localities in the south. In Wyre it is confined to a relatively small area of hilly forest. Its biology is entirely unknown except that the flying adults are attracted to the inflorescence of the wood spurge. The larval stage, as far as is known, has never been collected. Here is a chance for a rewarding piece of research for a keen observant naturalist!

A GLITTER OF GLOW-WORMS

Glow-worms are beetles. They belong to a family, the LAMPYRIDAE, with a world-wide distribution of over 2,000 species, but of these only two species are to be found in Britain. These are the glow-worm, *Lampyris noctiluca*, and the very rare *Phosphaenus hemipterus*. The glow-worm was formerly widely distributed but local. I say 'formerly' because it has been claimed that they are now extinct in Britain. Fortunately, this is not so. The glow-worm is still abundant around the Forest, especially so in the Furnace Mill—Far Forest area. During the space of about an hour from when darkness fell, 13 males flew to the lit windows of The Newalls on 1st July 1968!

Glow-worms are strange, both in their habit and shape. In the first place we should say that in some accounts, only the female is referred to as the glow-worm. It is she who emits the strongest light, but the male can also be picked out in the pitchy blackness of the night by his luminescence, even if somewhat less spectacular than that of his mate. The male is typically beetle-like, which is more than can be said for the female. When at rest the head of the male is retracted under a thin shield-shaped prothorax so that it is invisible from the top, but when he is active the large black bulbous eyes, situated right at the front of the head, are easily observed.

The larvae of the glow-worm possess curved, sickle-shaped mandibles which are grooved. They feed on slugs and snails and when seized in the sharp jaws a digestive fluid passes down the groove into the luckless prey. It is thus digested externally and the fluids are sucked up by the larva. The head of the larva can be retracted completely within a chamber in the prothorax. It has a peculiar means of progression. Its legs are small but it is helped by the abdomen being curled under, then straightened

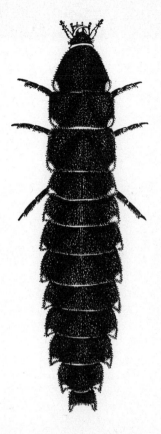

The larva of the glow-worm. It feeds on slugs and snails. The adult female much resembles it.

out which pushes the insect forward. The last segment of the abdomen is furnished with two projections which help it to do this. The larva, presumably one destined to become a female, will sometimes emit light from the apex of the abdomen.

The photogenic organ of the glow-worm consists of an outer layer which produces light by the oxidation of a material *luciferin*, and an inner reflective layer consisting of urate crystals. The luminous organ is under the control of the insect and can be switched on or off at will. This organ is well provided with air tubes on which it is dependent and is actuated by an enzyme working in the presence of water.

The glow-worm, often alluded to in our poetry and literature, seems scarcely ever to be mentioned in our modern times. But this extraordinary sight of the countryside of Wyre is worthy of our thoughts and quiet contemplation.

Looking at drawings of male glow-worms in various books I am driven to the conclusion that dead specimens provided the models.

The male glow-worm. The wing-cases gape apart.

The front end of the shield is transparent. The wing cases are full greyish black each with a pair of ridges and the apex is more yellowish. It is characteristic of this species that the wing cases do not meet along the middle line but always give the appearance of being partially open and the wing tips are always visible. The male flies well and is attracted not only to the luminescent female but to lighted windows and outdoor electric lighting, as mentioned above. This must have some appreciable effect in reducing the number of males available for reproduction.

The earth-bound females possess neither wing cases nor wings and, indeed, have very much the appearance of the immature larval stage. The separate segments of thorax and abdomen are distinct and rather scale-like. The head is small, and can also be retracted under the prothoracic shield, and the eyes are inconspicuous.

For Further Reading

BARRETT, K. E. J., 1968, A Survey of the Distribution and present status of the Wood Ant, *Trans. Soc. Brit. Ent.*, **17**(8):217–233.

BEAUFOY, S., 1947, *Butterfly Lives*, Collins, London.

BECHYNE, J., 1956, *Beetles, Open-Air Guide*, Translated and Edited by C. M. F. Von Hayek, Thames and Hudson, London.

BLATCH, 1901, *Victoria County History, Worcs.*, **1**:878.

CARPENTER, G. D. H. and FORD, E. B., 1933, *Mimicry*, Methuen, London.

CLEGG, J., 1952, *The Freshwater Life of the British Isles*, Wayside and Woodland Series, Warne, London.

COLLINGWOOD, C. A., 1955, Ants in the South Midlands, *Entomologists' Gazette*, **6**: 143–149.

COLLINGWOOD, C. A., 1958, A Key to the Species of Ants (Hymenoptera, Formicidae) Found in Britain, *Trans. Soc. Brit. Ent.*, **13**(5): 69–96.

CORBET, P. S., LONGFIELD, C. and MOORE, N. W., 1960, *Dragonflies*, Collins, London.

DONISTHORPE, H. ST. J., 1927, *British Ants*, 2nd Edition, London.

ELLIS, H. W. and MARTINEAU, A. H., 1908, *Entomologists' Record*, **20**: 56.

FRASER, F. C., 1949, *Handbooks for the Identification of British Insects, Odonata*, Roy. ent. Soc. Lond., **1**(10): 1–48.

FROHAWK, F. W., 1914, *Natural History of British Butterflies*, 2 vols., Hutchinson, London.

HICKIN, N. E., 1952, *Caddis—A Short account of the Biology of British Caddis Flies with special reference to the Immature Stages*, Methuen, London.

HICKIN, N. E., 1967, *Caddis Larvae*, Hutchinson, London.

HICKIN, N. E., 1968, *Insect Factor in Wood Decay*, 2nd Edition, Hutchinson, London. (Contains line drawings of nearly all British Cerambycid beetles.)

HUXLEY, T. H., 1879, *The Crayfish—An Introduction to Zoology*, Kegan Paul, Trench, London.

IMMS, A. D., 1957, *General Textbook of Entomology*, 9th Edition, Revised by RICHARDS, O. W. and DAVIES, R. G., Methuen, London.

JOY, N. H., 1933, *British Beetles*, Warne, London.

LANE, C., 1959, A very Toxic Moth: The Five-Spot Burnet (*Zygaena trifolii*), *Entomologists Monthly Magazine*, **95**: 93.

LINSSEN, E. F., 1959, *Beetles of the British Isles*, Wayside and Woodland Series, 2 vols., Warne, London.

McMILLAN, N. F., 1968, *British Shells*, Wayside and Woodland Series, Fredk. Warne, London.

MOSELY, M. E., 1939, *The British Caddis Flies (Trichoptera), A Collector's Handbook*, Routledge, London.

NEWMAN, L. H., 1948, *Butterfly Haunts*, Chapman and Hall, London.

NEWMAN, L. H., N.D., *Butterflies on the Wing*, Edmund Ward, Leicester. (Truth in a Tale Series for Small Children, with a series of beautiful illustrations by Miss N. C. Glegg.)

ROTHSCHILD, M., et al., 1961, 1963, 1965, Exhibits, *Proceedings of the Royal Entomological Society of London*, C, *Journal of Meetings*, **30**(1): 3 and **28**(8): 39 and **26**(6): 22.

STEP, E., 1932, *Bees, Ants and Allied Insects of the British Isles*, Warne, London.

SOUTH, R., 1906, *The Butterflies of the British Isles*, Warne, London.

SOUTH, R., N.D., *The Moths of the British Isles*, Wayside and Woodland Series, First and Second Series, Warne, London.

SOUTHWOOD, T. R. E. and LESTON, D., 1959, *Land and Water Bugs of the British Isles*, Wayside and Woodland Series, Warne, London.

STOKOE, W. J., N.D., *The Observer's Book of Butterflies*, Warne, London.

WITHYCOMBE, C. L., 1922, Notes on the Biology of some British Neuroptera, *Trans. ent. Soc. Lond.*, 501–594.

THE FISHES, AMPHIBIANS AND REPTILES OF WYRE

DOWLES FISHES

MILLER'S THUMB, *Cottus gobio*

Undoubtedly, the most abundant fish in Dowles is the miller's thumb or bullhead, or as it is called by the local children, the bull-knob. In the brook, but away from the fastest water, they are to be found under almost every stone. In our eyes, of rather ugly appearance, the head is disproportionately large. It is broad and

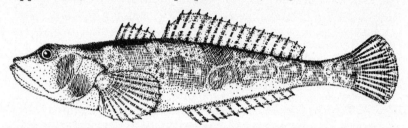

The miller's thumb in side view. It grows to three or four inches in length and spends most of its time resting on the stream bottom.

rounded in front and bears a strong spine, backwardly directed on the pre-opercle. The overall length of the fish is around three or four inches. In colour it is of a light brownish yellow, banded and spotted with a darker brown, and with a more or less pronounced greenish tinge. There are two dorsal fins which are large and fan-shaped, the one in front being more spinous. The ventral fin is spinous also. Whereas pectoral fins are large and rounded, the pelvics are small. The skin does not bear scales.

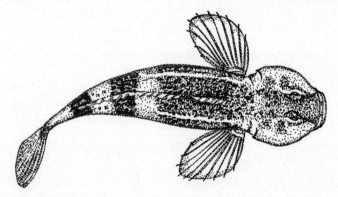

The miller's thumb is the most plentiful fish in Dowles. When seen from the top, the head is disproportionately large.

The miller's thumb is not a strong swimmer, spending a lot of time resting on the stream bottom or under a sheltering stone. When disturbed, however, it shoots forward with great speed to take up another position, although this burst of activity does not take it very far. Spawning takes place in March and April, when a cluster of large pink eggs is deposited in a cavity scooped out under a stone. Often, however, tins or glass jam-jars, which have found their way into the stream, are used as nests. The male fish guards the nest and if the stone covering the nest is lifted, he does not swim away. Some years ago, I lifted a Bovril bottle out of the brook only to find it full of miller's thumb eggs with the male fish present. I gently put the bottle back and the parent did not desert them. In spite of the spinous nature of the miller's thumb, the kingfisher will catch and eat them, or feed them whole to their young!

LAMPREY, *Petromyzon fluviatilis*

I once caught a lamprey in the little stream that runs into Dowles at the 'island'. I do not know whether this primitive and most curious of our fishes is still to be found in Wyre, but I see no reason why this should not be. There are so many strange

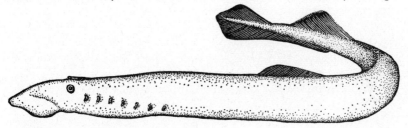

The lamprey has been found in Dowles and, no doubt, still occurs. It has a large bag-like mouth which it uses as a sucker.

and fascinating phenomena displayed by the lamprey that it is difficult to decide where to begin. Let us take two features of its anatomy first. It has no jaws. This is, with the exception of the closely-related hag fishes, unique amongst fish. Its several rows of strong teeth encircle the bag-like mouth on the inside of the cheeks. The mouth acts as a sucker and it can hold its position clinging to a stone in a fast-moving stream, or it can fasten itself onto a fish such as a salmon and rasp large lumps of flesh from its back. By this means also, the lamprey can be carried long distances by its unwilling travelling companion. The second anatomical point concerns its pineal gland. This gland arises from the roof of the forebrain and bears a strong resemblance to an eye. It appears to be light sensitive but its value to the lamprey is uncertain because it possesses a pair of apparently good seeing eyes.

The development of the lamprey is also strange. Its first three or four years of life are spent in a tube buried in mud, where it subsists on minute organisms and particles of organic debris in the mud or carried in the water currents. This is somewhat akin to a larval stage as it bears little resemblance to the form of the adult. The eyes are rudimentary and are covered with skin so that it is blind, teeth are absent, and the organic particles are carried along a canal until they are 'caught' by strings of mucus. The head bears a single median nostril. Altogether, it is a strange animal!

CHUB, *Leuciscus cephalus*

On a hot summer's afternoon schools of small chub, up to seven or eight inches in length, can be seen very near the surface in the small pools of Dowles. Presumably, as they grow larger they drop downstream until they swim into the Severn.

The top surface of the chub is a light olive-brown and is silvery beneath. The pelvic fins and the anal fin are reddish. The scales are fairly large in size and an important character distinguishing it from the dace, concerns the edge of the dorsal and anal fins. This is straight in the dorsal and convex in the anal, whilst in the dace it is concave in both cases.

It is said that the chub undergoes two phases in its diet; carnivorous when it takes small fish, frogs, worms and insects and their larvae, and vegetarian when it eats seeds, roots and buds of freshwater plants, as well as algae. In Dowles, however, it would have great difficulty in finding vegetable material other than algae and *Fontinalis* moss, yet the young fish are thought to feed more on vegetable than animal matter. But the chub has a large mouth and gape, its jaws are strong and the pharynx well supplied with teeth which points to the importance of the carnivorous content of its diet.

A few years ago, some small chub from Dowles were pan-fried and placed before me for my breakfast. As a result I can confirm the remarks of an unknown piscatorial gourmet who likened them to cotton-wool mixed with fine needles.

EEL, *Anguilla anguilla*

Large eels are sometimes found in Dowles. I have, myself, seen several. One large individual was disturbed at 'the island'; this was where the stream is crossed by the 'elbow path'. An attempt was made to put it on the bank in order to measure it—what a futile occupation! It was extremely strong and lived up to its reputation of slipperyness. In the end I was covered with slime and the eel had disappeared upstream where it was determined to go. I would guess its length at between two and a half to three feet. The migration of the eel is, of course, legendary. The very small eels, scarcely larger than darning needles, enter the Severn from the sea and are called elvers. In spite of the millions that are caught (it is recorded that three tons were collected in the Gloucester district, where they are boiled and eaten as a delicacy, in a single day in 1886), they make their way into the streams, lakes and ponds, travelling overland at night in rain and heavy dew in order to do this. There is some adaptation to breathing through the skin when this takes place, as scales would prevent it, but in the eel they are microscopic. There they live and grow, feeding on a wide variety of animal matter until, in October, changes take place in the shape of the head, and a change in colour from yellow to silver; then they slip downstream and out into the ocean to return to their breeding place. This is now known to be the area of the Western Atlantic, south of Bermuda. This entails a journey of some three or four thousand miles and is accomplished by the males at the age of some eight to ten years and the females from ten to eighteen years. When they have spawned they die and it takes the leaf-shaped young eels (called leptocephali) about three years to swim back across the Atlantic when they metamorphose into elvers and ascend the rivers of Europe.

SALMON, *Salmo salar* AND BROWN TROUT, *Salmo trutta*

The brown trout is abundant everywhere along Dowles, and they also make their way considerable distances up even the very small streamlets. But they are lean and hungry-looking fish, seldom larger than seven or eight inches in length.

I have never met anyone who has actually seen a salmon in Dowles, but it is certain they do ascend a few miles up from the Severn as the salmon parr are sometimes found. The salmon eggs hatch during the very early spring, but for the first month the fry or alevins, as they are called, remain on the stream bottom whilst nourishment is absorbed from the yolk sac. At the end of this period they are about one inch in length, but then grow three or four inches during the first year, and at the end of two years they are about six inches long. They are then known as parr and feed actively on aquatic insects and crustaceans.

The parr is bluish or purplish in colour and bears a row of from seven to eleven bluish 'parr-marks' along each side. The colour then changes to a bright silver and it is then known as a smolt and at this stage it drops downstream into the Severn and thence into the open sea.

THE AMPHIBIOUS FROG, TOAD AND NEWT

Only one species of frog, the common frog, *Rana temporaria*, is native to Britain although several species, including the edible frog, *Rana esculenta*, the marsh frog, *Rana ridibunda*, and the tree

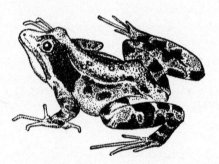

The common frog still common around Wyre.

frog, *Hyla arborea*, have been introduced and have become locally common. The edible frog is found in Norfolk (another authority considers Surrey, Middlesex and Kent), and the tree frog in the Isle of Wight. The marsh frog, *Rana ridibunda*, imported from Hungary in 1935 occurs commonly in the Romney Marsh district. When the males of this species are breeding, the chorus is deafening.

In the last few years fears have been expressed that the common frog has disappeared from a great part of Britain, and the view has been put forward that this may be due, at least in part, to the fact that the frog is a popular laboratory animal used in vast numbers for the teaching of zoology in schools. Even if the great diminution in numbers is due to some other cause, the time has surely come when the use of frogs, or for that matter any other of our native animals, should be discontinued. Two exceptions only should be allowable. Students in courses leading to degrees in medicine must obviously obtain the necessary skill in dissection. Animals used for dissection should be bred specially for the purpose, in ways that do not cause any interference with the numbers of our wild stock.

The frog possesses a smooth wet skin, although that of the female is rather rougher than that of the male. They are variously coloured in browns, yellows and greens, with a dark bar behind the eye, and with the legs more or less densely banded. Reddish or coppery-coloured frogs are not uncommon in Wyre.

Frogs breathe by two means. A substantial absorption of oxygen takes place through the skin of the body as well as the absorption by the internal lungs. Air is forced into the lungs by the 'buccal pump'. If a frog is watched it will be periodically seen to lift the throat region. This forces air which has been taken in through the nostrils, down into the lungs. There is no muscular development as in mammals which can suck in air by rhythmically contracting and expanding the lung chamber.

The life cycle of the frog must be known to everyone, the frogspawn having been collected by most small boys who watch the subsequent metamorphosis from external-gill bearing 'embryos' to the agile tadpoles. The development of legs and the subsequent absorption of the tail precedes the migration from the water to land.

There are two British native species of toad, the common toad, *Bufo bufo*, and the natterjack toad, *Bufo calamita*. Only the former species is found around Wyre, the natterjack being generally confined to sandy regions and thus more usually found in coastal or estuarine areas. This latter species is easily identified by a light-coloured stripe which runs down the middle of its back. Toads are readily differentiated from frogs by their very warty skin and shorter legs. Although able to make a succession of short hops toads are not nearly so agile as are frogs and prefer to walk or crawl than to jump.

The common toad is often met with around Wyre, especially in the local cottage gardens where they hide under loose stones during the day. Three inhabited the small paved area in front of The Newalls this summer (1968), venturing out at darkness to feed on slugs and other small animals. Like the frogs and the newts the toads make for ponds and lake-sides in the early spring. When they pair the male clasps his mate tightly during

The toad. Abundant around the forest.

the whole of the rather protracted spawning operation. Unlike the frog spawn, that of the toad is in the form of a long rope which usually gets wound around the water weeds. For the first month the young toad tadpoles possess external gills but these are then absorbed and thereafter breathing takes place by internal gills. The hind legs appear at about seven weeks and when the forelegs appear they leave the water, the tail having by this time almost disappeared. The young toads do not breed until they are five years old.

Three species of newt are found in Britain, the great crested newt, *Triturus cristatus*, the smooth newt, *Triturus vulgaris*, and the palmated newt, *Triturus helveticus*. The two former species are commoner in the east than in the west, but the palmated newt is uncommon, or local, in the east and much more common in the west. Our species in Wyre is the palmated newt and I know of a small water-filled pit in the centre of the forest where literally hundreds of this, the smallest British newt, a mere three inches in length, congregate in spring to breed.

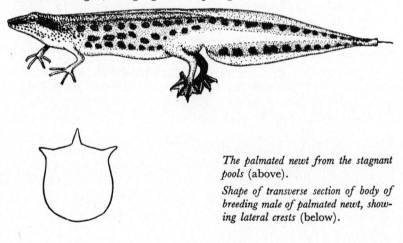

The palmated newt from the stagnant pools (above).

Shape of transverse section of body of breeding male of palmated newt, showing lateral crests (below).

In most accounts of our newts, the smooth newt is described and then the palmated is dealt with by comparing it with the former. So let us describe our own palmated newt and compare the smooth newt with it. Perhaps the most distinctive feature concerns the tail of the male; it ends in a bristle-like projection, rather accentuated in the breeding season but always present. It is not present in the smooth newt. Secondly, the hind feet of the male are very strongly webbed and black in colour, again most distinctive in the breeding season; the web more or less disappears when the newts come on land in the autumn, and again this palmation is absent in the smooth species. The head of the male is a beautiful golden-brown covered with a close reticulation of darker olive-brown. The male produces a crest in early spring which starts just behind the head and gradually enlarges until it is deepest somewhere before half-way along the tail. There is, in addition, a lateral crest on each side of the main crest. In the smooth newt, the crest is undulating and there are no lateral crests. The throat of the palmated newt, both male and female is plain whereas that of the smooth is spotted. These characters should serve to distinguish the two species, although it will be noted that the identification is much more easily performed in spring and early summer.

THE LIZARD OF THE STONY PATHS

The brown and spotted lizard of the stony paths, walls, banks and heathy hill rides of Wyre is the common lizard, *Lacerta vivipara*. It exists in delightful profusion throughout the forest, as

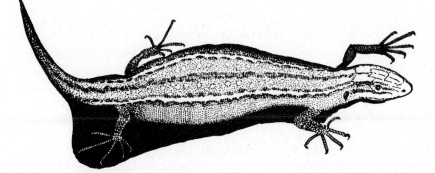

The common lizard—abundant throughout the forest. The stumpy tail signifies a female. The male has a long and graceful tail.

all of keen observing sight and hearing can testify. The scintillating watchful eyes on a scaly head emerging from a rocky bank, or the rustle of dried leaves on a hedge bank, signal their presence. That is not to say that invariably they are found in situations of exceptional dryness. Indeed, if a place was to be chosen where the lizard could be found with certainty then, I think, that point in Dowles path would be chosen where a marshy area of rushes and sedges marches alongside the hard trodden path. When the lizards seek shelter from the harsh vibrations of human footsteps they slip into the impenetrable green lushness of the marsh. But it is the sunny places that are so attractive to them and, of course, these are most usually the dry places, the sandy, stony and rocky spots, and only those where the sun is seen and felt for most of the light-long day. The common lizard is a sun-basker. In front of our cottage there are a number of old oak stumps partially covered with creeping jenny, and here the lizards love to feel the sun as they lie stretched out along the gnarled wood. They have learnt not to heed human movement.

The common lizard attains a length of some seven inches in the female and six in the male—usually they are a little less in length than this. The rather stumpy appearance of the tail denotes the female, that of the male being more slender and graceful. The 'vivipara' of the specific name refers to the hatching of the eggs which takes place at the moment of laying. The inch-long, nearly black young fend for themselves immediately after birth and there are some six to twelve born together. They feed on various insects and spiders and their general abundance surely denotes an abundance of their prey!

SLOW-WORM, *Anguis fragilis*

If we look upon the names of creatures in Nature to be more or less descriptive of their appearance or behaviour, then in the case of the slow-worm we shall be disappointed. Take its Latin name first which the great Swedish classifier, Linnaeus, gave it— *Anguis fragilis*. *Anguis* is the Latin word meaning a snake but our slow-worm is not a snake; although it possesses no legs, the bones of the skull declare it to be a lizard. The two halves of the lower jaw are joined at the front and other lizard-like characters shown by the slow-worm are its eye-lids which no snake possesses, and also the notched tongue where snakes have a truly forked one.

The slow-worm has a strap-shaped notched tongue. It is completely harmless and devours large numbers of slugs.

The other common name by which it is widely known is blind-worm. I have no idea why this name should have been bestowed upon it in the past because one does not require exceptional eyesight to observe its brilliant black shining eyes. There are in other parts of the world lizards with no legs. On the other hand, although there are no snakes with functional limbs, there are some species with rudimentary pelvic girdle. The python of Africa and Asia is an example of this.

To return to our *Anguis fragilis*, the specific component of the name is descriptive of an interesting phenomenon displayed not only by the slow-worm but by many other lizard species besides. This concerns the fragile nature of the tail. It readily breaks off if firmly held, obviously a great advantage if caught by a predator, enabling escape into the vegetable litter of the hedge-bank. Then taking its popular names, it certainly is not slow in motion. It certainly basks in the sun, but its movement is sinu-ously purposeful and often so rapid that only the rustle of leaves displays its whereabouts.

The maximum length to which the slow-worm grows is 18 inches but this would be a giant. One 12 inches in length would still be a large one. The head is small and, in fact, narrower than the body nearest to it; the eye is quite close to the upper jaw. Both jaws are provided with backwardly pointing teeth that come in very useful for dealing with the slippery prey. The tail which is longer than the combined length of head and body is longer in the male. It tapers rather gradually before ending abruptly with a point at the tip. At the time of writing I have one with a very blunt tail-end but it appears to be growing a new one. The regeneration of a broken tail is very common in slow-worms and a good job is made of it, although the scaling at the joint does not always appear to fit very well. Generally, the scales of the body are small but they overlap so beautifully that one is unaware of their basic pattern of movement. If a slow-worm is held in the hand, the pressure exerted by the bending of the body is very pronounced, in fact it seems impossible to hold them without gripping them so intensely that there is a danger of hurt to them. One cannot feel the roughness of the scales; incidentally, those of the head are rather larger than those of the body.

In colour, the slow-worm is a light greyish-brown but in young specimens there is a black line down the middle of the back and also a thinner line along the side. The underside is generally lighter in colour, but the individual scales are often more strongly marked with bluish black and sometimes appear somewhat iridescent.

The food of the slow-worm consists of small insects and other small invertebrates such as spiders and perhaps more especially slugs. The greyish white slug, *Limax agrestis*, a special pest of lettuce growers, is recorded as constituting a mainstay of its diet.

The young slow-worms hatch from the eggs on being laid, or very shortly afterwards. They are silvery in appearance and there is a black line down the centre of the back.

From six to twelve young are produced in August or September and break the egg shell as they are born. The young slow-worms are about two inches in length and are much like the parents except that they are much lighter in general colour, but have a pronounced black line running the length of the centre of the back. They are quick and agile and feed upon small insects, worms and slugs.

Slow-worms hibernate, often several intertwined together, in a cavity under a large stone in vegetable litter, or in the deep recesses of a bank.

THE SNAKES

Two species of snake are to be found in Wyre, the grass snake, *Natrix natrix*, and the adder, less commonly known as the viper,

Vipera berus. The grass snake is rather longer and more slender than the adder and is usually to be found in damper situations. It averages about 26–34 inches, although Edward Step, in his *Animal Life of the British Isles* states that females average four feet in length and the males a foot less. He also says that exceptional examples are a little short of six feet. The grass snake is very easily distinguished by two yellow or orange patches at the back of the long narrow head which gives the appearance of a collar. Immediately behind the collar there are two black patches which sometimes join together in the middle. The ground colour of the upper part of the body is greyish, brownish, or olive, and there are two rows of small black spots and a row of vertical bars along the side. The broad, plate-like scales of the underside are mainly dark grey or black splashed with white. The grass snake hibernates under old coppice stumps (in which Wyre abounds) and in spring and summer they feed on frogs, toads, newts, mice, and small birds. It readily enters the water to catch newts; indeed, fish are also known to be taken.

The scales at the top of the mouth of the grass snake allow the tongue to be everted for smelling, without the mouth being opened.
The tongue of the grass snake is used for 'smelling' objects in its near vicinity. The forked tip is vibrated extremely rapidly.
Drawn from a photograph by Leonard J. Appleby and published in Country Life.

The eggs are laid in a long string of from one to four dozen usually among rotting vegetable matter, manure often being chosen for the cradle. This occurs from mid-summer to early autumn and the eggs hatch in from six to ten weeks. The young grass snakes are from six to eight inches in length and before feeding they shed their skins, a process which is repeated four or five times annually for the rest of their lives, perhaps ten years or more.

If captured the grass snake produces a strong, garlic-smelling secretion, objectionable enough to put off most of its captors.

In recent years I have only seen two grass snakes in Wyre. One had been run over at Sturt Common. John Betts, however, records seeing a number in the grounds of Goodmoor Grange.

ADDER, *Vipera berus*

By far the commoner of the two snakes in Wyre is the adder and they are really abundant. They are most often seen by the sharp-eyed observer curled up in a sunny spot at the side of the path, not in the dense woodland, but where rocky scree forms the banks and where there is a tangle of bilberry, bramble and heather. They are very alert and agile and when moving along through the rough herbage one only catches the slightest glimpse although the loud rustlings of their movement is easily heard. But when coiled in the sun they often appear reluctant to move

A female adder. Note the zig-zag pattern down the middle of the back, the row of spots on each side, and the rough scaling.

away. Sometimes they are met with crossing the open timber paths which they do at great speed and with considerable agility.

The adder is not a difficult snake to identify. The 'ace of spades' head is quite different in shape from that of the grass snake. Behind the eyes the head broadens and it is flatter. The body is short and thick and the tail is very short compared with that of the grass snake. The average size for a male is given as 21 inches, and for a female 24 inches. The ground colour, and to some extent the colour pattern, shows considerable variation and there is, in addition, a sexual difference. The ground colour is usually grey, brown, creamish or olive, but occasionally it is black which obliterates the patterning. The latter consists of a dark zig-zag pattern down the centre of the back with a row of spots on each side. The zig-zag pattern finishes at the back of the head like an arrowhead. A black band stretches backwards from the eyes. The eyes are worthy of comment in that they are copper coloured with black vertical slit-like pupils. These are typical of eyes that can see in the dark yet it is not known whether it is a nocturnal animal.

The males are generally lighter in colour than the females and the male's throat is usually black or if it is white the scales are usually edged with black. In the female the chin is yellowish white sometimes with a reddish tinge.

The adder is rather more tolerant of cold weather than is the grass snake and will emerge from its hibernation when the temperature rises above 8°C (46°F). In Britain, the adder usually hibernates for about 135 days—from October to March. It does not burrow like the grass snake but uses crevices in rocks or under tree stumps and spends the winter about one foot below the surface of the ground.

On 26th January 1969, David and Verney Naylor found a 21¾ inch adder coiled on a path near Shelf Held Coppice. It appeared rather torpid.

The manner of hatching of the young adders is very different from that of the grass snake. The five to twenty eggs are ruptured on the point of laying so that there is no external incubation, the young seemingly being born alive. They subsist on insects at first then turn their attention chiefly to small rodents such as wood mice and bank voles but will also take frogs and toads.

The adder usually glides away if confronted with danger and they seldom attack people. But it does happen sometimes quite accidentally, and I know of two instances where men have been bitten in the Forest of Wyre. Firstly, Paul Cadbury gave an account of being bitten in the finger as he scrambled up the bank from Dowles Brook. Thinking that it was a wasp sting he found two tiny punctures that started to bleed. When his hand and arm began to swell he went straight down to the Kidderminster District Hospital where he was given an injection of anti-venom serum from the Pasteur Institute in Paris. This caused the swelling to subside rapidly and after staying in hospital for 24 hours as a precautionary measure he was discharged without any ill-effects. Six years previously a man had been admitted to Kidderminster Hospital with an adder bite which was more serious because he did not seek help immediately.

Secondly, the late Spencer Oliver was bitten by an adder in the leg a few years ago. This was in the little field where he lived on his own, near the old Wyre Forest railway station, and he would then be about 70 years of age. He said that as he walked through the grass which he had been cutting he thought that he had trodden on a stick which then stuck in his leg. But it was an adder which he had trodden on! However, he refused to go to hospital or even to see a doctor in spite of the earnest advice of his good neighbours. His gravest fear was that he would be separated from the forest by some bureaucratic intrigue, and who can blame him! He insisted that nature must take its course, as he expressed it, but this resulted in a savage suppurating wound. Miraculously, he gradually recovered and he lived for some years afterwards.

For Further Reading

BURTON, M. and BURTON, R., General Editors, 1968, *Purnell's Encyclopedia of Animal Life*, No. 1, Paulton, Somerset.

CADBURY, P. S., 1967, *Bitten by a Snake*, Bournville Works Magazine, **65**:311.

CLEGG, J., 1952, *The Freshwater Life of the British Isles*, Wayside and Woodland Series, Warne, London.

JENKINS, J. T., 1925, *The Fishes of the British Isles*, Warne, London.

MACAN, T. T. and WORTHINGTON, E. B., 1951, *Life in Lakes and Rivers*, New Naturalist Series, Collins, London.

NORMAN, J. R. (revised by GREENWOOD, P. H.), 2nd Edition, 1963 (1st Edition, 1931), *A History of Fishes*, Benn, London.

STEP, E., 1921 (and later editions), *Animal Life of the British Isles*, Wayside and Woodland Series, Warne, London.

THE BIRDS OF DOWLES

The Dowles Brook bisects the forest into its two halves and is the county boundary for the five miles or so of its length which stretches from Furnace Mill on the west to the river Severn, one mile above Bewdley, on the east. Throughout its length it runs over slab-like shelving rock with frequent swift runnels and swirls through gaps in dams of old alder trunks brought down in the early spring floods. Sandy spits and deep mud-bottomed pools also occur as the brook twists around the deep steep-sided valleys. But the outstanding feature of the brook is that except for the last few yards of its length it flows under dense tree foliage. When I was a young man this was the foliage of the common oak, the small-leaved lime, the hazel, and directly on the brook edge, the alder.

Today, much of the common oak has been removed by the band-saw, replaced by spruce, and here and there larch. In the last few years alder has been levelled and poplar planted in its place; poplar festooned with polythene bags to scare the deer off its succulent but aromatic shoots. But it still remains that the brook flows coldly and swiftly under an arch of green with but few little open meadows to let the sun and its light onto the water.

Four bird species use the brook, not only as a highway but for their food gathering and breeding—two species almost exclusively. These are the dipper and the kingfisher. They are seldom to be seen more than a few yards from the narrow streak of water. Two other species, the grey wagtail and the redstart use the brook as their living space but stray further from it, although usually keeping to the tributary brooklets.

DIPPER, *Cinclus cinclus*

The dipper is a plump, somewhat stumpy, wren-shaped bird something the size of a blackbird, but the tail is short. It is dark-brown in colour with a white throat. Beneath the white 'bib' is a chestnut-coloured area which gradually darkens towards the legs. In its fast whirring flight, however, the bird appears almost slatey black especially along Dowles where the light is poor under the thick foliage.

There are two ways to see the dipper and both should be enjoyed. First, one quietly walks along the Dowles path keeping eyes fixed on every glimpse of the brook, observing every stone

The dipper confines its flight to Dowles and the tributary streams unless the latter are barred by embankments.

that projects from the water like a little island. These are favourite perches, slabby pieces of rock a couple of inches or so above the water level and in area of about one to two square feet. The white marks of their droppings signify these stones. But when a quiet and careful search of the brook is made it may be approached as it rests on its favourite mid-stream stones. Secondly, one may wait near a favourite perching place hidden behind alder or hazel and just wait and wait until suddenly the dipper arrives. Then a careful scrutiny of the bird may be made with binoculars and the extraordinary sight of its eye-cleaning or eye-drying, observed. Periodically, as it stands on its stone, it bobs or dips, making little curtsies in various directions. As it does so, the eye is momentarily obscured by a yellow membrane. This is referred to as its 'blinking' and the exact mechanism of its functioning is still argued by scientific ornithologists. Some assert that the blink is performed by the pigmented nictitating membrane moving vertically downwards, whilst others are equally positive that it is the yellowish upper eyelid which blinks, just as a human eye would do. But it is extraordinary to watch even though one is uncomfortably crouched behind an alder and the wood ants are biting!

There is another interesting habit of the dipper which concerns its feeding. Although its more usual method is to peck about around the stones in the shallow stream where the water just covers the legs, it will sometimes submerge completely and walk along the stream bottom with the head stretched forward and making swimming movements with its wings. It searches for small aquatic insects, crustaceans and molluscs such as caddis and mayfly larvae, water shrimps and water snails. I have not observed the submerging habit in Dowles but leaning over Ludford Bridge at Ludlow, idly enjoying the scene, a dipper flew downstream towards and directly underneath me, settled on a bankside stone and walked straight into the water.

Harthan thought that about 30 pairs were resident in the county and he quotes Elliott's estimation of ten pairs along Dowles Brook. (Jannion Steele Elliot lived at Dowles Manor from 1903 to 1942.) It is unlikely that ten pairs still remain as, . unfortunately, their nests are robbed and the young have been observed to be inexpertly ringed. It can only be hoped that the recent more positive legislation and the certificate for ringing now required from the Natural Environment Research Council will give these remarkable birds of the wild running streams greater freedom from harassment and disturbance.

KINGFISHER, *Alcedo atthis*

The kingfisher is, without doubt, and, indeed, as acclaimed on all sides, the most beautiful of all British birds. Not much different from a sparrow in size yet the brilliance of its colouration is such that the bird appears much larger, as though there was some aura around it. Its scintillating brilliance is such that no authorities can agree on a description of its colouration. In Witherby's

The kingfisher successfully bred in Wyre in 1969.

Handbook of British Birds it is stated of the bird's upper parts, in one place, that they are dazzling cobalt blue and in another, that they are dark greenish blue, each feather with a bright blue sub-terminal band but the back, rump, and the upper tail coverts are brilliant glossy blue or greenish blue. But then there is a footnote to the effect that if the bird is '*held*' with bill towards the light the whole of the upper parts appear deep blue, not greenish. The italics are mine—what an extraordinary statement that this bird could or should be held in the hand! This dazzling living ball of emerald has a wing-whirring flight of astonishing swiftness only a few feet above the rippling surface of the water.

The kingfisher feeds on fish and other aquatic creatures which it captures with a sudden devastating plunge into the water, capturing the prey with its long dagger-like beak. When a fish is captured it is given a few blows on the perch then swallowed whole, head first. It is sometimes shaken or thrown into the air then recaught to get to this position.

A long quiet day spent along the brook is usually rewarded by the sight of the kingfisher.

REDSTART, *Phoenicurus phoenicurus*

Although the redstart is found throughout a great part of its range in many types of woodland and parkland, including open hilly country with loose stone walls, in the forest it is mostly at home along the brook and little streams. It is continually swooping or fluttering after insect food and even when sitting on a twig between such activities its restlessness is exemplified by its bobbing and tail quivering.

The redstart. A nestbox was occupied by redstarts at Far Forest for fifteen years without a break.

It is robin-like in size as well as in general flight and behaviour. But its red, orange-chestnut and flicking tail is characteristic **and** it cannot be mistaken for any other bird. The male redstart has a black face and throat and its breast and flanks are orange too, like the tail, and when it arrives, sometimes as early as the first week of April, it is by no means shy.

For several hours one day at the edge of the forest, a cock redstart was fighting his own reflection on the polished chromium hubs of my car.

It nests in old oak stumps, but so far, its pale blue eggs have not been laid in my nest-boxes, although they are commonly recorded as using these artificial nest sites. But the redstart delights us along the banks of Dowles and when it is disturbed and flits to the next bush its orange tail never fails to make my heart miss a beat or two.

GREY WAGTAIL, *Motacilla cinerea*

The grey wagtail is only to be seen along the brook during the spring and summer months. In winter it migrates downstream to the broad river lands and water meadows. But when the garlic-odoured ramsons burst into bloom, sheeting the banks of Dowles with the myriad star-like flowers then the grey wagtails

The grey wagtail might be attracted to use a nestbox if placed under a culvert, a bridge, or let into a wall near or over water. An R.S.P.B. open-type nestbox of standard size might be proved suitable.

come flitting back. They fly from stone to stone using the self-same dipper stones and they seem everywhere at once. The grey wagtail is the possessor of the longest tail of all the wagtails and in typical wagtail fashion it continuously oscillates as though steadying itself after its quick run along the ground. Wagtails are slender, dainty and graceful birds, and of the two species with much yellow in their colouration, the 'grey' has blue-grey upper parts whereas in the 'yellow' wagtail the upper parts are greenish. The tail of the yellow wagtail is not nearly so long as that of the grey and the yellow is much less aquatic in its habits than the grey. That is not to say that the grey never wanders away from the brook during the summer. Indeed, it favours the shady field corners where the cows stand and is delicately expert at quickly tripping up to a cowpat and picking up a fly.

PIED FLYCATCHER, *Muscicapa hypoleuca*

This entrancing little bird is a summer visitor to our land and when it reaches our southern shores it flies north-west to Wales and northern England. The nearest nesting areas on their migration lines are in north-west Worcestershire, principally the Dowles valley in Wyre. The history of this species as a Worcestershire bird is only available in fragments. In 1828 Edwin Lees, writing in the section on Birds in Hastings' *Illustrations of the Natural History of Worcestershire* stated that the pied flycatcher was an inhabitant of the woods near Eardiston. By 1900, in the *Victoria County History*, Tomes, who wrote the bird section, added 'Near Worcester, Spetchley and Malvern'. Harthan stated that the only definite records of nesting were at the Rhydd on the

The cock pied flycatcher. Sooty black above and white below, with a white wing-bar.

Severn in 1877, Malvern Wells in 1932, and near Bewdley in 1936, but he stated that it had probably done so in Wyre Forest occasionally. This latter note was probably due to J. Steele Elliot whose manuscript notes covering the years 1890–1916, he acknowledges. This is of particular interest to us because J. Steele Eliott lived in Dowles Manor, within the eastern fringe of the forest. I was always under the impression that it was due to this very practical naturalist, who set up a large number of nest boxes near Dowles Manor, that a number of pairs of pied flycatcher were attracted to spend their summer nesting period in Wyre. However, in the early 1960's they could usually be seen around the old orchards along Dowles. So far, I have been writing about the north side of Dowles, in Shropshire. Imagine my delight then in 1965, to find them using my own nest boxes in the orchard field at The Newalls near the old Wyre Forest railway station! These were well within Worcestershire on the south bank of Dowles, and a few pairs have nested with me each year since.

The male of the pied flycatcher is quite unlike any other of our small birds. On top it is sooty black or sooty brown and white beneath with a conspicuous broad white wing-bar. It also has a white patch immediately above the beak. This may be a bar or separated into two white spots. The female is not unlike a hen chaffinch, being olive-brown above and whitish below. A similarity can be seen between the pied flycatcher and the spotted flycatcher in the manner of flight and perching, although the former does not possess the habit of returning to the same perch after chasing and catching a fly, to anything like the same degree as does the spotted flycatcher. The pied, however, will fly to a flower, pick an insect off a petal without alighting and fly off again, which is a delight to watch.

The nesting site is said to be chosen by the cock bird before the arrival of the hen but the latter makes the nest. All the nests at The Newalls have had a base of old oak leaves then a 'mattress' of strips of honeysuckle bark, and finally a cup of hair. About half the nests made in nest-boxes remain unfinished without the hair cup and do not have eggs laid in them. I am not sure of the explanation of this. Perhaps, like the wren, two or more nests are constructed by a single pair and then a final selection is made. They are rather late in egg-laying as this seldom occurs before mid-May, and often not until the last week in May. This prompts other nest-boxers to cork the entrance to the nest box until half-way through May to prevent the use of the box by tits. It is quite tame at nesting time and will often perch only a few feet away from the observer, but when the nestlings have fledged and flown they rove away from the nesting area and seemingly disappear amongst the by now leafy oaks and the heavy alder foliage along Dowles.

It is interesting to speculate as to the sensory perception which stimulates or activates this small bird to fly over what are apparently similar nesting areas in Kent, the home counties and the South Midlands, before finally reaching the acid woods of the durmast oak. The pedunculate oak, *Quercus robur*, the oak of the heavy clay of southern England has no attraction.

BIRDS OF THE DUSK

One of the most restful and, indeed, refreshing qualities of the forest is the sense of quietness. Birdsong can be appreciated and enjoyed with a background only of silence. Notes and cadences can be identified within the woods. In the sunny hours, these are mostly delicate and discreet, such as those of the willow and wood warbler, and on the woody fringes the song of the pied flycatcher and the chaffinch is sweet in the higher octaves. We must except the robust cuckoo, the fluting blackbird and the tremulous songthrush. In some years too the nightingale's day song leaves no doubts. But when the sun drops down diurnal metamorphoses into nocturnal, birds of the day drowse into their roosting places and the birds of the dusk and night stretch themselves and launch into the air. The little owls call, perch on the wires and telegraph posts around Worralls, then fly into the night on their diminutive rounded wings. The woodcock 'rode and groan' along their flight lines of habit around Brown's Bank and back again, and the tawny owls commence their far-carrying cries. The nightingale sings on from day into the night unaware that light has turned to dark.

But, for me, the principal bird of the dusk is the churring nightjar (*Caprimulgus europaeus*). More rarely is it heard now, at

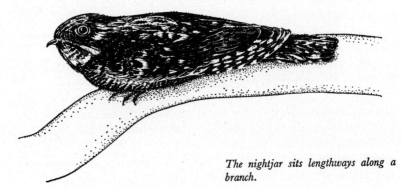

The nightjar sits lengthways along a branch.

least, towards the western end of Wyre where I am now most likely to find myself when the summer light disappears. What a noisy dusk must have fallen in the summer of 1930 when J. Steele Elliot estimated that there were about one pair per hundred acres of Wyre. Of course, the forest was much more open then. The steep sloping railway embankments running down to Dowles were covered with young silver birch and bracken, with here and there a patch of bilberry or heather. When I was a schoolboy I asked an older boy what it was that made the noise and he told me it was the bracken-clock which I thought somehow must be an insect, but I was very puzzled that it was so loud. Later, I saw a bird drop off a broken and dead oak branch some 20 feet up an oak and it flicked around making acrobatic convolutions, and in the almost total darkness I was able to watch it silhouetted against the silver sky. This, then, was the bird of many names; the nightjar, descriptive of its time of activity and its 'song', alias fern owl, descriptive of its habitat and near relatives, alias goatsucker, descriptive of myth and legend concerning its habits. I have also presumed that its generic name *Caprimulgus*, used by Linnaeus means the same but is in Latin.

The nightjar is a medium-sized bird somewhat the size of a thrush but its neckless head appears large in proportion. Its beak is small, but its gape is relatively enormous, cleaving the whole of the head, and fringed with bristles. In colour, it is of grey leaves and brown bracken in a disruptive design of great beauty.

The nest or scrape is on the ground amongst the ferny litter so that this cryptic colouration serves well its purpose of self effacement. The two white eggs would be viewed with ease did not the bird sit tight with its large lustrous eyes shut, except the thin slits. It noiselessly slips off only at the last tread.

The nightjar is a summer visitor reaching us in May from the first week onwards, but sometimes it may be early June. They leave from the middle of August until the end of September, when they migrate to the southern half of Africa. We have barely three months in which to enjoy their presence. Their food consists of moths (the ghost swifts in the family HEPIALIDAE seem to be especially favoured), crane flies and caddis flies, and their strange clapping and twisting flight at dusk demonstrates their dexterity in trapping them in the net of their throat. Returning to its watching point on the oak branch, it perches lengthways with head outwards so that even at dusk it becomes invisible as crouching to the branch it assumes the shape of a broken stump.

When the overhead sky deepens to purplish black and only a long streak of pinkish silver rides over Clee, the owls are calling. It has been sometime since the little owls slipped away from the dense hollybush by Spencer Oliver's old place and now we strain our ears to the far-carrying cries of *Strix aluco* the tawny owl and *Asio otus* the long-eared owl. The tawny's hoot is prolonged in separate syllables, but grouped in twos and threes on a long cadence, then there is a considerable pause of some three to seven seconds, a faint low 'oo', a brief pause then the long quavering 'hoooooo'. The tawny sounds from far and near and often very near, and they wing over the cottage gateposts, but the long-eared is a more remote bird preferring isolation from human activity. We must listen for a 'long-drawn out cooing moan' and not a hoot. These are individual notes but not grouped in syllables, but spaced equally, one every third second. It is said that it can be heard over half a mile away, but I venture that for the exceptional sound-carrying properties of Wyre this is not an over-estimate.

The long-eared owl is attracted to the coniferous woodland but was to be found in Wyre even when conifers were present only in isolation.

The long-ears are hard to find by day, sitting upright and close to the trunk of a dark spruce. The only nest I have found in Wyre was a dusty space amongst the roots of a spruce and that was years ago, but I now sometimes startle a large golden-buff freckled bird from the larch and pine copse, and so far have not been able to position myself for the viewing in order to see the ears before it has swept down in front of me and glided and flapped up the valley of the little stream.

THE SECRET OF THE CUCKOO, *Cuculus canorus*

> *'Some say that when the young cuckoo grows it ejects the other young birds, which then perish. Others say that the foster-mother kills them and feeds the young cuckoo with them, for the beauty of the young cuckoo makes her despise her own offspring.'*

So wrote Aristotle in his *History of Animals* about 350 B.C. Very little had been added to our knowledge concerning the cuckoo, not only on the behaviour of the newly hatched parasite, but also on how the introduction of the egg was effected, and other aspects of the cuckoo's life, until Edgar P. Chance carried out a series of detailed observations and egg translocations over a period of four years before he published his first book on the subject. This was *The Cuckoo's Secret* and the greater part of the work was carried out in the Wyre Forest area. The celebrated photographer of natural history, the late Oliver G. Pike, made a film of the cuckoo's method of egg-laying at Pound Green for Edgar Chance, and a number of slow-motion sequences are illustrated in the book.

Like many other birds the cuckoo selects a territory on arrival after the migration flight and returns year after year to the same area. At least this is true for the female and might be true also for the male, but on this there is some controversy to which we will refer later. The hen exhibits a strong preference for a particular species which she will parasitise, and which will become the host (or the fosterer in rather more anthropomorphic terms). The cuckoos which Edgar Chance studied at Pound Green used the meadow pipit, although 50 different bird species are known as fosterers; next to the meadow pipit the hedge sparrow, reed warbler, pied wagtail, robin and sedge warbler are most commonly victimised.

The cuckoo is expert in the ways of the bird species in whose nests she will lay her eggs. From a suitable position, usually in a

Many times Edgar Chance watched the cuckoo glide down to the nest of the meadow pipit, remove an egg with its beak, lay an egg in the nest, and then fly off with the meadow pipit's egg in its beak, all within ten seconds.

tree, she waits and watches then, when she knows the victim has just laid her second or third egg, she glides down to the nest. She then picks up one of the eggs, turns around and immediately lays her own egg in the nest, and then flies off. She usually eats the fosterer's egg. Although the cuckoo will wait quietly for several hours she is at the nest for only about ten seconds. If the entrance to the nest is such that she cannot lay directly into it from the top she appears to eject the egg into it. In this case, the egg does not always roll into the nest and if it fails to do so it is never pushed in with the beak. The cuckoo usually lays about 12 eggs although Edgar Chance describes one cuckoo that laid 25 eggs in one season and 21 the following season. This was accomplished by the provision of artificial nests, but the following year she laid 15 only with less suitable nests available. Normally, the cuckoo lays an egg on alternate days, that is if fosterer's nests are found. If the cuckoo cannot find a fosterer's nest at the point when the eggs are being laid she will destroy nests where incubation has started so that a new nest will be constructed and a new clutch started.

One of the most remarkable facts about the cuckoo concerns the colouration of the eggs. There is an extraordinary similarity in colour between the egg of the cuckoo and those of the fosterer. No really satisfactory explanation exists for this but Chance thought that there were different 'races' of the cuckoo; the 'meadow pipit race' would lay eggs similar to those of the meadow pipit and so on. For this to be true the male bird similarly must be of the same race. Chance thought that the cuckoo mated for life but there has been much controversy about this.

The one-day old cuckoo nestling, hatching first, ejects all other eggs from the nest.
Drawn from a photograph by F. H. Lancum.

Another strange piece of behaviour relates to the young cuckoo when it has been hatched a day or two. The incubation period is 12½ days so that as this is usually shorter than that of the fosterer's eggs, the cuckoo hatches first. The naked and blind nestling exhibits a strong ejection impulse and for a few days it pushes anything in the nest outside so that the fosterer's eggs are removed. It then remains alone in the nest to be fed by the foster parent for about three weeks.

The adult cuckoos leave for central and southern Africa early in July, but the young ones do not leave until August and the first half of September.

WOODCOCK, *Scolopax rusticola*

The woodcock is about the size of a wood pigeon but there the similarity must end. The head is disproportionately large and the front slopes up steeply, and then at the crown almost as abruptly slopes down. The eye is large and lustrous and is situated high up near the crown. The beak is long and straight and the top mandible terminates in a softish down-turning protuberance. It is a pale silvery colour underneath faintly barred with russet. The top of the head, back, wings and tail are mottled, striped,

The woodcock breeds in Wyre Forest. It is a bird of strange and mysterious habits.

barred and marbled with russet, deep chocolate, brown, silver-grey and brownish grey. Altogether this is the colour of the open forest floor when the oak leaves lie in little drifts amongst the dead bracken. He is a competent observer who espies a wood-cock on the ground! I have seldom ever accomplished this. Usually the woodcock flies up at one's feet when one is not expecting such an occurrence, and the heart beats fast at this confrontation.

The woodcock is said to feed only at dusk, which it does by probing its long stout beak into soft mud. But the beak tip is softish and has a sensory patch; perhaps it is the mud-dwelling creatures which activate it? Worms are its principal food which it swallows without withdrawing the mandibles from the mud—quite a feat! By day it hides in woodland of a rather open type but feeds in boggy open country at night. Feeding during day-time, however, does take place and often the woodcock is flushed from wet patches along the rides and paths in the forest, as well as swampy fields around its edge.

Flight between the daytime resting places and the feeding sites follow well-defined paths and is regularly-timed. It is fortunate that one of these flight paths follows the little stream forming the boundary of The Newalls for a quarter of a mile. Sitting outside the cottage at dusk, the woodcock can be watched coming up from the forest over Dowles. Along the edge of the forested bank they rise to a considerable height and then continue over Worral's Farm towards Far Forest. Unfortunately they occasionally hit the overhead electricity cables and are found dead beneath them.

The so-called 'roding' flight of woodcock is one of the strangest flights of all birds. Only the males take part and they fly a circular route at a height of about 100 feet above ground. It goes on for about an hour starting at sunset, usually from March till August. This is a fast flight but the wing beats are said to be owlish. Of course, the woodcock has rounded wings as have the owls, but the strange thing about the 'roding' flight is that every so often the wing beats miss and at that precise moment a peculiar sound is uttered by the bird and variously described as a croak or a groan followed by a high-pitched whistle. Whereas the hen makes the whistle on occasion, she never groans or croaks! These are strange sounds of the summer night, full of natural mystery, like many another common phenomenon of the countryside, and Ludwig Koch failed to record them though he tried, and he has written quite unashamedly that the human ear is superior to his recording instruments.

Then there is the strange chick-carrying habit. It seems certain, although not all observers have reported it, that the woodcock carries its chicks from the daytime woodland territory to the boggy feeding areas. The chick is carried between the legs and the body, but may be partially supported in this position by the tail or the bill, and the adult makes several journeys to bring up all the members of the brood.

Another type of flight occurs during courtship, when 'they flit around one another with butterfly-like flight.' This, the writer has seen in the forest and it is a remarkable display of flight. Generally, there is little room for aerobatics, but the courting woodcock slip and glide around the trees and shrubs with the round wings strangely cupped whilst they carry out their evolutions within a few feet of the ground, flying no higher than the young Scots pines that line the path.

The woodcock nests in Wyre Forest and Harthan states that

there is perhaps one pair per 200 acres. The numbers are increased during winter by migrants.

There is much fascination, mystery and conjecture about the everyday life of the woodcock. One is left with the fact that it is an extraordinary bird.

THE WOODPECKERS

He would be blind and deaf, or at least unobservant and hard of hearing, who walked for a mile or so around Wyre and failed to see or hear a woodpecker. All our three native British wood-peckers are to be found in Wyre but the largest, the green woodpecker, is by far the commonest and is an abundant bird. Its appearance, flight and voice is characteristic. It is almost as large as a pigeon and its green back and red crown make it un-mistakable. But it is more often seen in flight and looking at it from behind, the colour appears quite a bright yellow, due to its greenish yellow rump. If one is near enough to observe, the tail feathers are dark in colour and strangely pointed. Indeed, all three woodpeckers possess these special tail feathers and one has only to see the birds making their short, jerky jumps up the tree to realise how important these feathers are to the bird in helping it to maintain balance on the tree.

GREEN WOODPECKER, *Picus viridis*

A common species around Wyre on account of its liking for ants. The large wood ant is exceptionally abundant in Wyre and sometimes the green woodpecker is interrupted in scratching out the ant nests from heaps of forest floor debris. Indeed, the green woodpecker is commonly found on the ground wherever ants are likely to be seen. This is quite different from the case of the two species of spotted woodpeckers; they are seldom seen on the ground.

The flight of the green woodpecker is characteristic. There are three or four quick wingbeats followed by a long swoop with the wings tightly pressed to the body. But the most easily recognised evidence of the presence of the green woodpecker in any locality is the loud ringing yaffle, or laughing call, which gives the bird its name of 'yaffle'.

The nest-hole is pecked out of the main trunk of a tree and those in Wyre that I have seen were about seven or eight feet from the ground. An old silver birch or an old cherry, apple or

The green woodpecker. The largest British woodpecker. The tail feathers are pointed and help the bird to maintain position on the tree trunk, although this species is often seen on the ground where it searches for ants.

damson, seems a favourite choice. There is no nesting material, the five, six or seven whitish, translucent and oval eggs being laid on a few wood chips only.

Like the pigeon, food is passed to the young in the form of a white, milky paste.

GREAT SPOTTED WOODPECKER, *Dendrocopos major*

This bird advertises its presence mostly by its conspicuous black and white barred plumage, reddish under-tail coverts and, in the case of the male only, a crimson nape patch, as it flies swiftly from tree to tree. Its sharp sounding cry of 'tchick, tchick', when

The greater spotted woodpecker is a robber of nestboxes. Its long tongue is shown reaching down to newly-hatched pied flycatchers.

once heard, can be identified from afar but the sound made by the great spotted woodpecker which has caused the greatest interest, is the 'drumming'. The manner of production of this loud vibrant sound excited controversy for many years. Both sexes drum on suitable sounding boards such as the base of a broken branch by a series of rapid blows at something like eight to ten per second, made with the bill. The duration of the drum is usually about one second.

The nest-hole of the great spotted woodpecker is rather like that of the green, but somewhat smaller and is usually made higher up the tree trunk, seldom being found at less than ten feet from the ground. In Wyre they are often found in an unsound silver birch, and a whole succession, one above the other, are sometimes seen.

The eggs are like those of the green, but smaller, and also rest on a few chips of wood. But unlike the green, the young are fed on insects brought in the beak of one of the adults.

Two or three years ago I found a ring of feathers of a great spotted woodpecker—all that was left of a bird struck down and eaten, most probably, by a sparrow-hawk.

LESSER SPOTTED WOODPECKER, *Dendrocopos minor*

A very small bird, not much larger than a sparrow and the whole of the wings and back are barred. The male has the front of the

The lesser spotted woodpecker. Only the size of a sparrow. Note that in all woodpeckers two toes point forwards and two backwards.

head a dull crimson, but in the female it is white. This, our smallest woodpecker, is never very much in evidence but is more usually to be seen in old orchards, but it is known also to look for its food amongst the topmost branches of oaks, and other broad-leaved forest trees. Here it can be watched fluttering from branch to branch, but over longer distances it shows the same undulating flight as in the other woodpeckers.

Like the great spotted woodpecker it drums and, indeed, its drumming cannot always be distinguished from that of its larger relative.

The nest-hole is often in a decayed branch high in the tree.

THE WARBLERS

It is one of the great delights for those of us who live in Britain to experience, from the end of March to the middle of May, the great influx of migrant birds into our countryside. Amongst these is a throng of small brownish or greenish yellow birds of many species, generally with sweet song, known as the warblers. There are abundant species occupying a comparatively wide variety of habitats, whilst there are less abundant species often occupying a specialised habitat. Finally, there are many rare species, a few individuals only reaching our shores.

Some warblers can be identified with relative ease, the white-throat and the blackcap are examples. Others offer extraordinary difficulties in this regard, only the specialist being able to separate some species with certainty, and then only when the bird is in his hand. In addition to the two species just mentioned, three warblers to be found in and around Wyre are the chiffchaff, the willow-warbler and the wood-warbler, but these can be separated on sighting only with the greatest of care. Fortunately they sing different songs so that it is usually necessary to hear them in order to say definitely to which species they belong.

CHIFFCHAFF, *Phylloscopus collybita*

The first of our Spring migrants to arrive. Its characteristic and unmistakable song of two notes often repeated, one note higher pitched than the other, and rather irregular is considered by the bird-lover as the first real sign of spring. This is rendered as chiff-chaff-chiff-chaff-chiff-chaff, etc. for about 15 seconds, whilst the bird moves amongst the tree foliage, generally well up. It resembles the willow-warbler, rather like a smaller and dingier edition of it, but it is less yellow underneath and its legs are much darker, almost inclined to black.

The chiffchaff is a bird of the woods and old hedges and is said to be more dependent on trees than the willow-warbler. W. B. Yapp who has made an extensive study of birds in woods, and especially in Wyre Forest, thought that the chiffchaff requires a thick shrub layer associated with tall trees, but this was not invariably the case. Although it is found in central Europe associated with coniferous woodland in Britain this is seldom the case, but when it does occur larch is usually the tree species preferred. In Wyre, Yapp states that the chiffchaff was almost absent from the woods of birch and oak. It is present, however, in the old orchards and in the more scrubby woodland.

The flight of the chiffchaff is not long-sustained and is said in Witherby, to be somewhat jerky and flitting. When it can be seen amongst the foliage it is observed to move with restless activity, frequently flicking its wings and tail, and constantly darting or fluttering about to capture an insect.

WILLOW- WARBLER, *Phylloscopus trochilus*

A bird very much like the chiffchaff but it is larger, its legs are light brown not blackish, it is more greenish above and more yellowish below. Its habitat is much more varied than that of the chiffchaff and it may be found in virtually any open woodland or bushy areas. The willow-warbler is also rather less active and restless than the chiffchaff and is frequently observed much lower in the shrubby layer or hedgerow than the latter.

The willow warbler. A bird of scrubby woodland. The most common warbler of Wyre.

Witherby states that when in song no other distinction is needed for its identification. It is a simple, pleasing, continuous rippling phrase of closely similar notes, usually faint and low at first but gaining loudness and emphasis, then sinking away again to a fainter, but more distinctly phrased, ending. It has been rendered as 'se—se—se—see—see—sü—sü—süit—süit—sueet—sueetew'. It lasts from three to five seconds and is delivered from four to eight times per minute.

Yapp found this to be the most common species in his study area of oak underplanted with beech. In the peak years of 1955 to 1962, 24 contacts per hour were recorded in May. Although there has been some falling off in numbers in the period 1963 to 1967, there were still 14 contacts per hour.

WOOD-WARBLER, *Phylloscopus sibilatrix*

Found in mature woodland of beech and oak especially, but is also to be found in poorer woods of oak and birch. Generally, where this bird occurs, secondary growth such as from coppicing is sparse or absent. It is rarely found in coniferous or mixed woods in Britain although in central Europe it is commonly to be found in such a habitat.

The wood warbler. Larger than the chiffchaff and the willow warbler, and more contrasting coloration than these latter species.

It can be distinguished from the chiffchaff and the willow-warbler; firstly by its larger size, which is about five inches in length compared with the four and a quarter inches of the two other species, and secondly by its more contrasting colouring. The wood-warbler is more yellowish green above, the eye-stripe is most prominent (it is least prominent in the chiffchaff), whilst the throat and upper breast is bright sulphur yellow and the lower breast and belly are gleaming white (in the other two species these parts are greyish). In addition, in the wood-warbler the edging of the inner wing-feathers is broad and distinctly yellowish. As far as habit is concerned it often holds the wings in a drooping position so that the tips show below the body, but it never flicks the tail as do the other two species.

The wood-warbler sings two songs. Firstly, a single note which is repeated at increasing speed until it ends on a 'shivering trill'.

This takes about three seconds with about seven second intervals. Secondly, a note which has been described as a plaintive liquid 'püü' repeated about seven to fourteen times at brief intervals.

Yapp recorded that the wood-warbler decreased in numbers as the beech plantations thickened, but an increase was observed when a clearance took place.

For Further Reading

BAYNE, C. S., 1944, *Exploring England*, Collins, London. (Illustrated by C. F. Tunnicliffe.)

CHANCE, E. P., 1922, *The Cuckoo's Secret*, Sidgwick and Jackson, London.

CHANCE, E. P., 1940, The Truth about the Cuckoo, *Country Life*, London.

FISHER, J., 1966, *The Shell Bird Book*, Ebury Press and Michael Joseph, London.

FISHER, J., 1967, *Thorburn's Birds*, Ebury Press and Michael Joseph, London.

HARTHAN, A. J., N.D., *The Birds of Worcestershire*, Littlebury, Worcester.

JOCH, L., N.D., General Editor, *Encyclopaedia of British Birds*, Waverley Book Company, London.

WITHERBY, H. F., JOURDAIN, F. C. R., TICEHURST, N. F. and TUCKER, B. W., 1941 (and other editions), *Handbook of British Birds*, 5 vols., Witherby, London.

YAPP, W. B., 1962, *Birds and Woods*, Oxford University Press, London.

YAPP, W. B., 1969, The Bird Population of an Oakwood (Wyre Forest) over eighteen years. *Proceedings of the Birmingham Natural History Society*, **21**(3): 119–216.

THE MAMMALS OF WYRE

HEDGEHOG, *Erinaceus europaeus*

It is a matter of concern to us that we are really only aware of the abundance of the hedgehog by the frequent occurrence of their dead and mangled bodies on our roads. On the rapid approach of a dangerous situation the hedgehog has only one instinctive reaction and that is to roll into a ball and tuck its unarmoured head and limbs into its belly, which presents a sharp spinous exterior to its enemies. But that, unfortunately, is not a sufficient defence against the motor car. The hedgehogs of the suburban gardens, and they are surprisingly common, suffer more on the main roads, than those of our woods, where roads used by fast-moving transport are less frequent. This is, therefore, a good argument, I think, for restricting motor traffic in the forest and I certainly believe, in the interests of all wild creatures that must cross the road, that no further extension of motor traffic should be permitted on the forest roads.

The eyes of the hedgehog are fairly large although it is thought that its sight is poor and it has a moist black nose like a dog.

The hedgehog, *Erinaceus europaeus*, is a member of the order INSECTIVORA in which it is joined in the British fauna by the mole and the shrews. This group of mammals is relatively unspecialised and, indeed, many primitive features are shown. Generally, throughout the world, insectivores are well distributed but in Britain we only have one species of hedgehog, one mole, and five species of shrews. The hedgehog is to be found in some abundance throughout the British Isles although it is uncommon in the Highlands of Scotland and also occurs in the main islands. Generally, it is said not to frequent dense woodland yet in Wyre it appears to be a regular inhabitant of this type of country. Wherever it is found, however, there must be sufficient woodland litter, leaves, and debris, to give shelter during the daytime and during the winter months. The hedgehog is mainly nocturnal, usually being seen at dusk and it is often the custom, where it occurs in gardens, to put out a plate of bread and milk for it.

Except for man's motor car and his dog, the hedgehog can have few enemies today when it is living in suburban gardens and parks. In woodland conditions, however, the fox and the badger prey upon it and the hedgehog skin, more or less neatly turned inside out, can be found along the woodland edge or forest path. Presumably, in Wyre, this is the work of the fox, as the badger is not to be found so commonly. The tawny owl is also said to take the hedgehog. No doubt the owl's scaly legs and sharp beak are an easy match for the hedgehog's spines.

The food of the hedgehog is mainly invertebrates such as insects, slugs, and earthworms, but it will also take the eggs of small birds and perhaps also their young too. A little vegetable matter in the form of acorns and berries is also taken, but this is probably only a very small proportion of the whole. The most spectacular item of food, however, is the adder and there must have been a number of accounts of such encounters. The hedgehog rushes in and bites the reptile then immediately rolls up, then after a time repeats this until the reptile is dead. The hedgehog has been the victim of much persecution in the past mainly because it was thought to take the eggs and young of game birds. This is, however, discounted today.

The hedgehog passes the winter months in a nest of dried grass and leaves in a pile of woodland litter or leaves. In gardens and parks the rubbish pile or compost heap is often chosen. It is not until the late autumn, however, that the winter sleep is undertaken, but this is only a light hibernation and during good weather they will uncurl and carry out a certain amount of exploration before settling down again.

One of the most remarkable but little known aspects of the behaviour of the hedgehog was called by Maurice Burton 'self-anointing'. I am not sure whether this habit has been observed in the wild but a hedgehog in captivity, after chewing on a piece of leather, will then cover itself with a frothy saliva which is even placed on its spines.

Because the males are fecund from early April to late August and pregnancies occur from May to October, it has been put forward that two litters each year are possible. But here again is a case of one of our most common animals of the countryside about whose biology we know so little. Gestation occupies 31 to 32 days and about five young are usually born. They are born blind, their eyes opening after 14 days. In just over three weeks they commence to leave the nest when they follow the mother around during her foraging, but the male takes no part in this.

In one interesting but extremely important way, the hedgehog serves man. They are used in experimental work on virus research as they are able to carry the viruses responsible for foot and mouth disease, influenza and yellow fever.

MOLE, *Talpa europaea*

It is extraordinary that we know so little about the mole, one of our most abundant furry mammals. Even though it spends the whole of its life, or nearly the whole of it, just beneath the surface of the ground, one would have thought that by now a wealth of information would have been built up concerning it. What has happened, of course, is that a wealth of myth and ignorance has been built up instead, and much of it persists today. The number of researchers who have studied the mole can almost be counted on the fingers of one hand. Perhaps the reason for this is that until very recently few have been able to keep and observe this strange little animal in captivity.

Most country folk have seen a dead mole, either because it had been trapped or found dead on country paths, usually during periods of drought when the mole sometimes finds difficulty in getting enough to eat.

The mole, *Talpa europaea*, is a medium-sized animal larger than a mouse but smaller than a rat, and extremely modified for tunnelling underground. The head is rather pig-shaped and merges directly into the shoulders, there being no neck although, of course, the neck vertebrae are present. The shoulders, however, are extremely powerful and the forelimbs are immensely strong serving as burrowing tools. These forelimbs are turned outwards and they cannot be brought underneath the animal for walking as in all other British mammals. The forefeet or 'hands' are very specially modified for digging, scraping, and pushing. They are turned outwards, are flat and spade-like, and furnished with five very strong claws. The hindlegs are specially modified. The trunk is cylindrical and terminates with a stumpy tail which narrows near the base and is always held vertically upwards. The degree of acuteness of the senses possessed by the mole has puzzled many people, mainly perhaps because the eyes are very small and there appear to be no ears. Generally, the eyes are hidden being covered by the fur. The hair around the eyes is

under the control of the mole who can 'radiate' the hair away
from the eyes so that it can expose them at will. However, its
vision at best cannot be very acute. There is not much con-
vincing evidence concerning the mole's ability to see and the
most recent research workers came to the conclusion that the

*The eyes of the mole are generally invisible as they are covered by the fur, and the tail is
upright to keep contact with the tunnel roof. Thus, its tail is of more value to it than sight
in its direction finding.*

mole could only distinguish light from darkness. An ear is present
but as the external pinna is absent, it has often been thought that
the mole was devoid of hearing. In fact, the ears are situated near
the shoulder region and consist only of an aperture slightly less
than a tenth of an inch in circumference and generally covered
by the fur. It is not thought that the hearing of the mole is
exceptionally acute although the anatomy of the ear structure
has led one investigator to assume this. On the other hand,
moles have experimentally been found to appreciate sounds at a
much lower oscillation frequency than can man. Moles can
utter two kinds of sounds which can be heard by man. Firstly,
there is a soft twittering which accompanies the mole's exploring
activities and, secondly, loud squeaks are produced when they
fight.

It is known, however, without any doubt, that the tactile
sense, the sense of touch, is highly developed in the mole. This
appears to be concentrated in the snout where it is hairless and
where a number of special sensory organs, known as Eimer's
organs, are situated. These appear as small conical projections.
They are richly supplied with nerves and blood vessels, and as
well as being specially sensitive to pressure are also thought to be
used by the mole for detecting differences in temperature and
humidity. In addition to these, there are a number of tactile

hairs on the chin, the snout and the cheeks. It is interesting also that the tail is believed to play a part in the mole's general sensory perception. It is always held upright and maintains contact with the roof of the tunnel. The sense of smell of the mole is not much developed and does not appear to play a part in finding its food.

The food of the mole consists of practically all the invertebrates it can find in the soil; insects, earthworms and slugs, therefore, figure largely in the menu, and it is of interest to note that these are eaten by being grasped, or rather held down by the forefeet whilst being consumed, and the hind legs straddle the floor of the tunnel. Its food is found when the mole is exploring the tunnel system, or whilst it is actively tunnelling. A very small part of its food is taken above ground. Perhaps one of the most interesting aspects of the mole's behaviour concerns its so-called 'larders'. Sometimes when mole-runs are dug up, collections or knots of earthworms are found. On examination, these are seen to have the head-end bitten, or otherwise damaged, and the explanation is put forward that they are caught when abundant and stored, after being paralysed by the mole, and eaten when food becomes hard to find.

One aspect of the mole's tunnelling is worthy of mention. It has been generally supposed that when the new excavated earth is pushed to the surface that this is done by the mole lifting it upwards with the snout and head. However, it has been proved that this is accomplished by the forelimbs, each used alternately.

The mole is a deep sleeper like the dormouse, and can sometimes be handled before it wakes.

SMALL FURRY ANIMALS

The small mouse-sized and mouse-like animals of the forest belong to two quite distinct groups of the fur-bearing mammals. Firstly, there are the carnivorous insectivores which include the hedgehog, the mole, and the shrews, and here we shall concern ourselves with the shrews, or the genus *Sorex*. Secondly, there are the gnawing RODENTIA which comprises the most abundant in species of all the orders of mammals and here we shall deal with the voles and with two species of mice.

Wherever in the forest there is ground cover, whether of plants, tree litter, or tussocky grass, then the small furry animals

are exceptionally abundant. Yet a casual observer may be unaware of their presence although when sitting still if his hearing
be keen, he could not fail to sense the continual high-pitched
squeaks and twitters of these tiny mammals as they go about
their business. If, however, one makes a careful examination of
the ground surface, it is found to contain a bewilderingly complex
system of tunnels amongst the plant debris. Let us describe five
of these mouse-like animals found in Wyre, two insectivores and
three rodents, all very common except the smallest of the rodents,
the diminutive harvest mouse.

The shrews are characterised by their small size, long snouts,
fine velvety fur, and their teeth, which are situated in a continuous row along the jaw, and are tipped with red enamel.

COMMON SHREW, *Sorex araneus*

A rather smaller animal than the house mouse and its fur is light
to darkish brown on top and greyish white underneath. A
creature of intense activity it is forever hunting for small insects
and other invertebrates on which it subsists. It is active throughout day and night, fairly long periods of activity alternating with
short rest periods. Ground beetles, flies and spiders, appear to be
most commonly eaten, but it will eat carrion and even dead
bodies of its own kind. There have been a number of estimates
of the amount of food taken each day. This appears to be about
three-quarters of its own weight. It swims well.

Except in the breeding season they are solitary, although a number may inhabit a single tunnel system, but they show fight and
utter shrill 'screams' when they meet. The common shrew rarely
lives more than a few months more than one year and most
usually breeds in the spring after the year of birth, although a
few females mature late in the summer of their year of birth.
The period of gestation is not known with certainty but is thought

The common shrew.

to be between 13 and 19 days. The number of embryos usually lies between five and nine but there is about 20 per cent foetal mortality. The number of litters in the season is most commonly two, but one litter only is not uncommon, whilst numbers up to five have been reported from continental Europe. Development in the nest is slow and the eyes do not open until a day or so before weaning at 18–21 days and the young stay in the nest until they are almost fully grown.

Such a numerous mammal attracts many predators, including the fox, and the feral domestic cats which are common in the forest. The weasel hunts the burrows and the tawny owl and kestrel search for them by night and day. They sometimes enter The Newalls, gaining entrance through cracks in the masonry at below ground level, and they breed regularly under the stone slabs of the garden, cheek by jowl with the bank voles. There is some suggestion that the shrews are distasteful to carnivores, and their untouched dead bodies are quite commonly found.

PYGMY SHREW, *Sorex minutus*

Not so common as the previous species but even so is still an abundant animal around the forest. It is smaller than the common shrew but the tail is relatively longer. The colour of the coat on the top side is rather sandy brown and lacks much of the variation in colour found in the common shrew. The tail is also rather more densely haired than in the latter species. It has been found from trapping experiments by Crowcroft that pygmy shrews accounted for four per cent of shrews caught in woodland, whereas in open grassland the per-

The pigmy shrew.

centage of pygmy shrew rises from 10 to 16 per cent. Like the common shrew it is an animal of great activity but appears to be much more of a climber, being sometimes found in the upper stories of buildings, as I have myself found them at The Newalls.

An interesting point concerning its habits is the fact that it lives in the same tunnel systems as the common shrew but is expert in keeping out of the way.

Two litters are produced during the summer as in the common shrew and in many other respects the two species show many similarities.

BANK VOLE, *Clethrionomys glareolus*
Easily identified from the other little furry animals in the forest by its blunt muzzle and short tail. The tail is only about half the length of head and body. The coat is chestnut coloured above, and silvery grey beneath. It appears to be the commonest of the small mammals, at least around The Newalls, where it often leaves its tunnels and crevices in the garden rock-work, and the grassy banks, to survey its human observers. This attractive little animal is said to be most abundant in deciduous woodland and scrub, and its voice consists of chattering and squeaking. Like shrews, it is active throughout the twenty-four hours. A

The bank vole.

little more is known concerning its breeding cycle than for some other species. The breeding season starts from mid-April and may proceed until December in some years. The gestation period is just under 18 days and the number of litters each year is probably around four to five. The young are born at a weight of about 15 to the ounce, they are weaned at about two and a half weeks and are sexually mature in four to five weeks! For food, the bank vole consumes more vegetable material than animal, with a high proportion of green plants. When snow has melted, the position of the tunnels is easily made out by the apical parts of grass leaves which have not been eaten, and the extensive nature of the tunnel system comes as a great surprise.

WOOD MOUSE OR LONG-TAILED FIELD MOUSE,
Apodemus sylvaticus

This mouse can be separated from the voles by the pointed muzzle, large ears and long, relatively hairless, tail. The latter is equal in length to that of head and body. It is rather larger than the house mouse and the coat is brown, mixed with yellow, becoming more yellow along the flanks, but is white below. The eyes, and especially the ears, are prominent. It occupies complex tunnel systems in the ground litter, and in the rough fields around the grass tussocks, by the forest. The wood mouse moves rapidly with little leaps, scurrying here and there, but unlike shrews and voles, only forages at night. Often enters buildings and stays if house mice are not present.

Wood mice.

Breeding occurs in March and usually continues until October, although in some years it may continue throughout winter. Gestation is about 25 days and the number in the litter is between five and six, but the number of litters per season is not known. The young are weaned at about 21 days, but they first leave the nest at 15 to 16 days.

Vegetable matter probably constitutes the major part of the wood mouse's diet, seeds being especially prominent in stomach contents, but insects are also eaten, as well as green plant material.

HARVEST MOUSE, *Micromys minutus*

The smallest of our rodents, being much smaller than the house mouse. It is 'foxy-red' in colour on top, white below, and its tail is long and prehensile. It is usually to be found in long grass or cornfields, but in winter usually burrows just below the surface.

Its nest is woven of grass, about the size of a cricket ball, and is to be found above ground. Gestation takes 21 days and the litter is recorded as being from four to nine. After 15 days the young are independent and reach adult weight at 24 days. The length of life is thought to average from 16 to 18 months in the wild, but about two years in captivity.

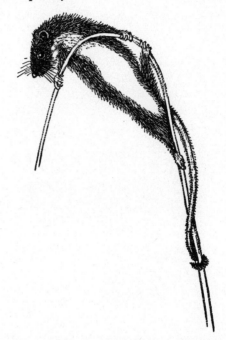

The harvest mouse.

The food of the harvest mouse is said to consist of grain, fruits, green vegetable matter and insects. It seemed quite common some years ago, but is now much less frequently seen. It is active throughout the day and night.

A DORMOUSE'S DORMITORY

Imagine the surprise when looking into a bird nest-box at the end of April this year to find a dormouse rolled up into a ball and fast asleep! Woodmice sometimes use nest-boxes but they jump out with great speed the moment the box is touched. But the dormouse never appeared to lose a wink's sleep and the lid of the box was gently closed. It seemed that a great or blue tit had laid the foundations of a nest as a customary inch layer of green moss had been placed in position. The dormouse must have exercised considerable agility in order to enter the entrance hole of the box, and with some confidence too, as it was sited about 12 feet above ground level. The box was on an oak tree growing on the bank of a streamlet, only about 50 yards from Dowles, so just that much inside the boundary of Worcestershire. The nest-box was found to be empty when we looked inside a fortnight later.

The dormouse has a body of an almost infinite number of shapes and when it sleeps it rolls up into a tight ball, with its bushy tail wrapped around it.

Finding the dormouse immediately solved a mystery. In the spring of the previous year, one of the southern owl boxes was found to contain a large quantity of the finely stripped bark of honeysuckle and as the pied flycatcher makes its nest of this material it was thought at first that this beautiful little black and white bird had gathered it in. Pied flycatchers had made three nests within a few yards of the owl box so that our thoughts naturally ran in this direction. On looking at our animal books, however, it was learnt, as I should have known, that the dormouse is also very fond of honeysuckle bark and makes its nest of this material when it is available. It appears to be shredded rather more finely than the pied flycatcher will accomplish and it makes a soft but springy mattress and the dormouse is able to weave it to some extent. The southern owl box consists of a tunnel made of rough-sawn one inch planks, three feet long and one foot wide, with the base filled in except for drainage holes. The dormouse nest was found in one 12 feet from the ground, but similarly placed on an oak tree at the side of the streamlet, but on the other side of the old railway line. The nest was not disturbed or the mystery would have been solved a year earlier.

A point of great interest concerning the presence of the dormouse in Wyre is the general belief that in Britain it is in an overall decline. The map of its distribution given by Lawrence and Brown (see 'For Further Reading') shows the dormouse to be very rare throughout the Midland counties. Indeed, except for the southern and south-eastern coastal counties, where it is given as not common, elsewhere it is shown as rare.

The dormouse, *Muscardinus avellanarius*, is about the size of a mouse but generally appearing stouter. The muzzle is short with a distinct 'Roman nose', the ears are prominent, and the eyes are large and lustrous. The most characteristic feature of the dormouse, however, is the tail which is much stouter than that of a mouse, blunt at the tip and quite bushy. The colour of the coat of the Wyre specimen was a rather rich mustard colour with the longer hairs black and the belly whitish, but the coat colour is usually given as 'bright foxy'.

In habit, the dormouse is almost entirely nocturnal and usually forages above ground. Its food consists of nuts and similar fruits and seeds. The most usual habitat is an oak wood where there is an understory of hazel. The nuts of the latter which have been eaten by the dormouse are said to be quite characteristic. There is a small hole in the shell neatly gnawed out and the nut is expertly removed by the tongue. It is also sometimes found in beech and sweet chestnut woods.

About four is the usual number of young in a litter and the life span is usually about four years, although they have lived for six years in captivity. At one time dormice were often kept as pets but now that they have become much rarer this practice has ceased.

RED SQUIRREL, *Sciurus vulgaris*

One of the most pleasurable features of a walk through the forest when I was a boy (and now that was many years ago), was the sighting of a red squirrel. Often they would be seen quite close, as near as ten or fifteen feet. For a few seconds they would cease all movement, peer and stare at the human interferer with

The red squirrel is distinguished from the grey by its smaller size and particularly by the long ear-tufts and its generally reddish coloration.

their large dark eyes, then with a series of leaps they would disappear from sight amongst the leafy oak foliage.

What caused their virtual disappearance from the South and the Midlands of England during the middle 1920's is largely a matter of conjecture, but it is certain that no recovery in their numbers has taken place. Of course, it was commonly believed that it was the presence of the more belligerent grey squirrel that drove away the 'reds', but as the latter disappeared even where the 'grey' had not been seen, some other cause must be sought to account for it.

The most recent authoritative work describing this phenomenon has been given by A. Baqueriza in *Country Life* for 17th April 1969. Red squirrels occur in a few situations in Shropshire but in one locality they became diseased and started to die in 1960. A local naturalist, Mrs. Eatough, and a veterinary friend, F. B. Edwards, studied this epidemic closely, and perhaps the first point of significance was that grey squirrels had appeared in the locality about a fortnight before the onset of red squirrel disease. The 'reds' died out and within two years the 'greys' were firmly established. From tests that were carried out it seems probable that a virus of influenza type was responsible for the disease and that also the virus can exist within a squirrel population without causing disease. Some other factor, therefore, must be present and it has been suggested that this was a 'stress' due to changing habitat. It is difficult to define this but urbanisation of the countryside, and noise, could have been the cause.

The red squirrel, *Sciurus vulgaris*, is an arboreal rodent with a bushy tail a little smaller than the grey squirrel and distinguished from the latter by its reddish colour and its long hairy eartufts. During the moult in summer, the long tail hairs and the eartufts are shed, and at this period the colour of the coat is at its lightest so that identification may present difficulties to the inexpert. The red squirrel has a voice which is said to be a rasping chatter followed sometimes by a hoarse call or whine. It is most active in the early morning and at dusk. Inclement weather conditions during winter inhibit activity to some extent although there is no true hibernation.

The drey is spherical, generally placed at the junction of branches with the main trunk and is of twigs lined with moss, leaves and shredded bark. In the south there appears to be two breeding periods, firstly, from January to April and, secondly, from the end of May to August, and the average litter size is three although up to six is known. The most important single item of diet is the seeds gnawed from Scots pine cones. Other tree seeds are taken such as beech mast, acorns, hazel nuts and sweet chestnut. Much other vegetable matter, such as bulbs, buds and fungi is also part of the diet. Only occasionally are birds eggs and young birds taken. Food is sometimes buried to be recovered later, probably being found by scent.

The red squirrel is very much at home in coniferous woodland so that if substantial decline in grey squirrel numbers took place we might well see the 'reds' again in Wyre.

REYNARD THE FOX

The fox is now the largest of our carnivorous land mammals and even today it remains a common animal of the countryside. It holds an important place in literature. From our earliest recollections in fairy stories and fables, the fox is associated with craftiness and cunning and certainly this reputation has been earned even though the involved and circuitous wilyness described in the fables of Aesop and La Fontaine cannot be taken literally. To exist in such numbers, even in the suburbs of our great cities, means that the fox must possess a plastic behaviour pattern enabling it to fit into new situations and allowing it to find its

The long thin muzzle, flat mask, and the long bushy white-tipped tail are sufficient to identify the fox even in the failing light.

food, breed, and hide away even in the closest proximity to man. Around Wyre, however, the fox lives out its life in the wooded countryside in the manner which it has followed perhaps for several centuries. There is one particular exception to this however; the myxomatosis epidemics have meant that the rabbit has disappeared for a few months in a varying pattern of its localities and the fox has had to look elsewhere for its food.

It would seem to be unnecessary to describe the fox because its appearance is so well known to so many people. But although it is often abroad by day its usual peak of activity is at dusk and the early part of the night. Usually it keeps out of the way and, ironically, although the lone countryman sometimes comes upon a fox, when it is intent on stalking, it is the motorist who most often sights it. The fox habitually keeps to particular beats and even in the beam of the motor-car headlights he will leap a hedge and bound across the road. Often he is seen at the litter-bins around picnic spots when the crowds have gone.

The fox is glimpsed momentarily so that the outstanding characters for identification are worth stating. The colour is a yellowish to brownish red, 'foxy' in fact, and the underparts are greyish white. The back of the ears and the lower parts of the legs are black. The ears are large, almost always pricked, and triangular in shape. The face or 'mask' is flattish with the cheek hairs pointing outwards whilst the muzzle is narrow and pointed, with a small black, wet, nose. The muzzle and the face is white underneath. Apart from the general gait and poise of the animal, however, the most distinctive character for identification is the large bushy tail with a white tip. This is known as his 'brush'.

The food of the fox is very varied and it is probably the great variety which makes the fox so successful in exploiting a large range of habitats. Historically, the rabbit figured largely in the fox's menu, but with myxomatosis they came harder to come by, although many an infected rabbit was put out of its misery by the fox. Availability is stated to be the main factor in the formation of the fox's diet. Fruit is taken in the autumn (it would be of interest to know whether our new British vineyards are ever raided by the fox). Mice and voles are often of importance and they are sometimes scraped out of their burrows and then swallowed whole. Birds and their eggs are taken too. The feathers of the wood pigeon are often found in Wyre—all that is left of a forest meal! It must be mentioned also that the remains of a Rhode Island red or a white Leghorn are often to be found in the forest. Insects, especially beetles, are eaten and their wing cases are to be found in the long and tapered castings.

The pad marks of the fox show hair traces in soft ground.

The tracks of a fox are difficult to distinguish from those of a small dog except on soft mud. Here the long hairs between the pads can often be made out. They are absent in the tracks of a dog.

BROCK THE BADGER

The badger is not nearly so well-known as the fox. Yet, the badger is widely distributed in Britain and found in every county of England and Wales. It is, however, nocturnal, seldom being seen abroad during daylight hours. These latter are spent underground. The sleeping place of the badger is known as the 'set' and is usually excavated in sloping ground in woodland, but adjacent to pasture. Sets are extensive and are occupied over many years. The tunnel system is often complex and entrances are numerous. The sleeping chambers are lined with a dry bedding of grass, moss, straw and leaves which is brought out to air on sunny mornings. The badger set may also house foxes, rabbits or rats, usually keeping out of each others way. During winter there is not a true hibernation and although it can survive without food for a considerable time it often emerges from the set, even in midwinter.

It is the nature of the set which determines the type of country in which badgers are to be found. Generally, in Wyre, the ground is much too rocky and friable making an extensive set difficult for the badger to construct. This is certainly the reason why the badger is not common in Wyre although they do occur in at least one area where the soil is deep on the forest edge.

In early spring the adult male (known as the boar) will wander far afield to seek a mate. At this time he leaves his characteristic pad marks along the soft earth at the wood's edge. This shows a large 'palm' and the five digit pads in a shallow arc in front. The tracks of the forefeet are larger than those of the hinder.

The black and white striped head, grey, shaggy coat and squat appearance easily identify the badger.
The pad marks of the badger shows the five digits in a shallow arc. (The dog and the fox show only four.)

The badger possesses a scent-gland near the tail and when abroad the boar marks his path with his scent, and in this way is able to retrace his steps homeward, followed by his new mate. This animal is a squat, heavy, wedge-shaped, medium-sized species which cannot be mistaken for any other animal, even at a distance. The most easily distinguishing character, however, is the face marking. Two conspicuous broad black stripes extend from the muzzle to the neck with white in the middle line and beneath, and the ears are white around the margins. The back is grey and shaggy in appearance but the short legs and under-side of the belly are dark, almost black. The claws are very strong and those of the forefeet are especially large. The individual hair from the badger's back is quite characteristic and can often be collected from the lowest strand of barbed wire. The hair is light in colour at the base and then a dark area occurs until nearer the tip, when it is light again. All of us rather old-fashioned people who still shave with a blade, either safety or otherwise, and apply lather with a brush, should be aware of this because, historically, the badger bristle has been an important component of the shaving brush. The tail of the badger is only about four inches in length but the weight of the animal is extraordinary. The average length, tail included, is about 36 inches, but the average weight of a male is about 27 pounds, and a female 24 pounds. Not unusually, the weight is over 40 pounds and some are known of over 60 pounds. Compared with this, the average weight of a fox is 15 pounds (dog) and 12 pounds (vixen).

With regard to the food of the badger, it will eat almost anything available in season which it can tackle or reach, both animal and vegetable. Earthworms figure to the largest extent in its diet and, formerly, young rabbits were important too. In addition, it will eat most small animals such as mice, rats, hedgehogs, voles, moles, shrews, frogs, toads, as well as slugs and snails. Insects are eaten, especially the larger ones, and wasp nests are often clawed out and the grubs consumed. Unfortunately for brock (his Anglo-Saxon name), he will sometimes take poultry but this is not typical. But carrion is eaten from time to time including young birds, such as rooks, which have fallen from the nest, and dead lambs are known to have been taken. As far as vegetable matter is concerned they will dig up roots, bulbs and rhizomes, and forage for a variety of fallen fruits such as apples and plums, as well as acorns and beech mast. Indeed, it is reported that acorns make up a considerable part of the diet in autumn in good acorn years. Grass is eaten in winter together with other green food.

The breeding cycle of the badger is remarkable. Mating will take place from February to October, although chiefly from February to May, but there is a long period of delay in the implantation of the fertilised egg-cells. This delay may be as long as nine months and implantation takes place in December. The young (from one to five) may be produced any time from January to May and they remain underground for about eight weeks and are weaned at about twelve weeks. During this latter stage the female (called the sow) starts to feed her litter on food which she regurgitates and they stay with her until the autumn, and sometimes over winter with her.

OTTER, *Lutra lutra*

When I was a boy and camped on the banks of Dowles Brook at the Island, often I was woken by the splashings of otters and the strange noises that go with them—the whistles, murmurings and whickering, sometimes so human that I found it too difficult to sleep through it. This was added to when the brook seemed alive with the gurgling, trickling and swirling sound of the water. But I was never privileged to see one at that time in Dowles, although one late evening, an entrancing half-an-hour was spent at Welford-on-Avon watching a bitch otter playing with her cubs in the water. A quite sizeable fish was thrown into the air and then a game of exciting ottery water polo took place until it was too dark to follow.

When the otter fled in alarm down the dried-up stream he appeared to bound on his hind legs only. The hair of the otter aggregates into spikes when wet or muddy.
The track of the fore-foot of an otter on soft mud, showing the extent of the webbing.

Then, five years ago, I saw an otter in the forest within a few yards of where I used to hear them at night. He was really more surprised than I and made his exit in such an extraordinary manner that he obviously considered himself at a distinct disadvantage at the encounter. Walking over the culvert at the 'island', where the stream runs under the Forestry Commission road there was a tremendous flurry and commotion. An otter simply flew out of the culvert and disappeared down the narrow almost dry stream in the direction of Dowles. It happened in a flash but my impression was that it was mainly running bipedally —on its hind legs only.

One might wonder whether sufficient food could be found in Dowles for its subsistence? There is a note in the literature concerning a half to three-quarters grown otter that ate from 12 to 20-lb of food per week, but whether this food was easily come by (which I suspect), we are not told. It is known, however, that eels can be a substantial component of the diet, and crayfish too, and although no actual record of the bull-head as an article of diet can be traced, doubtless if hunger drives they would be taken also. I had almost forgotten our own rather thin trout and if to these are added the minor food items which the otter is known to take, such as frogs, birds, rodents, newts, slugs, earthworms and insects, it appears certain that otters could find an adequate living in Dowles if they ranged far afield—which, of course, they are known to do.

The common otter, *Lutra lutra*, has a wide distribution, being found throughout Europe and temperate Asia, but merges into a closely related species in the tropical Indo-Malayan region. The otter found throughout Canada is also very similar to the European species. Until very recently the otter was to be found throughout the British Isles more commonly in areas where there were large rivers, but they are also to be found in coastal districts in the absence of rivers, especially in the northern isles. Again, until very recently it was hunted and it was thought generally that there was one otter for each six miles or so of stream. However, after a stretch of stream had been worked for some time it would be abandoned. Like so much of our native fauna, little is really known about the otter and its movements, but it is thought that it will travel long distances when seeking 'pastures new'.

The signs of an otter's presence should not be hard to find by a competent field-naturalist or, indeed, by a good observer. The otter uses the same feeding place which could be a rock in midstream or a grassy bank with good cover around, and here will be found the remains of its meals, fish-heads and tails with the claws of crayfish (those likely to be present along Dowles), but in Severn and its large tributaries, the broken shells of the swan mussel would most likely be included. Another sign of the otter on the stream bank are the 'spraints', the faecal matter, and these are also usually deposited in regular places. The spraints are cigar-shaped from one to three inches in length and vary in number from one to four. They can be easily identified when fresh as they possess a peculiar musty odour; they are exceedingly mucilaginous and black in colour, and characteristically contain fishbones and scales. The droppings of mink which have now become established in some parts of Britain, originating from escapes, will also often contain fish-scales and be deposited on the stream bank, but they are much smaller, seldom exceeding an inch in length—somewhat greenish when fresh and the odour very unpleasant.

Normally, otters are solitary and nocturnal only coming together for breeding. The male is called a 'dog', the female a 'bitch' and the two or three young are 'cubs'. Very little is known about the breeding cycle of otters, but it is probable that only one litter each year is produced and the dog takes no part in rearing the cubs. The period of gestation is usually taken to be about 62 days and a nest of grass and moss is made in the holt which may be at some distance from the main feeding area. The cubs stay in the breeding holt for about a couple of months, thereafter they stay with the bitch for some considerable period travelling long distances around the countryside.

Now there is disquieting news about the otter population, and it is widely reported that their numbers have dropped to the extent that they are absent from many parts where they were formerly abundant.

THE PIPISTRELLE AND THE LONG EARED BAT

A bat is just a bat to most people, something with an eerie reputation flittering around old country churchyards at dusk. But thirteen different species of these highly adapted small mammals are to be found in the British Isles, although two species are very rarely observed (the mouse-eared bat, *Myotis myotis*, could be a rare winter immigrant or possibly a local rare resident. It is a large bat up to nearly 18 inches wing span, whilst the parti-coloured bat, *Vespertilio murinus* is a rare vagrant in Britain only having been seen three times over the last 150 years.) Bats, however, have never attracted many students to study their natural history and, no doubt, when this comes about many more fascinating facts will emerge. One point, of the greatest importance about bats, that has been ascertained in recent years concerns the remarkable flight in conditions near to darkness. Their ability to avoid objects has been remarked upon for centuries, but it was as recently as 1920 that it was discovered that bats find their way about, and secure their prey, by what is called 'echolocation'. Short-wave pulses in the form of minute squeaks are emitted and the nature of their reflection, or echoes, gives information concerning the position and nature of objects in the path of the waves. In the family RHINOLOPHIDAE, containing our two species of horseshoe bats, pulses of constant frequency are emitted through the nose and the peculiar horse-shoe shaped skin folds cause the beams to be unidirectional. In the family VESPERTILIONIDAE to which all the remaining British species belong, the pulse-repetition rate reaches about 60 a second when the bats approach a stationary object, and in some species it increases to about 200 per second when the bat is pursuing an insect. Each pulse lasts only two five-hundredths of a second.

Apart from this extraordinarily precise method of navigation, the mechanism of the flight of bats is also of the greatest interest. The bats constitute the only group of mammals that have mastered aerial flight, indeed, of the vertebrates only the birds have accomplished this. We have, of course, to except Man, who has conquered the air, not by adaptation of his own body, but by his technological achievements. This has concerned the manipulation of his environment to the extent that from it he fashioned craft to journey into outer space.

Bats constitute the order CHIROPTERA and it seems that they have evolved from the order INSECTIVORA represented in Britain by the hedgehog, the mole, and the shrews. Everyone would be able to recognise a bat when its wings are stretched, although when at rest with its wings folded alongside its body, looking like any small furry animal, this would not be so easy. The fore-limbs of bats are highly modified, the forearm being very long and curved, and the digits are exceptionally long and slender except for the thumb which is short and hooked. The wing stretches from the shoulder to the thumb then to the tips of the elongated digits, thence to the ankle and then joins the slender tail at some point. There are differences, according to the species, but when the wing is extended everyone would recognise it as a bat's wing.

Although the pelvic girdle supporting the articulation of the hindlimbs is relatively weak, the pectoral girdle and chest, both bones and muscle, are strongly developed. The ears of bats also show important modifications especially so in the vespertilionid bats, where there is a large upwards extension of the base of the ear called the 'tragus'.

We need a careful study of the bats of Wyre and of the nearby Severn, but two species are very common. These are the pipistrelle, Britain's smallest bat, and the long-eared bat which is exceptionally abundant.

PIPISTRELLE, *Pipistrellus pipistrellus*

This species is found everywhere in Britain and is the commoner species. The wing span is about eight inches reaching up to ten inches, but the weight is only up to approximately six grams, less than a quarter of an ounce! When not in flight it is to be found in buildings, holes and crevices in trees and rocks, and a characteristic of this species is that it will crawl into confined spaces.

Long-eared bat in crawling position. The ears act as tactile organs and are well endowed with blood vessels. The thumbs are used to pull the bat along. The nostrils are bare and warty outgrowths occur behind them.

It will also find its way into a roof-void by creeping through the cracks under distorted tiles. Its high-pitched squeaking can be heard in flight. Its flight is often jerky and regular beats are often used.

The pipistrelle hibernates from the end of October till early March, but when the temperature rises above 40°F it will often emerge from its hibernaculum for a short flight. The gnats constitute the larger part of its food, but moths are eaten in addition, the latter being taken to a resting place and the wings bitten off before being consumed. Copulation takes place in autumn but the female stores the sperm as she does not ovulate until May when fertilisation takes place. After a gestation period of about 44 days the single young is born from about the second week of June.

LONG-EARED BAT, *Precotus auritus*

This is another common and widely distributed species in Britain. It is thought to be especially abundant in the Midlands, and this is certainly true in Wyre.

The long-eared bat in hibernation position. Note that only the earlets (tragus) extend downwards. The true ears are folded under the wings.

The exceptionally long ears are usually sufficient to identify it and the fur of the upperside is from a medium to a greyish brown, whilst that of the underside is yellowish white to yellowish brown. The wing span is around ten inches. It appears to hibernate in buildings around Wyre and on warm winter days it will emerge for a short flight and even feed on hibernating small tortoiseshell and peacock butterflies. The ears, as well as being large, are also complex and are tucked away when the animal is at rest, along the side of the body, but the ears will sometimes be partly unfurled sideways on occasion, when they have been likened to rams horns.

THE FOREST FALLOW

Four species of deer are now generally considered to have attained the status of 'British' in one degree or another. These are as follows: the red deer, *Cervus elaphus*, an indigenous British species. Fallow, *Dama dama*, which although mentioned in the Domesday Book as well established, seems not entirely to have gained the distinction of being a British species. Roe, *Capreolus capreolus*, an indigenous British species, once widely distributed then of narrow range when the forests were depleted; now increasing again and recorded from sixteen English counties. Sika, *Cervus nippon*, an introduction around the mid-19th century is now established in eleven English counties (but neither Worcestershire nor Shropshire). In addition to these, however, a few other deer species, having escaped from captivity, seem to have established themselves locally. Chinese muntjac, *Muntiacus reevesi*, or its hybrids with the closely-related Indian muntjac, *Muntiacus muntjac*, are to be found occasionally in the Midland counties, including Worcestershire. Chinese water deer, *Hydropotes inermis*, is to be found in counties around Woburn, where it was introduced at the beginning of the century and in woods around Walcot Park, Shropshire, where it had also been introduced from Woburn.

The Deer of Wyre are the fallow. The presence of no other deer species has so far been authenticated. This seems surprising as the extensive woodland of such varied types, and the comparative isolation, would seem to offer sanctuary to several other species.

The deer has traditionally been the most noble quarry of the hunter. During the last few years, however, two facts have become apparent. Deer have become an important amenity of the countryside to be enjoyed by an increasing number of people who, because of our increasing mobility and, indeed, greater leisure time, are able to travel into the countryside.

Unfortunately the fallow deer of Wyre are, to all intents and purposes, invisible unless one hides up in special places at dawn or dusk. It is only rarely that one comes upon them by accident. In the thick woods one sometimes is aware of hurried scurrying as a party of fallow make a rapid departure or a small group may be seen in the half-light along the field side of a favoured wood. For many generations they have been harried and hunted, and not always in a humane manner, but although views have changed concerning our relationships with wild deer, they still remain out of sight. Perhaps it may not be many years before the Wyre fallow allow themselves to be seen as they graze unconcernedly through the forest glades for all to enjoy their grace.

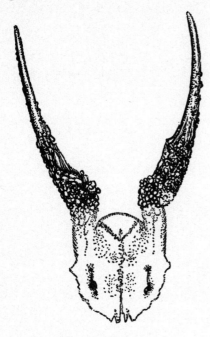

The first head, the second year of a Wyre pricket. These measured 8½ inches in length which are much above average.

The male of the fallow is a buck and the female is a doe, contrasting with the red deer stag and the female hind. Only the buck bears antlers. In January, about nine months after being dropped as a calf, the first antlers commence to grow and these consist of single spikes and are covered with velvet until from the end of July to the middle of August when it is stripped off. The young buck in his second year with his first head of antlers is known as a pricket. These small spike-like antlers are usually from six to eight inches high. The second head is shed at about late April and the third head is then developed. In this, brow and trey tines are well-developed and about two inches in length, whilst the palmation is now well marked with about half an inch spellers or fingers. The spellers at the top and the 'spur', the lowest at the back of the palmation, should be half as long again as the other spellers.

Fourth head of a Wyre fallow buck (fifth year). Weight 3½ lb. Brow tines 4⅞ inches in length, 18 inches from boss to middle speller.

Fifth head of a Wyre fallow buck. Circumference of bosses 6 inches and 6¼ inches.

The fourth head develops as soon as the third head is shed, between the middle of April and the middle of May, and the velvet is cleaned off between the middle of August and middle of September. The palm is now heavy and supported by substantial beams. The spellers of the palm are now conspicuous with the spur and the fore-top over two inches in length. For the following three years development takes place with the brow and trey tines lengthening, thickening, and growing upwards. After that, succeeding years show a regression in their form and weight which is known as 'going back'.

THE BREEDING CYCLE

The buck spends the summer on his own or in small parties of the same sex whilst the antlers develop, but about the second week of October the does begin to assemble with them. The mating period is known as the rut and mating takes place in a traditional area which is marked out by the oldest or most virile buck. This he does by fraying young trees and urinating around them. In this way, it is stated, the secretion from the post-orbital gland and the scent of the urine gets transferred to the antler palms and thus gets widely dispersed. Aggressive challenging takes place accompanied by 'rhythmic mixture of bark and grunt' and as the does come into season he covers them. The rut lasts about four weeks, at the end of which the buck is in bad condition but fairly quickly recovers. The period of gestation is given as seven and a half months (de Nahlik) and as eight months (Southern), and the single fawn (or occasionally twins) is born in May or June. There is high mortality amongst the fawns probably due, in part, to foxes but they also get caught in wire fences.

THE SIGNS OF DEER

Even if, at the present time, we seldom sight the fallow, the observant eye sees many signs, not only of their presence, but also of what they have been doing. One cannot walk far into the forest before the tracks of fallow show in the muddy patches. Their maximum size is about two and a quarter inches in width at the heel, and the outer edge and 'heel' is longer than inside the hooves, so that when walking on hard ground the track consists only of the outer edges. When walking on more or less even ground the tracks of front and hind feet roughly register. Groups of four show that the animal is galloping. Droppings will often be seen where the deer are at all numerous. Sometimes the pellets adhere together much like those of sheep but more usually they are separate. Those of the buck are pointed at one end and concave at the other, whilst those of the doe have no concavity but a marked point. The pellets are roughly half-an-inch in length. The fraying bushes can sometimes be found; indeed, when the buck has really thrashed them, the light colour of the unbarked twigs makes them conspicuous against the darker background.

THE GREAT BUCK OF WYRE

It is an extraordinary fact that in wild fallow deer the master buck or 'great buck', as he has been called in the English language for many centuries, is seldom seen by human eyes. He is an elusive creature of exceptional powers of hearing, smell and sight, but to these must be added patience of a superhuman intensity. He literally never puts a foot wrong, preferring to keep still without even an ear-flick on the flimsiest evidence of human nearness. He has become nocturnal, the periods of daylight during which he moves at all can be measured only in minutes at dawn and dusk. He avoids his own kind throughout the year except at the rut in October when the hinds gather around him

The great buck of Wyre. Antlers from the front.

and as they come into season they solicit the attentions of this muddy-backed, strong-smelling, grunting and groaning, antlered master. The depth of his affection sometimes kills the young hinds.

On 17th November 1965, a great fallow buck crowned with massive antlers, stepped into an open glade in Hawkbatch. It could not perceive that it was under the observation of Edwin George of the Forestry Commission. It was almost blind. A large growth emerging from the brain through a small hole near the base of the right antler had pushed one eyeball completely out of its socket. It could not have lived much longer and its life was mercifully ended just where it stood. It was a dun-coloured animal of poor body-weight, grallocked, it weighed only 114 lb compared with a normal 190 lb. During the rut the master buck does not eat but rapidly comes into condition again at the resumption of normal feeding. This, on account of his, by now, rapidly deteriorating health and failing sight was not possible.

Edwin George estimates his age as about eight years and his antlers (his seventh) show him to be a fallow buck with few peers in any wild company. The antler of a fallow buck consists essentially of a central trunk, the 'beam', which arises from the skull with two side branches, whilst the distant end of the beam is flattened into the 'palm'. The palm is concave, bulging outwards. This latter is edged by a number of finger-like projections which vary to a very great extent. Indeed, it can be said that no

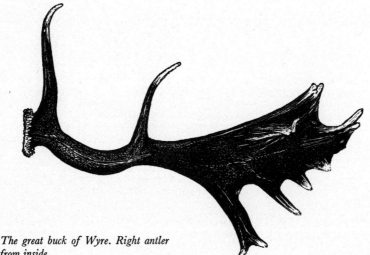

The great buck of Wyre. Right antler from inside.

two pairs of fallow antlers are identical. Fallow bucks are like human beings in that each can be separately identified by their individual characteristics.

The beam enters the skull and is continuous with it, in the form of white bone where it is covered with flesh, but at the point of emergence from the head the beam is ringed by a protrusion which is variously beaded. This is known as the burr, and the beads where they are light in colour are called the 'pearling'. The first two branches from the beam project forwards then upwards and are generally somewhat circular in cross-section. They are called 'tines', the one nearest the head is the 'brow-tine', whilst the one furthest from the head is the 'trey-tine'. The front edge of the palm is slightly curved forwards and the top edge and the upper part of the back edge bears a number of projections or tines. These tines are somewhat

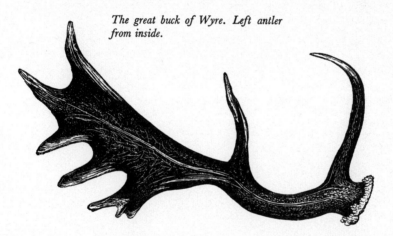

The great buck of Wyre. Left antler from inside.

flattened but often with a thickening at the base. Between the tines the indentations may be shallow, the tines being small, or may be deep if the tines are long.

Because these antlers are outstanding for a wild fallow I have illustrated and measured them in detail. There must be many heads of fallow decorating the walls of our homes around Wyre and, indeed, much further afield, and it is hoped that perhaps their owners may be persuaded to measure them in the manner which is described below so that we may help fit the pieces together and build up the story of the Wyre fallow. Increasing interest is being shown in this large wild animal of great charm and beauty, but much remains to be learnt of it.

There is one very special point, however, which needs explanation. For a natural history specimen of any sort, whether a butterfly in a cabinet, a pressed flower, or the antlers of a deer, to have any scientific or documentary value, it must bear a record of certain essential data. Without this such specimens are virtually valueless. The necessary information can be divided into three parts, first, the date, the day, the month, and the year; secondly, the place, which should include the name of the parish and the county. Names of certain locations of a more general nature, however, would be acceptable, such as Wyre Forest or Malvern Hills. The third part consists of the name of the captor or person who actually collected the specimen and recorded the previous information. This data should appear on the skull attachment to the antlers in indian ink, on the front face, so that it is visible with ease to anyone examining the antlers.

The antlers have, since historical times, been trophies of the chase and there has evolved a system of measurement in order to assess their value. A. J. de Nahlik has recently given a summary of the methods of measurement which I have endeavoured to follow in examining the antlers of the great buck of Wyre, with some difficulties I must add. However, measuring total antler length from the bottom of the burr to the tip of the longest tine on the palm and pressing the tape to the outside of the beam, this was found to be $26\frac{1}{4}$ inches for the right and 25 inches for the left. If, however, we take the length to the depression at the base of the first palm tine, this gave an antler of $23\frac{1}{4}$ inches for the right and $22\frac{1}{2}$ inches for the left. The circumference of the right burr was $7\frac{3}{4}$ inches and the left was 8 inches. The circumference of the beam at its thinnest point was $4\frac{1}{8}$ inches for the right, both for the lower beam and the upper, above the trey tine. In the case of the left antler, however, whilst the circumference of the lower beam was the same, that of the upper beam, at $4\frac{3}{8}$ inches, was a little larger.

The brow and trey tines are of exceptional development. In the right antler these were $7\frac{5}{8}$ and 7 inches, respectively, whilst in the left they were $9\frac{1}{8}$ and $6\frac{1}{2}$ inches. De Nahlik states that the brow tines will rarely be longer than six to seven inches unless exceptionally good conditions prevail and, of course, the trey tines are somewhat smaller. Well-developed palm tines are present also. In the right antler the lowest palm tine is bifurcated and of the exceptional length of $4\frac{1}{4}$ inches.

There is also a double-pointed button growing on the flat of the palm to the inside. There are six principal tines on each palm but on the right three are bifurcated; indeed, one of these, the fore-tine, has a small third point. The lowest palm-tine of the left is bifurcated. The tips of the third and fifth palm-tine of the left have been broken off.

The skull has been cut to the 'short nose' and the hole in the skull near the base of the right beam is oval and almost a quarter of an inch at its longer diameter. The colour of the antlers is a dark chocolate-brown, the tips of the tines being light. The tips of the left brow and the right brow and trey tines are polished like ivory, especially the left brow tine. This latter must have been put to good use and is like a dagger, but has somehow protected its trey tine.

Altogether these antlers of the great buck are a splendid trophy of our wild Wyre fallow, but it is now certain that this is not the only tangible thing remaining of this great buck. He has passed on his blood and already another buck shows promise of being the image of his father, so that we may have, in the herd, many another splendid animal in the future.

MAN THE DOMINANT ANIMAL

Man not only now dominates the earth, but has now commenced to dominate the moon. Having set foot on the moon no doubt it will not be long before he commences to use its resources, although at the time of writing, the indications are that these do not include living organisms, at least, in our sense of the word.

The domination of man over all other living things and, to a great extent, over his physical environment, has been brought about not only by his technological skills but also by sheer weight of numbers! Over great areas of our earth man certainly dominates the landscape. Flying over many areas of the world's land surface, his tilled lands and planted forests are almost always in evidence. Even when the appearance is of virgin tropical or temperate forest it is often that timber trees of economic value have already been removed. The deserts too are relics of land once fertile that have now been despoiled through ignorance of the principles of conservation.

It is staggering to find that it was only in 1969 that the science of nature conservation, using the word 'conservation' in the widest sense, has been recognised. The scientific journal *Biological Conservation* is still in its first volume and in the July issue this is

The yellow-rattle, Rhinanthus crista-galli, *abundant around Wyre, is a parasite of various grasses and other herbs to which it attaches itself by the roots. The flowers are yellow and the calyx is lime-green and compressed. The square-sectioned stem twists through a right-angle between each node and the seeds rattle in the dried flat calyces when it is made into hay.*

the title of an important article by L. K. Shaposhnikov, the director of the Central Laboratory of the Nature Conservation, U.S.S.R. The conservation and, indeed, renewal of natural resources has been given a new name 'Sosiecology' and really it adds another dimension to the meaning usually given to nature conservation, this is—'the study of the conditions required for satisfactory human existence'. This is an all embracing subject without a doubt! It must include man's psychological requirements—his entertainment and amusement, his recreation and his refreshment, not only bodily, but that of his mind also.

Those of us to whom the conservation of Wyre as an area of great beauty is of paramount importance believe so for many reasons. Some of us are filled with interest in the intricate, small things, such as the small moths or groups of tiny creatures which have only been catalogued with Latin names and, so far, have not been noticed in our ordinary prose. For others it is the wild flowers, the shrubs and the mosses on the trees, and, indeed, those things that give some indefinable look to our English countryside. Yet, for others, it is the forest quietness, noticing the dappled sunlight on the path where the sun has penetrated, and the foliage of the oak.

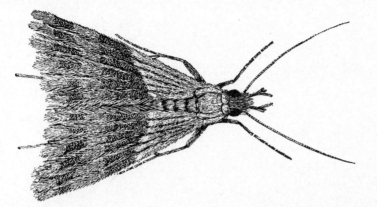

The many-plume, Orneodes hexadactyla, *is a small brown and speckled moth common around Wyre wherever the honeysuckle is to be found. The pink-coloured caterpillars live inside the unopened flower buds and eat the pollen. The moths emerge in August when, after a period of flying around at night, they hibernate in creepers and hedgebottoms and are often found in outhouses. When active they display their feather-like wings rather like a fan.*

But for all of us it is a happy place enveloping its quests with a mantle of pleasure. The mean and the sordid must not intrude and that is why the task of the conservation of Wyre is such a worthwhile task. It is possible for us now to make Wyre a place where many others may share this mood.

For Further Reading

GODFREY, G. and CROWCROFT, P., 1960, *The Life of the Mole*, Museum Press, London.

LAWRENCE, M. J. and BROWN, R. W., N.D., *Mammals of Britain—Their Tracks, Trails and Signs*, Blandford, London.

DE NAHLIK, A. J., 1959, *Wild Deer*, Faber & Faber, London.

PIKE, O. G., 1950, *Wild Animals in Britain*, Macmillan, London.

PITT, F., 1938 (and other editions), *Wild Animals in Britain*, Batsford, London.

PITT, F., N.D., *British Animal Life*, Westminster Press, London.

STEP, E., 1921 (and later editions), *Animal Life of the British Isles*, Wayside and Woodland Series, Warne, London.

SOUTHERN, H. N. (Editor), 1964, *The Handbook of British Mammals* (Mammal Society of the British Isles), Blackwell, Oxford.

VESEY-FITZGERALD, B., 1949, *British Bats*, Field Study Books, Methuen, London.

WHITEHEAD, G. K., 1964, *The Deer of Great Britain and Ireland*, Routledge and Kegan Paul, London.

Index

(*Page entries in italic indicate illustrations*)

otter, 257–9, *257*
Oxbind Coppice, 12, 37

Panther, *113*
Pararge aegeria, 155–6, *156*; *megera*, 157–8, *157*
parasol mushroom, 110, *113*
peacock, 145, 148, *148*, 262
Pedicularis sylvatica, 95, *95*
Pentatomidae, 124
periwinkle, 69; greater, 70; lesser, *69*, 70
Perla, 131
Perry, W. G., 74
Petromyzon fluviatilis, 201–2, *201*
Phallus impudicus, *112*
Philopotamidae, 134
Phlogophora meticulosa, 173, *174*
Phoenicurus phoenicurus, 218–9, *218*
Phosphaenus hemipterus, 196
Phylloscopus collybita, 234–5; *sibilatrix*, 236–7, *236*; *trochilus*, 235–6, *235*
Picea abies, 38, *39*
Picus viridis, 230, *231*
Pieridae, 139–145
Pieris brassicae, 143–5, *144*; *napi*, 145, *146*; *rapae*, 142, *142*
Pike, Oliver G., 225
pine, Corsican, 33; Scots, 34–7, *36*
Pinus sylvestris, 34–7, *36*
Pipistrellus pipistrellus, 261
Pitt, William, 88
Pitts, Alderman Edmund, 14, 15
Plectrocnemia conspersa, 136
plum, 175
Polygala serpyllifolia, 90–1, *90*
Polygonia c-album, 149–51, *150*, *151*; hutchinsoni, 150
Polygonum, 171
Polyommatus icarus, 169, *169*
Polypodium vulgare, 108, 109
polypody, 108; common, 108, 109; three-branched, 108
Polyporus betulinus, 29
Pontia daplidice, 140
poplar, 215
Populus tremulosa 20–1, *21*
Potamobius pallipes, 121, *121*
Potamophylax latipennis, 137
Pound Bank, 163

Pound Green, 2, 225; Common, 9; Coppice, 9
Powis Castle, 31
prickly-toothed shield fern, 109
Prunus avium, 26, *27*; *cerasus*, 28; *padus*, 27
Pseudotsuga taxifolia, 31–3, *32*
Psyllidae, 102
Pteris aquillina, 109
Pulicaria, 80
purple loosestrife, 66–8, *67*
purple hairstreak, 163–5, *164*
Pustularia rosea, 114
Pyrola media 53–4, *53*
Pyrrhosoma nymphula, 130
Pyrus domestica, 17
Quale, Mrs., 53
Quercus cerris, 4, 12–14, *14*; *ilex* 12; *pedunculata*, 3; *petraea*, 4–5, *5*, 12; *robur*, 3–4, *4*, 12, 222; *sessiliflora*, 4

Rabbit, 253, 256
ragwort, *178*
Ramsbottom, J., 111
ramsons, 59, 60, *61*
Rana esculenta, 204; *ridibunda*, 204; *temporaria*, 204, *204*
Ranunculaceae, 49, 50 52
Ranunculus ficaria, 49–50, *50*
Raphidia, 126; *xanthostigma*, 127, *126*
rat, 256
Rea, Carleton, 110
Rea, Miss Violet, 113
Rea River, 110
red admiral, 155
red ant, 192
red squirrel, 250–2, *250*
redstart, 215, 218–9, *218*
Rhagium mordax, *194*, 194
Rhamnus catharticus, 139; *frangula*, 44
Rhinanthus cristagalli, 272
Rhinolophidae, 260
Rhyacophila dorsalis, 136
Rhyacophilidae, 134
Rhyssa persuasoria, *185*, 186–9
Rhyssella curvipes, 189
Ribbesford Woods, 2, 3, 58, 110
ringlet, 159–62, *161*
robin's pincushion 103